Calorie Chart

BREADS, CEREAL, RICE AND PASTA

Food Item	Calories	Total Fat
Bagel, 3-inch	155	1
Blueberry muffin, 2 1/2-inch	110	4
Bread, 1 slice	65	1
Crackers, 4 small	60	0
Dinner roll, 1 average	145	2
English muffin, 1 plain	135	1
Flour tortilla, 8-inch	140	3
Oatmeal, cooked, 1/2 cup	75	1
Pancake, 4-inch	100	0
Pasta, cooked, 1/2 cup	100	0
Pretzels, 1 ounce	110	1
Ready-to-eat cereal, 1 cup	120	1
Rice, cooked, 1/2 cup	105	0

VEGETABLES

Food Item	Calories	Total Fat
Asparagus, cooked, 1/2 cup	25	0
Beets, cooked, 1/2 cup	35	0
Broccoli, cooked, 1/2 cup	20	0
Carrots, cooked, 1/2 cup	35	0
Corn, canned or frozen, 1/2 cup	65	0
Green beans, cooked, 1/2 cup	35	0
Iceberg lettuce, 1 cup	10	0
Peas, cooked, 1/2 cup	60	0
Potato, baked, 1 medium	130	0
Tomato, 1 medium	40	0
Tomato juice, 3/4 cup	30	0

FRUITS

Food Item	Calories	Total Fat
Apple, 1 medium	80	0
Apple juice, 3/4 cup	90	0
Apple sauce, unsweetened, 1/2 cup	50	0
Banana, 1 medium	110	0
Blueberries, 1/2 cup	40	0
Cantaloupe, 1/2 medium	95	1
Grapefruit, 1/2 medium	40	0
Grapes, 1/2 cup	55	0
Orange, 1 medium	60	0
Orange juice, unsweetened, 3/4 cup	75	0
Peach, 1 medium	40	0
Pear, 1 medium	100	1
Pineapple, 1/2 cup	40	0
Strawberries, 1/2 cup	25	0

MEAT, POULTRY, FISH, DRY BEANS, EGGS AND NUTS

Food Item	Calories	Total Fat
Almonds, 1/4 cup	210	19
Beef rib roast, cooked, 3 ounces	210	13
Beef sirloin, cooked, 3 ounces	155	4
Beef tenderloin, cooked, 3 ounces	175	8
Chicken breast, broiled with skin, 3 ounces	125	5
Chicken drumstick, fried, with skin, 3 ounces	200	11
Crabmeat, canned, 3 ounces	85	1
Dried beans and lentils, cooked, 1/2 cup	120	0
Egg, cooked, 1	75	5
Fat-free cholesterol-free egg product, 1/4 cup	25	0
Ground beef, extra-lean, cooked, 3 ounces	176	8
Ground beef, regular, cooked, 3 ounces	260	19
Halibut, broiled, 3 ounces	100	1
Ham, fully cooked, 3 ounces	150	8
Hot dog	140	13
Lamb loin chop, cooked, 3 ounces	175	8
Peanut butter, 2 tablespoons	190	16
Peanuts, 1/4 cup	210	18
Pork loin chop, cooked, 3 ounces	180	8
Pork tenderloin, cooked, 3 ounces	140	4
Salmon fillet, broiled, 3 ounces	135	5
Scallops, steamed, 3 ounces	100	1
Shrimp, batter-dipped, 3 ounces	200	9
Tuna, water-packed, 3 ounces	100	1
Turkey, roasted, no skin, 3 ounces	160	6
Veal loin chop, cooked, 3 ounces	140	5

MILK, YOGURT AND CHEESE

Food Item	Calories	Total Fat
American cheese, 2 ounces	230	18
Cheddar cheese, 1 1/2 ounces	175	14
Cheese spread, 2 ounces	120	8
Milk, Fat-free (skim), 1 cup	85	0
Milk, Low-fat (2%), 1 cup	120	4
Milk, Whole, 1 cup	150	8
Mozzarella cheese, 1 1/2 ounces	120	8
Parmesan cheese, grated, 1 1/2 ounces	90	6
Ricotta cheese, part skim, 1/2 cup	170	10
Yogurt, fat-free, 1 cup	135	0
Yogurt, low-fat, 1 cup	155	8

FATS, OILS AND SWEETS

Food Item	Calories	Total Fat
Butter, 1 tablespoon	100	12
Chocolate bar, 1 ounce	145	9
Cola, 12 ounces	150	0
Cooking spray	2	0
Cream cheese, 1 ounce	100	10
Jam or preserves, 1 tablespoon	50	0
Jelly beans, 10	110	0
Margarine, 1 tablespoon	100	11
Mayonnaise or salad dressing, 1 tablespoon	100	11
Sherbet, 1/2 cup	135	2
Sour cream, 1 tablespoon	30	3
Vegetable oil, 1 tablespoon	120	14

Betty Crocker's
Eat and Lose Weight

IDG Books Worldwide, *An International Data Group Company* • Foster City, CA • Chicago, IL • Indianapolis, IN • New York, NY

IDG BOOKS WORLDWIDE, INC.
An International Data Group Company
919 E. Hillsdale Boulevard
Suite 400
Foster City, CA 94404

For general information on IDG Books Worldwide's books in the U.S., please call our Consumer Customer Service department at 800-762-2974. For reseller information, including discounts and premium sales, please call our Reseller Customer Service department at 800-434-3422.

Library of Congress Cataloging-in-Publication Data

Crocker, Betty.
   [Eat and lose weight]
   Betty Crocker's eat and lose weight—3rd ed.
     p. cm.
   Second ed. published under title: Betty Crocker's new eat and lose weight.
New York : Macmillan USA, 1996.
   Includes index.
   ISBN 0-7645-6205-3 (alk. paper)
   1. Reducing diets—Recipes. I. Crocker, Betty. New eat and lose weight. II. Title.
RM222.2 .C749 2000
641.5'635—dc21   00-058191

UPC: 785555037670   EAN: 9780764562051

GENERAL MILLS, INC.
Betty Crocker Kitchens

Manager, Publishing: Lois L. Tlusty
Editors: Kelly Kilen, Cheri Olerud
Recipe Development: Janet Sadlack, Grace Wells
Food Stylists: Nancy J. Johnson, Cindy Syme

Photographic Services
Photographer: Valerie J. Bourassa

IDG BOOKS WORLDWIDE, INC.

Cover and Book Design: Michele Laseau
Photography Art Director: Brent Bentrott
Junior Designer: Holly Wittenberg

For consistent baking results, the Betty Crocker Kitchens recommend Gold Medal Flour.

Manufactured in the United States of America
10 9 8 7 6 5 4 3 2 1
Third Edition

Cover photos: Roasted Red Pepper Bruschetta (page 22), Vegetarian Cannellini Bean Lasagna (page 172), and Chocolate Soufflé Cakes (page 218)

Dear Friends,

Ready to lose weight and feel great? Then say good-bye to strict diets and trendy eating plans! In our newest edition of *Betty Crocker's Eat and Lose Weight*, we've created an easy-to-follow, two-step plan that combines healthy eating with an active lifestyle. As you'll see, each step is geared towards maximum results with minimum effort.

Our easy plan begins with *Step 1: Eating Smart.* Learn the basics for creating a sensible diet that will not only help you lose weight, but give you the know-how to build a lifetime of healthy eating. Worried about being carried away by cravings? We help you fight temptation with our Smart Food Choices Chart. And because it's so important to lose weight sensibly and safely, we give you the truth behind the trends when it comes to fad diets.

When it comes to *Step 2: Staying Active*, it doesn't matter if you're a student, a stay-at-home mom, or a busy parent on the run—everyone needs to get moving! We help you get started—and keep going—with exercise tips and techniques that really work.

But the best part is the food! Nearly 150 delicious recipes make losing weight so satisfying. You'll love Beef Medallions with Pear-Cranberry Chutney, Creamy Corn and Garlic Risotto, Zesty Autumn Pork Stew and Mocha Angel Cake—and so will your family. Want more good news? Every recipe is paired with an Eating Smart and Staying Active tip to keep you motivated and inspired along the way.

So are you ready to get started? Then do the two-step with me—the easy way to lose weight, feel great and enjoy every single meal!

Betty Crocker

P.S. Here's to a new you!

Contents

The Easy Two-Step Guide
to Losing Weight and Feeling Great, *6*

Chapter 1: Quick-Fix Appetizers and Snacks, *16*

Chapter 2: Favorite Breakfasts, *42*

Chapter 3: Soups, Sandwiches and Main-Dish Salads, *68*

Chapter 4: Sensational Poultry, Fish and Seafood, *94*

Chapter 5: Great Beef, Pork and Lamb, *130*

Chapter 6: Easy Meatless Meals, *156*

Chapter 7: Savory Breads, Vegetables and Side Dishes *188*

Chapter 8: Delicious Desserts, *214*

A Week's Worth of Menus, *235*

Extra Charts, Tables and Helpful Tips, *238*

Index, *247*

Rio Grande Turkey Soup (page 71)

Losing Weight and Feeling Great!

Trying to lose weight, but don't want to sacrifice your favorite foods? You don't have to! Successful weight-loss programs are those that you can (and want to) continue with for a lifetime.

With *Betty Crocker's Eat and Lose Weight* cookbook, we transform the old-fashioned concept of dieting into a new-fashioned healthy lifestyle. In addition to the great-tasting recipes you'll find inside, we've packed this book with lots of nutrition and exercise tips to help you lose weight and keep it off—for good!

To make losing weight as easy as it can be, we've put together an ultra manageable plan with just two steps to success. They are:

Step 1 Eating Smart

Step 2 Staying Active

By balancing what you eat (step 1) with how active you are (step 2), you'll be well on your way to a healthy weight and can forget about dieting—forever! So let's get started.

Getting Started

Before beginning any weight-loss program, the first two questions to ask yourself are: Do I need to lose weight? and How much should I lose? Wait—don't run to the scale for the answer to the first question. A healthy weight goes beyond the numbers on the scale. A scale tells you how many pounds you weigh, but it doesn't tell you how much of that weight is fat or where the fat is located on your body. It's the extra body weight from fat that increases your risk for developing heart disease, high blood pressure and certain types of cancers.

Where your body stores fat can also affect your health. People who carry most of their weight around the waist are called "apples," and those who carry their weight around the hips and thighs are called "pears." As a rule, it's healthier to be a "pear"—fat around the waist is associated with an increased risk of certain health problems. To determine your shape, calculate your *Waist-to-Hip Ratio*. Measure your waist at its narrowest point and your hips at their widest point. Divide your waist measurement by your hip measurement. For a woman, a ratio greater than 0.80 indicates an apple shape. Men are apples if this number is greater than 1.0.

Besides the bathroom scale, a weight-height table such as the Gerontology Research Center Table (page 249) can offer you yet another clue. One drawback to tables like these is that they don't take into consideration individual characteristics such as your age, sex and frame size. And, like your scale, they can't tell you whether or where you are carrying too much fat.

Another, and perhaps more valuable, tool is the Body Mass Index (BMI), which estimates how much mass, including fat, you have. It relates your weight to the health risks of being overweight better than a scale can. Use the table on page 250 to find your BMI. Generally, a person with a BMI of 27 or more is considered moderately overweight, and anything over 30 is considered seriously overweight. Because the BMI doesn't account for the increased weight of those who carry a lot of muscle weight, it's possible to be physically fit and have the same BMI as someone who is truly over-weight. It's best to check with your doctor if you have questions about your ideal weight.

Setting a Goal Weight

You've checked the charts, figured your BMI and decided it's time to shed some extra pounds. Now what? The next step is to set a healthy goal weight. Thankfully, you can forget about a "magic" number. A specific body weight is not always the best goal in a weight-loss program. Many who have successfully lost weight—and maintained that loss—have opted to throw out their scales. As foreign as this seems to veteran "dieters," monitoring weight without a scale allows you to get in touch with your body. Remember, the number on the scale is only one of many factors influencing your health and body image. Do your clothes fit better? Do you have more energy? Both are signs that you're on your way to a healthy body weight. Keep it up!

Also consider *set point* and *heredity* as you develop weight-loss goals. The theory that each body has a pre-determined "set point" means that two people of the same height and body frame may function best at different weights. Weighing significantly more, or less, than where your body wants to be can make you more tired, disrupt your menstrual cycle and even depress your immune system. As for heredity, look to your genes for clues as to what you can realistically expect to weigh. If you have overweight parents, this doesn't mean you, too, will be overweight. It may just mean you aren't meant to be model-thin.

So relax. With good food choices and exercise, you will soon reach your goal as the inches melt away. Now, on to our easy two-step program!

Goal Setting—The Long and Short of It

Weight-loss plans benefit from setting long-term and short-term goals. Long-term goals are made possible by achieving the short-term goals, and the short-term goals are what speed us toward our long-term goals. Here are some examples:

Short-Term Goals

- Take a walk around the block after dinner.
- Take the stairs instead of the elevator—wherever you go—for one week.
- Park at the far end of the parking lot when you go shopping.
- Try one new, low-fat recipe each week.
- Attend a low-fat cooking class.
- Switch from full-fat to low-fat milk (or cheese or sour cream or . . .).

Long-Term Goals

- Establish healthy eating habits—that you enjoy!
- Stick with a regular exercise program.
- Maintain a healthy weight.

Setbacks and Rewards

We're all human, and we all have setbacks along the way. Whatever you do, don't let set-backs stop you. Get back up, dust off the cookie crumbs and continue moving toward your goals. When you reach your goals (and you will!), reward yourself by celebrating. This will moti-vate you toward future success.

Step 1 Eating Smart

Now that you've set a realistic weight-loss goal, let's get to the heart of the matter and take a closer look at how to go about losing weight.

Eight Basics for Eating Smart

Step 1 begins with the basics—your diet. The following guidelines, provided by the U.S. Department of Agriculture, will help lead you down the path to losing weight while building a solid foundation for a lifetime of healthy eating.

Let the Pyramid Guide Your Choices

No one food contains all the nutrients you need for good health. The greater the variety of foods you eat, the better for your body. Eating according to the Food Guide Pyramid (page 251) is a super start to keeping calories in line. Writing down everything you eat for a week and comparing your list to the Food Guide Pyramid is helpful. Are you getting enough food from each group? Are there groups from which you tend to overeat? Are your serving sizes too large or too small?

Choose a Variety of Grains Daily, Especially Whole Grains

Foods made from grains (like wheat, rice, corn and oats) are naturally low in fat, plus they are loaded with fiber and many of the vitamins and minerals that your body needs. For maximum fiber and nutrients, whole grains are your best bet.

Choose a Variety of Fruits and Vegetables Daily

We're so often told what not to eat in order to lose weight. But here, experts tell us to eat *more!* Fruits and veggies are packed with vitamins, minerals and fiber. Fruits and vegetables differ in their nutrient content, so be adventurous and try a variety of colors and kinds.

Keep Food Safe to Eat

A vital part of healthy eating is keeping foods safe from harmful bacteria, parasites and chemical contaminants. *Safe* means the food poses little risk for foodborne illness. By following safe handling procedures, you can keep your food safe to eat at home or away.

Choose a Diet That Is Low in Saturated Fat and Cholesterol and Moderate in Total Fat

Although cutting back on fat is one of the most effective ways to slash calories, no one is suggesting that you eliminate all the fat from your diet. Fat contributes to the taste and satisfaction of food, and your body needs fat to function properly. However, some kinds of fat, especially saturated fat, can raise blood cholesterol levels. Saturated fats, found mostly in meats, eggs and dairy products, should make up no more than 10 percent of calories per day. As for total fat intake, aim for no more than 30 percent of your daily calories.

What about cholesterol? The cholesterol in the foods we eat is called *dietary cholesterol*. The cholesterol in our bloodstream comes from two sources: the foods we eat and our body's own manufacturing process. Dietary cholesterol is found only in animal foods: meats, poultry, dairy products and seafood. Note that most foods high in cholesterol are also high in saturated fats. While experts have yet to agree on dietary cholesterol's effect on the body, it's generally accepted that you should limit your intake to 300 milligrams per day.

Choose Beverages and Foods to Moderate Your Intake of Sugars

We've all heard the rumors about the evils of sugar. It's true that sugar-rich foods are often empty-calorie foods, which means they contribute few nutrients to a healthy diet. But just the same, sugar is a carbohydrate, and it won't jeopardize weight-loss plans if eaten in moderation. In fact, sugar is a valuable energy source. Balancing a moderate sugar intake with other nutrient-rich foods keeps your energy levels up and running.

Choose and Prepare Foods with Less Salt

While cutting back on salt and sodium doesn't necessarily help you lose weight, eating lots of salty foods can cause water retention and bloating, making you *feel* heavier. In addition, sodium has been associated with high blood pressure, particularly for those individuals who are sensitive to the level of salt in their diets. Because only a small percentage of us fit into that category and there isn't a way to predict "salt sensitivity," moderation is recommended for everyone (2,400 mg per day). You can keep high-sodium foods to a minimum by reading labels and tasting your food before adding salt. Experiment with herbs and other flavorings when you cook, relying on salt only to enhance the natural flavors of your food.

If You Drink Alcoholic Beverages, Do So in Moderation

Alcohol contributes calories but little else to a healthy diet. Too much alcohol can also lower inhibitions and increase your appetite, causing you to eat more than planned. However, some studies have shown that low to moderate amounts of red wine may be good for the heart.

When Considering Calories, Are All Foods Created Equal?

The fuel your body needs to function comes from calories, but not all foods are created equal. Gram for gram, some foods are more concentrated sources of calories than others. (One gram is about the same as a regular paperclip.)

Eating more calories than your body needs as fuel—whether they come from carbohydrates, protein or fat—will be stored away as fat, which ultimately results in weight gain.

Energy Source	Calories per Gram
Carbohydrates	4 calories per gram
Protein	4 calories per gram
Fat	9 calories per gram

The Truth About Fad Diets

Fad diets are just that: fads. Unfortunately, many people think they need to rely on a fad diet to lose weight, only to find the pounds right back on again. Described below are the pitfalls of some of the most popular diets.

Very-Low-Calorie Diets

Weight loss is based on calorie restriction with extremely limited amounts of food (fewer than 800 calories per day). Concerns include:

- Daily nutrient guidelines not met.
- Initial rapid weight loss is water weight; the weight will come back.
- Low calorie intake deprives you of energy.
- Difficult to maintain for a lifetime.
- May cause menstrual problems.

Liquid Diets

One, two or three meals a day are replaced with a powder or liquid beverage. Concerns include:

- Most people quit due to lack of variety.
- No chance to develop healthy eating habits.
- Can cause constipation.
- May cause menstrual problems if calorie level is too low.
- Very low calorie liquid diets cause large amounts of water to be lost. When dieter goes back to normal eating, the body compensates by retaining massive amounts of fluid, diluting potassium stores and causing abnormal heart rhythms.

High-Protein/Low-Carbohydrate Diets

This is similar to an inverted Food Guide Pyramid with animal protein at the base and carbohydrates at the top. High-protein (and often high-fat) foods, such as meat and cheese, are emphasized; carbohydrates are often restricted. Concerns include:

- May cause weakness, headaches and dizziness.
- Can increase blood fat and cholesterol levels.
- May cause menstrual problems.
- Can result in ketosis, a condition where the body breaks down muscle tissue to get energy. Over time, ketosis can lead to serious health

problems, such as kidney damage, increased risk of osteoporosis and gout—a painful inflammation of the joints.

- Dramatically limits food choices, making it difficult to maintain for a lifetime.

Single-Food Diets

Only one type of food—grapefruit or rice, for example—is allowed. Concerns include:

- Daily requirements for nutrients are either not met or exceeded.
- Most people quit due to lack of variety.
- No chance to develop healthy eating habits.

Herbal Supplements, Diet Pills and Other Diet Drugs

Taking supplements and/or beverages in place of or in addition to regular meals. Products claim that they increase metabolism, suppress appetite or block fat absorption. Concerns include:

- Death has resulted from mixing some supplements with prescription medications.
- Fat blockers may inhibit absorption of fat-soluble nutrients.
- No chance to develop healthy eating habits.
- May develop a dependence on a weight-loss product.
- Heart conditions—sometimes fatal—have been linked to certain diet drugs.
- May cause weakness, headaches, insomnia, irritability and high blood pressure.

Eating Disorders: Walking a Thin Line

The portrayal of an ultra-thin body size in popular culture has contributed to a rise in eating disorders, especially among young people. Two well-known disorders are *anorexia nervosa*—excessive weight loss—and *bulimia nervosa*—binge-eating followed by a pattern of purging.

If your child or someone you know needs to lose weight, make sure he or she follows a nutritionally sound diet. Most importantly, show your children the joys of a healthy lifestyle with your own good eating and exercise habits.

So What Does Work?

While there are no overnight, instant or magic cures for weight loss, here are a few more tips that may help trim your waistline:

Group Support

Many people who have lost weight credit group support with their success. The support you get from a group can help you lose weight and maintain healthy eating and exercise habits. Because everyone is different, group programs may not work for everyone. But if you find one that stresses healthy eating habits along with the benefits of exercise and attention to changes in behavior, it may give you the support you need.

Plan It Out

Busy lifestyles can make a healthy diet seem nearly impossible. With a little planning, it doesn't have to be that way. Rather than dine-and-dash at the local fast-food restaurant, take a few minutes the night before to pack your lunch with healthy foods you enjoy. If mid-afternoon munchies are a problem, stash an apple in your briefcase so you don't turn to the vending machine. To make meal planning easier, check out the menus in the back of the book (pages 247 to 248) for a week's worth of meals at your fingertips.

Write It Down

Recording what and how much you eat will make you more aware of your current eating habits. Also, recording when, where and how you feel when you eat will give you some valuable insights. Other benefits to recording what you eat? When you know you need to write it down, you may choose to eat less. Looking back at what you've eaten throughout the day can also reveal patterns, allowing you to correct or avoid situations where you tend to overeat.

Enjoy Your Food!

This may be the most important key to a successful weight-loss plan. Too often we eat on the run. Eating while rushed or preoccupied prevents us from fully enjoying food. Take time to savor your food. When you've truly enjoyed a meal or snack, your urge to overeat will lessen.

Smart Food Choices

Successful weight-loss plans balance what you eat with how much you eat. Although no food is off-limits in a healthy eating plan, weight loss is accelerated by choosing foods that have more of the good stuff and less of the not-so-good stuff. Start by stocking your pantry and fridge with low-calorie, low-fat foods that you like to eat.

Food Type	Instead Of	Go For
Breads, Cereals	Croissants; butter rolls. Presweetened cereals. Cheese crackers; butter crackers; fried tortilla chips.	Whole-grain breads such as whole wheat, pumpernickel and rye; breadsticks; English muffins; bagels; rice cakes; pita breads; tortillas. Oatmeal; whole-grain cereals; polenta. Saltine crackers; graham crackers; whole-grain crackers; low-sodium pretzels; air-popped popcorn; baked tortilla chips.
Rice, Pasta	Egg noodles.	Brown and white rice; pasta; Asian noodles.
Baked Goods	Frosted cakes; cookies; pastries; doughnuts; sweet rolls; coffee cakes.	Angel food cake; low-fat whole-grain muffins.
Fruits	Fruit pies.	Fresh, frozen and dried fruits.
Vegetables	Veggies prepared with butter or in cheese or cream sauce.	Fresh, frozen and canned vegetables.
Meat, Poultry, Fish	Fatty meat; organ meat; cold cuts; sausage; hot dogs.	Lean meat; skinless poultry; fish; shellfish.
Legumes (Beans, Peas and Lentils)	Refried beans; high-sodium canned beans.	White beans; black beans; red beans; kidney beans; soybeans; soy foods (tofu, tempeh, soymilk); split peas; lentils.
Eggs	Egg yolks.	Egg whites; egg product substitutes.
Dairy Products	Cream; whole milk; 2 percent milk; half-and-half; whipped toppings; nondairy creamers; sour cream. Full-fat cottage cheese; full-fat cheeses; cream cheese. Ice cream.	Low-fat milk (fat-free skim or 1 percent); fat-free or low-fat buttermilk; low-fat chocolate milk; fat-free or low-fat sour cream. Fat-free or low-fat cottage cheese; fat-free or low-fat cheese; fat-free or low-fat ricotta or cream cheese. Fat-free or low-fat yogurt. Sherbet; sorbet; fat-free or low-fat ice cream or frozen yogurt.
Fats, Oils	Saturated fats: coconut oil, palm oil, palm kernel oil, lard, bacon fat.	Monounsaturated and polyunsaturated vegetable oils: olive, canola, peanut, soybean, sunflower, sesame, safflower; cooking spray.
Spreads	Butter; margarine.	Fat-free and low-fat spreads; fruit butters.
Chocolate	Baking chocolate; candy bars; chocolate chips.	Baking cocoa.

Staying Active

Staying active is the second half of any successful weight-loss equation. By staying active, you burn calories. The more calories you burn, the more weight you lose. Yet, exercise isn't just about weight loss. Avid exercisers say they enjoy staying active simply because it feels good! An active person has more stamina, has a stronger immune system and tends to have a higher self-esteem. Not surprisingly, exercisers experience less depression than nonexercisers.

You needn't aspire to be an Olympic athlete to be "in shape." If you can run to catch a bus without getting winded or enjoy a fast-and-furious game of tag with your children, you know the joy of being fit.

What's your activity level? Size yourself up using The Activity Pyramid (below).

Many people have started exercise programs with the best of intentions, only to abandon them. This is less likely to happen if you find activities you enjoy. With the many exercise options available (see Activity Chart on the inside back cover), there's bound to be an activity that works for you. Even better, cross-train by combining a number of different activities.

Don't have much time? Research has shown that you can portion your exercise throughout the entire day. Half an hour of walking, for instance, can be divided into three 10-minute mini walks.

Don't forget that every little bit helps. No one is asking you to run a marathon or climb a mountain (unless you want to!), but a little bit of something is better than nothing. In fact, studies have shown that

The Activity Pyramid

Source: Institute for Research and Education Health System Minnesota. ©1997 by Institute for Research and Education. Reprinted with permission.

"fidgeters," those people who can never seem to sit still, may burn up to 400 calories a day with their foot-tapping, leg-jiggling and thumb-twiddling. Of course you'll have to do more than twiddle your thumbs to stay fit, but don't let unachievable fitness goals keep you from becoming—and staying—active.

The F.I.T. Principle

The F.I.T. Principle answers questions regarding the Frequency, Intensity and Time (or length) of your workouts. Following these guidelines will help you get your heart rate up and burn calories. Remember, before beginning an exercise program, visit with your doctor to find out about which activities will work best for you.

F: Frequency

How often should I work out? To lose weight, you need to exercise aerobically three to five times each week for anywhere from 15 to 60 minutes. Aerobic exercises are those that demand oxygen (*aerobic* means "with oxygen"), boost your heart rate and use large muscle groups. Walking, jogging, swimming, in-line skating and biking all are aerobic activities.

I: Intensity

How hard should I work out? To maximize your train-ing, you should be working at an intensity rate of 60 to 85 percent of your target heart rate. If you're a begin-ner, aim for about 60 percent. As your aerobic condi-tioning increases and you up the intensity of your workouts, you'll be more comfortable working in the 70 to 85 percent range. Monitor your heart rate using the Target Heart Rate Chart (page 14) or use Borg's Scale of Perceived Exertion (page 14) to track your intensity level.

T: Time

How long should I work out? Achieving cardiovascu-lar benefits and maximizing your calorie burn also depend on the length of your workouts. If you're exer-cising for weight loss, work up to sessions that last between 45 and 60 minutes. (This doesn't include warm-up or cool-down time.) Beginners may need to start at 5 or 10 minutes and gradually increase their exercise time. During this time, you should be working within your target heart rate zone.

Target Heart Rate

To make the most of your workouts, you need to know how hard to work. Contrary to popular belief, more is not always better. Check your pulse during a workout to find the point at which you maximize calorie burn and get your heart pumping.

Choose either your carotid or radial artery to check your pulse (see diagram below).

Your carotid artery (just to either side of the center of your neck).

Your radial artery (your wrist).

Apply light pressure with your fingers, but don't use your thumb. Count the beats you feel in 10 seconds. Refer to the Target Heart Rate Chart (page 14) to see if you're within your proper training range.

Target Heart Rate Chart (10-Second Count)

% Allowable Maximum

Age	60%	70%	75%	80%	85%
Under 20	21	25	26	28	30
20	20	23	25	27	28
25	20	23	24	26	28
30	19	22	24	25	27
35	19	22	23	25	26
40	18	21	23	24	26
45	18	21	22	23	25
50	17	20	21	23	24
55	17	19	21	22	23
60	16	19	20	21	22
65	16	18	19	21	22
70	15	18	19	20	21
75	15	17	18	19	21

Source: Stretching Inc., P.O. Box 768, Palmer Lake, CO 80133

Perceived Exertion

Another way to monitor exercise intensity is to use Borg's Scale of Perceived Exertion. Use this scale to find your "comfort zone" when working out. Your breath should be rhythmic and comfortable when exercising.

To use the scale, assign a number between 6 and 20 as your desired intensity, with 6 being extremely light and 20 being extremely difficult. A perceived exertion level between 11 and 15 means you are working at approximately 60 to 85 percent of your maximum heart rate.

You can also use the "talk test" to gauge how hard you are working. You should be somewhat short of breath while exercising, but if you can't carry on a conversation, you're working too hard.

Borg's Scale of Perceived Exertion

Desired Intensity	Perceived Exertion Level
6	Very, very light
7	Very, very light
8	Very, very light
9	Very light
10	Very light
11	Fairly light
12	Fairly light
13	Fairly light
14	Fairly light
15	Hard
16	Hard
17	Very Hard
18	Very Hard
19	Very, very hard
20	Very, very hard

Source: Guidelines for Exercise Testing and Prescription, American College of Sports Medicine.

Stretching, Flexibility—and Weight Loss?

Believe it or not, there is a link between stretching, flexibility and weight loss. Stretching bridges sedentary and active lifestyles; it helps make an active lifestyle possible. By stretching, you prepare your body for movement. Especially important for aerobic exercisers, stretching helps smooth the transition from inactivity to vigorous activity. Failing to stretch before and after a workout results in tight, inflexible, injury-prone muscles. Many people skip stretching to save time. But if their tight muscles lead to injury, exercise programs are put on hold indefinitely while they recover.

Stretching is peaceful, relaxing and noncompetitive. What better way to warm up for a workout? Stretching also adjusts to each individual; you do what feels right for you. Think you don't have time to stretch? Think again. You can't afford to *not* take time to stretch. The following ideas may help. You can stretch:

- Before you get out of bed in the morning
- At work to release nervous tension
- After sitting (or standing) for a long time
- When you're talking on the phone
- Before and after aerobic exercise
- Before you go to bed at night
- Whenever you feel stiff

Strength Training

Weight lifting is no longer solely for professional body builders. Studies have shown that muscle building increases calories burned at rest. The more muscle you have, the more calories you burn. Strength training also increases bone density, which can reduce your risk of osteoporosis and other debilitating illnesses.

For best results, try lifting weights two or three times each week. Sessions should last between 20 to 60 minutes. You don't have to belong to a gym to strength train. Inexpensive free weights and resistance bands make it possible to lift weights at home. Because injuries are more likely when people start lifting weights on their own, it's helpful to first find a trainer who can explain basic equipment and proper form. A trainer can also help tailor your workout to help you reach specific goals.

One Last Note

Before starting any weight-loss or exercise plan, it's a good idea to check in with your doctor. After an OK, start slowly and try not to expect to lose lots of weight quickly. Your best bet for permanent, safe weight loss is to lose one to two pounds each week. Be patient. It takes time to make lifestyle changes; they don't happen overnight.

Remember, a daily program of smart eating and regular activity is what works when it comes to losing weight. With a little time and patience, you'll find that our safe, easy two-step plan will give you the tools you need to maintain a healthy weight for a lifetime. Hang in there . . . you can do it!

Excercise Quickies

We're all busy. So how can we find time to exercise? The following list offers little ways to stay fit during a busy day. They may seem small, but they add up throughout the course of a day.

- Do yard work.
- Schedule walk breaks instead of coffee breaks.
- Wash your car by hand.
- Walk the dog.
- Make more than one trip carrying laundry up the stairs or bringing in groceries.
- Do housework to fast music.

Quick-Fix
Appetizers
and Snacks

1

Oven-Fried Chicken Chunks with Peanut Sauce, 18

Thai-Spiced Cocktail Shrimp, 19

Spinach Quesadillas with Feta Cheese, 20

Layered Vegetable and Aioli Appetizer, 21

Roasted Red Pepper Bruschetta, 22

Rosemary Focaccia Wedges, 24

Black Bean–Corn Wonton Cups, 25

Caribbean Salsa Bites, 26

Sun-Dried Tomato Biscotti with Basil–Cream Cheese Topping, 28

Easy Salmon Pâté, 30

Herbed Seafood Spread, 32

Asiago Cheese and Artichoke Dip, 33

Gingered Caramel and Yogurt Dip, 34

Sweet-Hot Salsa, 36

Lime Tortilla Chips, 37

Caramelized-Sugar Popcorn, 39

Crunchy Fruit Snack Mix, 40

Layered Vegetable and Aioli Appetizer (page 21)

Oven-Fried Chicken Chunks with
Peanut Sauce

PREP: 10 MIN; BAKE: 25 MIN | 8 SERVINGS

1 pound boneless, skinless
  chicken breasts

1 1/2 cups cornflakes cereal,
  crushed (1/2 cup)

1/2 cup Reduced Fat
  Bisquick®

3/4 teaspoon paprika

1/4 teaspoon salt

1/4 teaspoon pepper

Cooking spray

Peanut Sauce (below)

Heat oven to 400°. Line jelly roll pan, 15 1/2 × 10 1/2 × 1 inch, with aluminum foil. Remove fat from chicken. Cut chicken into 1-inch pieces.

Mix remaining ingredients except cooking spray and Peanut Sauce in 2-quart resealable plastic food-storage bag. Shake about 6 chicken pieces at a time in bag until coated. Shake off any extra crumbs. Place chicken pieces in pan. Spray with cooking spray.

Bake uncovered 20 to 25 minutes or until coating is crisp and chicken is no longer pink in center. Serve with Peanut Sauce.

Peanut Sauce

1/2 cup plain fat-free yogurt

1/4 cup reduced-fat peanut butter spread

1/2 cup fat-free (skim) milk

1 tablespoon soy sauce

1/8 teaspoon ground red pepper (cayenne), if desired

Mix all ingredients in 10-inch nonstick skillet. Cook over medium heat 3 to 4 minutes, stirring occasionally, until mixture begins to thicken.

1 Serving

Calories 120
(Calories from Fat 25)

Fat 3g (Saturated 1g)

Cholesterol 35mg

Sodium 240mg

Carbohydrate 10g
(Dietary Fiber 0g)

Protein 13g

% Daily Value

Vitamin A 4%

Vitamin C 2%

Calcium 0%

Iron 12%

Diet Exchanges

1/2 Starch

1 1/2 Lean Meat

1 Eating Smart • Peanut butter isn't just for kids anymore. Rich in vitamins, minerals and heart-healthy fat, peanut butter provides satiety; a modest amount prevents overindulging in other foods. Reduced-fat peanut butters are also available, but don't forget to read labels—reduced-fat spreads are still high in calories and should be enjoyed in moderation.

2 Staying Active • If you feel pain (beyond mild discomfort) while exercising, stop and rest. Listen to your body. People often ignore pain, aggravating the problem; full recovery can then take weeks or months.

Thai-Spiced
Cocktail Shrimp

PREP: 20 MIN; CHILL: 4 HR; BAKE: 12 MIN | 12 SERVINGS (5 SHRIMP EACH)

1 1/2 pounds uncooked peeled deveined medium shrimp (about 60)

2 medium green onions, chopped (2 tablespoons)

2 cloves garlic, finely chopped

2 teaspoons grated lime peel

1/4 cup lime juice

1 tablespoon soy sauce

1/4 teaspoon pepper

1/8 teaspoon crushed red pepper

2 teaspoons sesame oil

Mix all ingredients except oil in large glass or plastic bowl. Cover and refrigerate at least 4 hours but no longer than 24 hours.

Heat oven to 400°. Spray rectangular pan, 13 × 9 × 2 inches, with cooking spray. Arrange shrimp in single layer in pan. Bake uncovered 10 to 12 minutes or until shrimp are pink and firm. Drizzle with oil. Serve hot.

1 Serving

Calories 50
(Calories from Fat 10)

Fat 1g (Saturated 0g)

Cholesterol 80mg

Sodium 170mg

Carbohydrate 1g
(Dietary Fiber 0g)

Protein 9g

% Daily Value

Vitamin A 2%

Vitamin C 2%

Calcium 2%

Iron 8%

Diet Exchanges

1 Very Lean Meat

1 Eating Smart • Shrimp is a lean source of protein, containing only about 100 calories and 2 grams of fat per 3-ounce serving. To enjoy shrimp at its nutritional best, use a low-fat cooking method such as broiling, grilling, baking, microwaving, boiling or steaming.

2 Staying Active • Cross training can keep you motivated and help reduce your risk of injury. Instead of doing the same activity every day, mix it up with other activities you enjoy. Running one day and swimming the next gives your leg muscles and joints a much-needed rest between runs.

Spinach Quesadillas with
Feta Cheese

PREP: 15 MIN; COOK: 12 MIN | 16 APPETIZERS

4 fat-free flour tortillas
(8 inches in diameter)

1/4 cup soft reduced-fat
cream cheese with roasted
garlic

2 cups frozen chopped
spinach, thawed and
squeezed to drain

1 tablespoon finely chopped
red onion

1/4 cup crumbled feta cheese
(1 ounce)

2 tablespoons fat-free sour
cream

Cherry tomato halves,
if desired

Sliced ripe olives, if desired

Spread 2 tortillas with cream cheese. Layer tortillas with
spinach, onion and feta cheese. Top with remaining
2 tortillas; press lightly.

Spray 12-inch nonstick skillet with cooking spray; heat
over medium heat. Cook each quesadilla in skillet 2 to
3 minutes on each side or until light golden brown.

Cut each quesadilla into 8 wedges. Top with sour cream,
tomato halves and olives. Secure with toothpicks.
Serve warm.

1 Appetizer

Calories 45
(Calories from Fat 10)

Fat 1g (Saturated 1g)

Cholesterol 5mg

Sodium 130mg

Carbohydrate 7g
(Dietary Fiber 0g)

Protein 2g

% Daily Value

Vitamin A 12%

Vitamin C 0%

Calcium 4%

Iron 2%

Diet Exchanges

1/2 Starch

1 **Eating Smart** • Instead of topping each individual appetizer, you may want to offer bowls of sliced ripe olives, chopped tomatoes and fat-free sour cream on the side.

2 **Staying Active** • You'll burn more calories walking when you go for the hills. It's no surprise that you burn more calories walking uphill compared to walking on level ground. But because your body spends energy holding you upright, you'll also burn more calories walking downhill compared to walking on the level.

Layered
Vegetable and Aioli Appetizer

PREP: 15 MIN; BAKE: 20 MIN | 12 SERVINGS

4 ounces fat-free cream
cheese, softened

1/2 cup fat-free mayonnaise

1 teaspoon finely chopped
garlic

1/2 teaspoon grated lemon
peel

Dash of ground red pepper
(cayenne)

2 medium bell peppers
(green, red or yellow), cut
into 1 1/2-inch pieces

1 small red onion, cut into
1-inch pieces

1 cup mushrooms

Olive oil–flavored cooking
spray

2 tablespoons crumbled
chèvre (goat) cheese

2 tablespoons chopped fresh
basil leaves

Crackers, if desired

Heat oven to 450°. Mix cream cheese, mayonnaise, garlic, lemon peel and red pepper in medium bowl until smooth. Cover and refrigerate while preparing vegetables.

Mix bell peppers, onion and mushrooms in medium bowl. Spray with cooking spray 2 or 3 times; toss to coat. Spread in ungreased jelly roll pan, 15 1/2 × 10 1/2 × 1 inch. Bake uncovered 15 to 20 minutes or until vegetables are tender; cool slightly. Coarsely chop vegetables.

Spread cream cheese mixture on serving platter. Top with vegetables. Sprinkle with chèvre cheese and basil. Serve with crackers.

1 Serving

Calories 25
(Calories from Fat 0)

Fat 0g (Saturated 0g)

Cholesterol 0mg

Sodium 135mg

Carbohydrate 4g
(Dietary Fiber 1g)

Protein 2g

% Daily Value

Vitamin A 16%

Vitamin C 32%

Calcium 4%

Iron 0%

Diet Exchanges

1 Vegetable

1 **Eating Smart** • Aioli is an intensely flavored garlic mayonnaise from southern France. Traditionally high in saturated fat and calories, aioli can be lightened by replacing the high-fat mayonnaise and other dairy ingredients with their fat-free counterparts.

2 **Staying Active** • You'll get more from a stair climber by holding the rails lightly, just enough to avoid losing your balance. Leaning on the rail or front monitor means you work less hard and reduce the number of calories you burn.

Roasted
Red Pepper Bruschetta

PREP: 10 MIN; BAKE: 8 MIN | 12 APPETIZERS

4 slices hard-crusted Italian or French bread, 1/2 inch thick

1 jar (7 ounces) roasted red bell peppers, drained and cut into 1/2-inch strips

1 or 2 medium cloves garlic, finely chopped

2 tablespoons chopped fresh parsley or 1 teaspoon parsley flakes

2 tablespoons shredded Parmesan cheese

1 tablespoon olive or vegetable oil

1/4 teaspoon salt

1/4 teaspoon pepper

1 tablespoon capers, drained, if desired

Heat oven to 450°. Place bread on ungreased cookie sheet. Mix remaining ingredients except capers. Spoon onto bread.

Bake 6 to 8 minutes or until edges of bread are golden brown. Cut each slice lengthwise into thirds. Sprinkle with capers.

1 Appetizer

Calories 40
(Calories from Fat 20)

Fat 2g (Saturated 0g)

Cholesterol 0mg

Sodium 105mg

Carbohydrate 4g
(Dietary Fiber 0g)

Protein 1g

% Daily Value

Vitamin A 6%

Vitamin C 20%

Calcium 2%

Iron 2%

Diet Exchanges

1/2 Starch

1 Eating Smart • Bruschetta (pronounced "broo-SKEH-tah" or "broo-SHEH-tah") is traditionally made by rubbing garlic cloves on toasted bread and drizzling with olive oil. We've lightened up our version of this Italian favorite by decreasing the olive oil and adding lots of flavorful ingredients. Small portions of healthy appetizers can support weight loss by taking the edge off your appetite so you won't overeat at mealtime.

2 Staying Active • Regular, moderate exercise has been shown to boost immunity, increasing the body's ability to ward off colds and other illnesses. But more is not always better. Long, intense exercise may actually depress immunity.

Roasted Red Pepper Bruschetta

Rosemary
Focaccia Wedges

PREP: 15 MIN; BAKE: 12 MIN | 6 APPETIZERS

Olive oil–flavored cooking spray

1 can (10 ounces) refrigerated pizza crust dough

3 cloves garlic, finely chopped

1/2 teaspoon dried rosemary leaves, crumbled

1 large sweet onion (Bermuda, Maui, Spanish or Vidalia), thinly sliced and separated into rings

3/4 cup grated fat-free Parmesan cheese topping (3 ounces)

1/4 teaspoon salt, if desired

Heat oven to 400°. Spray cookie sheet with cooking spray. Roll or pat pizza dough into 13 × 9-inch rectangle. Sprinkle with garlic and rosemary. Arrange onion rings evenly over dough. Sprinkle with cheese.

Bake about 12 minutes or until cheese just begins to brown. Lightly spray focaccia with cooking spray; sprinkle with salt. Cut into 6 wedges. Serve immediately.

1 Appetizer

Calories 165
(Calories from Fat 20)

Fat 2g (Saturated 1g)

Cholesterol 5mg

Sodium 440mg

Carbohydrate 35g
(Dietary Fiber 3g)

Protein 5g

% Daily Value

Vitamin A 0%

Vitamin C 0%

Calcium 6%

Iron 8%

Diet Exchanges

2 Starch

1 Vegetable

1 Eating Smart • Save calories and fat by using flavored cooking sprays instead of butter or oil. Look for butter, garlic, olive oil, sesame oil and lemon flavors.

2 Staying Active • Pump up your treadmill workout by swinging your arms while walking. Studies have found that treadmill walkers who used vigorous arm movements could boost their calorie burn by about half. Swinging your arms also strengthens your upper body.

Black Bean–Corn
Wonton Cups

PREP: 25 MIN; BAKE: 10 MIN | 36 APPETIZERS

36 wonton skins

2/3 cup thick-and-chunky salsa

1/4 cup chopped fresh cilantro

1/2 teaspoon ground cumin

1/2 teaspoon chili powder

1 can (15 1/4 ounces) whole kernel corn, drained

1 can (15 ounces) black beans, rinsed and drained

1/4 cup plus 2 tablespoons fat-free sour cream

Heat oven to 350°. Gently fit 1 wonton skin into each of 36 small muffin cups, 1 3/4 × 1 inch. Bake 8 to 10 minutes or until light golden brown. Remove from pan; cool on wire racks.

Mix remaining ingredients except sour cream and cilantro sprigs. Just before serving, spoon bean mixture into wonton cups. Top each with 1/2 teaspoon sour cream.

1 Appetizer

Calories 45
(Calories from Fat 0)

Fat 0g (Saturated 0g)

Cholesterol 5mg

Sodium 90mg

Carbohydrate 10g
(Dietary Fiber 1g)

Protein 2g

% Daily Value

Vitamin A 0%

Vitamin C 4%

Calcium 2%

Iron 4%

Diet Exchanges

1/2 Starch

1 Eating Smart • Black beans, like other legumes, provide plenty of complex carbohydrates and soluble fiber. Both nutrients can help with weight loss by making you feel full. As well, soluble fiber, when consumed regularly, may help lower blood cholesterol levels.

2 Staying Active • Afraid you'll increase your appetite by exercising? Don't worry. If you exercise moderately, you'll still eat about the same amount as if you were inactive. And because muscle weighs more than fat, you're more likely to become fit and trim by exercising regularly even if your body weight stays the same.

Caribbean
Salsa Bites

PREP: 15 MIN | 24 APPETIZERS

1/2 cup thick-and-chunky salsa

1/2 teaspoon jerk seasoning (dry)

2 teaspoons lime juice

2 teaspoons honey

24 Lime Tortilla Chips (page 37) or reduced-fat tortilla chips

1/4 cup fat-free black bean dip (from 9-ounce can)

1/4 cup golden raisins

1/4 cup reduced-fat or fat-free sour cream

24 fresh cilantro leaves, if desired

Mix salsa, jerk seasoning, lime juice and honey.

Top each Lime Tortilla Crisp with about 1/2 teaspoon black bean dip, 1 teaspoon salsa mixture, 2 or 3 raisins and 1/2 teaspoon sour cream. Garnish with cilantro leaf. Serve immediately.

1 Appetizer

Calories 20
(Calories from Fat 0)

Fat 0g (Saturated 0g)

Cholesterol 0mg

Sodium 35mg

Carbohydrate 4g
(Dietary Fiber 0g)

Protein 1g

% Daily Value

Vitamin A 0%

Vitamin C 2%

Calcium 0%

Iron 0%

Diet Exchanges

1 Serving Free

1 Eating Smart • If you're trying to lose weight, be extra careful when eating with others. Studies have shown that the larger number of people at a meal, the more each person tends to eat. But don't let this ruin your party. Just be aware of what and how much you eat, and appreciate the conversation as much as the food.

2 Staying Active • When shopping for a new treadmill or stationary bike, ask if you can try out the equipment in the store. You might also want to ask about the store policies regarding trial use of equipment at home and returns.

Caribbean Salsa Bites

Sun-Dried Tomato Biscotti with
Basil–Cream Cheese Topping

PREP: 20 MIN; BAKE: 50 MIN; COOL: 40 MIN | 32 APPETIZERS

1/4 cup sun-dried tomato halves (not oil-packed)

1/2 cup fat-free cholesterol-free egg product or 2 eggs

3 tablespoons olive or vegetable oil

2 cups all-purpose flour

1/4 cup sugar

2 teaspoons baking powder

1/4 teaspoon salt

1/8 teaspoon garlic powder

Dash of ground red pepper (cayenne)

Basil–Cream Cheese Topping (below)

1/4 cup crumbled chèvre (goat) cheese (1 ounce)

Heat oven to 350°. Pour enough boiling water over dried tomatoes to cover. Let stand 5 minutes; drain, reserving 2 tablespoons liquid. Finely chop tomatoes.

Mix egg product, oil and reserved tomato liquid until well blended. Stir in flour, sugar, baking powder, salt, garlic powder and red pepper. Stir in tomatoes. Divide dough in half. Shape each half into rectangle, 10 × 3 inches, on ungreased cookie sheet.

Bake 25 to 30 minutes or until golden brown. Cool on cookie sheet 10 minutes. Cut crosswise into 1/2-inch slices. Turn slices cut-side down on cookie sheet.

Bake 10 minutes. Turn biscotti. Bake about 10 minutes longer or until crisp and golden brown. Remove from cookie sheet to wire rack. Cool completely, about 30 minutes.

To serve, spread each biscotti with about 1/2 teaspoon Basil–Cream Cheese Topping. Sprinkle with about 1/2 teaspoon chèvre cheese.

Basil–Cream Cheese Topping

4 ounces reduced-fat cream cheese (Neufchâtel), softened

2 tablespoons chopped fresh or 1/2 teaspoon dried basil leaves

Dash of garlic powder

Mix all ingredients until smooth.

1 Appetizer	
Calories 60 (Calories from Fat 20)	
Fat 2g (Saturated 1g)	
Cholesterol 5mg	
Sodium 90mg	
Carbohydrate 8g (Dietary Fiber 0g)	
Protein 2g	

% Daily Value	
Vitamin A 0%	
Vitamin C 0%	
Calcium 2%	
Iron 2%	

Diet Exchanges	
1/2 Starch	
1/2 Fat	

1 **Eating Smart** • Sun-dried tomatoes add color and flavor to this savory cookie. Be sure to choose sun-dried tomatoes that aren't packed in a bottle or jar of oil. If you like fresh tomatoes, garnish with chopped roma (plum) tomatoes.

2 **Staying Active** • On average, a 200-pound person walking a mile and a half a day will lose 14 pounds a year. And this is without a change in eating habits!

Sun-Dried Tomato Biscotti with Basil–Cream Cheese Topping

Easy
Salmon Pâté

PREP: 15 MIN; CHILL: 2 HR | 16 SERVINGS (2 TABLESPOONS EACH)

1 package (8 ounces) fat-free cream cheese, softened

1 can (14 3/4 ounces) red or pink salmon, drained and flaked

3 tablespoons finely chopped red onion

2 tablespoons chopped fresh or 1/4 teaspoon dried dill weed

1 tablespoon Dijon mustard

2 tablespoons capers

Assorted crackers or pumpernickel cocktail bread, if desired

Line 2-cup bowl or mold with plastic wrap. Beat cream cheese in medium bowl with electric mixer on medium speed until smooth. Stir in salmon, 2 tablespoons of the red onion, 1 tablespoon of the dill weed and the mustard. Spoon into bowl lined with plastic wrap, pressing firmly. Cover and refrigerate at least 2 hours but no longer than 24 hours.

Turn upside down onto serving plate; remove bowl and plastic wrap. Garnish pâté with remaining 1 tablespoon red onion, 1 tablespoon dill weed and the capers. Serve with crackers.

1 Serving

Calories 50
(Calories from Fat 20)

Fat 2g (Saturated 0g)

Cholesterol 10mg

Sodium 240mg

Carbohydrate 1g
(Dietary Fiber 0g)

Protein 7g

% Daily Value

Vitamin A 8%

Vitamin C 0%

Calcium 8%

Iron 0%

Diet Exchanges

1 Lean Meat

1 Eating Smart • Many packaged crackers are loaded with fat. If you want to see how much fat is in a cracker, but don't have access to the box, rub it with a paper napkin. Crackers that leave grease marks are probably high in fat, so you might want to eat them in small amounts.

2 Staying Active • We've heard it before, but it's worth repeating: spot reduction does not work. Studies show that people who regularly do as many as 100 sit-ups a day have no significant loss of abdominal fat. If you'd like to trim your waist or tummy, concentrate on aerobic exercise for fat burning and do sit-ups to help tone stomach muscles.

Easy Salmon Pâté

Herbed
Seafood Spread

PREP: 15 MIN; CHILL: 1 HR; BROIL: 6 MIN | 24 APPETIZERS

1/3 cup chopped sweet onion
   (Bermuda, Maui, Spanish
   or Vidalia)

1 tablespoon chopped fresh
   chives

1 tablespoon chopped fresh
   basil leaves

1 tablespoon chopped fresh
   mint leaves

1 tablespoon olive or
   vegetable oil

1 tablespoon lemon juice

2 small roma (plum) tomatoes,
   chopped (1/2 cup)

2 medium cloves garlic, finely
   chopped

1 can (6 ounces) crabmeat,
   drained, cartilage removed
   and flaked

1 can (4 to 4 1/2 ounces) tiny
   shrimp, rinsed, drained
   and chopped

1 baguette (about 24 inches),
   cut into 24 slices

3 tablespoons olive or
   vegetable oil

Freshly ground pepper,
   if desired

Mix all ingredients except baguette, 3 tablespoons olive oil and the pepper in glass or plastic bowl. Cover and refrigerate at least 1 hour but no longer than 4 hours.

Set oven control to broil. Place baguette slices on ungreased cookie sheet. Brush with 1 1/2 tablespoons oil; sprinkle with pepper. Broil with tops 4 to 6 inches from heat 2 to 3 minutes or until light golden brown; turn slices. Brush with remaining 1 1/2 tablespoons oil; sprinkle with pepper. Broil 2 to 3 minutes longer or until light golden brown.

Place seafood mixture in serving bowl. Serve with toasted baguette slices.

1 Appetizer

Calories 60
(Calories from Fat 20)

Fat 2g (Saturated 0g)

Cholesterol 15mg

Sodium 230mg

Carbohydrate 8g
(Dietary Fiber 1g)

Protein 4g

% Daily Value

Vitamin A 0%

Vitamin C 2%

Calcium 2%

Iron 4%

Diet Exchanges

1 1/2 Vegetable

1/2 Fat

1 **Eating Smart** • Fresh herbs bring out-of-this-world flavors to a low-fat kitchen. Add finely chopped parsley, chives, basil, mint or tarragon to low-fat sour cream or cream cheese for a savory dip or cracker spread.

2 **Staying Active** • Curious as to how quickly you walk? Assuming your stride is 3 feet long, count how many steps you take in a minute and divide by 30. For example, if you take 105 steps per minute, you walk 3 1/2 miles per hour.

Asiago Cheese and
Artichoke Dip

PREP: 15 MIN; BAKE: 15 MIN | 16 SERVINGS (2 TABLESPOONS EACH)

1 package (8 ounces) fat-free cream cheese

1/2 cup fat-free sour cream

2 tablespoons fat-free half-and-half or evaporated fat-free milk

1/4 teaspoon salt

3/4 cup shredded Asiago cheese (3 ounces)

1 can (14 ounces) artichoke hearts, drained and chopped

4 medium green onions, chopped (1/4 cup)

2 tablespoons chopped fresh parsley

Crisp breadsticks or crackers, if desired

Heat oven to 350°. Beat cream cheese in medium bowl with electric mixer on medium speed until smooth. Beat in sour cream, half-and-half and salt. Stir in Asiago cheese, artichoke hearts and onions. Spoon into 1-quart casserole or small ovenproof serving dish.

Bake uncovered 10 to 15 minutes or until hot and cheese is melted. Remove from oven; stir. Sprinkle with parsley. Serve with breadsticks.

Microwave Directions: Use microwavable casserole or dish. Microwave uncovered on High 1 to 2 minutes, stirring every 30 seconds.

1 Serving
Calories 45 (Calories from Fat 10)
Fat 1g (Saturated 0g)
Cholesterol 0mg
Sodium 220mg
Carbohydrate 5g (Dietary Fiber 1g)
Protein 5g

% Daily Value
Vitamin A 10%
Vitamin C 2%
Calcium 8%
Iron 2%

Diet Exchanges
1/2 Very Lean Meat
1 Vegetable

1 **Eating Smart** • A semi-firm Italian cheese with a rich, nutty flavor, Asiago is made from part-skim or whole cow's milk. Full of flavor, a little of this cheese goes a long way in satisfying you. Enjoy crisp breadsticks, raw veggies or baked pita or tortilla chips with this tasty, low-fat Asiago dip.

2 **Staying Active** • How often do you need to replace exercise shoes? Exercise shoes typically lose about one-third of their ability to absorb shock after 500 miles of use; they may also wear unevenly. Shock-absorption is an important factor in protecting your joints from injury, so don't go by appearance alone. Loss of cushioning in the shock-absorbent midsole occurs long before the outer or upper shoe shows signs of wear and tear.

Gingered
Caramel and Yogurt Dip

PREP: 10 MIN; CHILL: 30 MIN | 8 SERVINGS (2 TABLESPOONS EACH)

4 ounces fat-free cream
cheese, softened

1/2 cup vanilla low-fat
yogurt

1/4 cup plus 1 to 2 teaspoons
caramel fat-free topping

1 tablespoon chopped
crystallized ginger

Apple slices, if desired

Pear slices, if desired

Beat cream cheese in medium bowl with electric mixer on
medium speed until creamy. Beat in yogurt and 1/4 cup
of the topping until smooth. Cover and refrigerate at
least 30 minutes until chilled.

Spoon dip into small serving bowl. Drizzle with 1 to
2 teaspoons topping; swirl with tip of knife. Sprinkle
with ginger. Serve with apple and pear slices.

1 Serving

Calories 60
(Calories from Fat 0)

Fat 0g (Saturated 0g)

Cholesterol 0mg

Sodium 120mg

Carbohydrate 12g
(Dietary Fiber 0g)

Protein 3g

% Daily Value

Vitamin A 8%

Vitamin C 0%

Calcium 6%

Iron 0%

Diet Exchanges

1 Starch

1 Eating Smart • Most store-bought dips are usually
high in saturated fat, calories and sodium. They contain,
on average, three times the calories and ten times the fat
of homemade dips made with low-fat dairy products
such as yogurt or reduced-fat cream cheese.

2 Staying Active • Stand up! By sitting down, you
burn only about 1 calorie per hour for every 2.2 pounds
of body weight. You can increase this number significantly simply by standing or, better yet, taking a walk.

Gingered Caramel and Yogurt Dip

Sweet-Hot
Salsa

1 medium papaya, peeled,
  seeded and chopped
  (1 1/2 cups)

1 small cucumber, peeled and
  chopped (1 cup)

1 small carrot, shredded
  (1/3 cup)

1 small jalapeño chili, seeded
  and finely chopped

1 tablespoon lime juice

1 tablespoon white vinegar

1/2 teaspoon sugar

1/4 teaspoon salt

Mix all ingredients in glass or plastic bowl. Cover and refrigerate at least 4 hours to blend flavors but no longer than 2 days. Stir salsa before serving.

1 Serving

Calories 30
(Calories from Fat 0)

Fat 0g (Saturated 0g)

Cholesterol 0mg

Sodium 90mg

Carbohydrate 7g
(Dietary Fiber 1g)

Protein 1g

% Daily Value

Vitamin A 16%

Vitamin C 70%

Calcium 2%

Iron 0%

Diet Exchanges

1/2 Fruit

Eating Smart • Papayas, once considered exotic, now appear regularly in mainstream grocery stores. Low in calories (about 25 per cubed 1/2 cup), papayas are nearly fat free. They also provide plenty of fiber and vitamins A and C—nutrients essential to good health.

Staying Active • Walkers, take note—walking on sand or soft dirt will boost your energy expenditure by as much as one-third. More energy expended means more calories burned and better conditioning.

Lime
Tortilla Chips

PREP: 10 MIN; BAKE: 10 MIN | 6 SERVINGS (8 CHIPS EACH)

1/2 teaspoon grated lime peel

Dash of salt

2 tablespoons lime juice

2 teaspoons olive or
  vegetable oil

2 teaspoons honey

4 fat-free flour tortillas
  (8 inches in diameter)

Heat oven to 350°. Spray large cookie sheet with cooking spray. Mix all ingredients except tortillas. Brush lime mixture on both sides of each tortilla. Cut each tortilla into 12 wedges. Place in single layer on cookie sheet.

Bake 8 to 10 minutes or until crisp and light golden brown; cool. Store in airtight container at room temperature.

1 Serving

Calories 100
(Calories from Fat 20)

Fat 2g (Saturated 0g)

Cholesterol 0mg

Sodium 230mg

Carbohydrate 18g
(Dietary Fiber 0g)

Protein 2g

% Daily Value

Vitamin A 0%

Vitamin C 0%

Calcium 0%

Iron 2%

Diet Exchanges

1 Starch

1 **Eating Smart** • Use the grated peel, or zest, of citrus fruits to bring fat-free flavor to spreads, marinades, dips, dressings, baked goods and sauces. For an additional fat-free flavor boost, combine grated peel with the juice of the same fruit.

2 **Staying Active** • Your mind is your most powerful piece of exercise equipment. If you believe there's no way you'll ever shed extra pounds, you won't. Believe you can achieve, and you will!

Snack Attack

Snacks are not diet-busting demons. In fact, snacks are now considered essential to healthy weight loss. Keeping energy levels up—and the urge to overeat down—is easier when you eat nutritious snacks. Curb between-meal hunger with any of these high-energy, low-cal foods, all weighing in at **100 calories or less**. So what are you craving? Something . . .

Crunchy

- 1 cup baby-cut carrots
- 2 cups raw broccoli and cauliflower flowerets
- 1 bag (4 ounces) fat-free caramel rice cakes
- 3 cups air-popped popcorn with 1 tablespoon grated fat-free Parmesan cheese topping
- 50 thin pretzel sticks (2 1/4 inches)
- 5 low-fat whole-grain crackers
- 10 baked potato chips with 2 tablespoons fat-free dip
- 9 animal crackers
- 3 graham cracker squares (2 1/2 inch)
- 6 reduced-fat vanilla wafers
- 2 small gingersnap cookies

Chewy

- 1/2 bagel with 1 tablespoon fat-free cream cheese
- 8 dried apricot halves
- 2 tablespoons raisins or dried cranberries

Creamy

- 1 carton (6 ounces) unsweetened applesauce
- 1/2 cup fat-free ice cream or frozen yogurt
- 1/2 cup fat-free yogurt
- 1/2 cup sugar-free pudding (made with fat-free milk)
- 1 cup sugar-free hot chocolate with 8 mini marshmallows
- 1/2 cup low-fat cottage cheese

Caramelized-Sugar
Popcorn

PREP: 10 MIN; COOK: 5 MIN | 10 SERVINGS (1 CUP EACH)

1/4 teaspoon salt

10 cups hot-air-popped popcorn

1/2 cup sugar

2 teaspoons margarine or butter

Sprinkle salt over popcorn in large bowl; set aside.

Place sugar in 4-quart Dutch oven. Heat over medium heat, shaking Dutch oven occasionally (do not stir), until sugar starts to melt. Reduce heat to low. Add margarine. Heat, stirring constantly, until sugar is completely melted and golden.

Remove Dutch oven from heat. Immediately add popcorn, stirring to coat. Quickly transfer to large bowl; cool. Store in airtight container at room temperature.

1 **Eating Smart** • Because 1 cup of air-popped popcorn has a mere 30 calories, downing 3 or 4 cups of popcorn will fill you up for about 100 calories! Another way to look at it: You can eat only 20 potato chips for the same number of calories found in 6 cups of popcorn.

2 **Staying Active** • Cross-country skiing is a fantastic exercise in terms of all-around aerobic benefits. Burning as many as 900 calories an hour, cross-country skiers use muscles in their shoulders, back, chest, stomach, buttocks and legs. Cross-country skiing also spares your legs the wear and tear that comes with joint-jarring activities such as running.

1 Serving

Calories 75
(Calories from Fat 10)

Fat 1g (Saturated 0g)

Cholesterol 0mg

Sodium 70mg

Carbohydrate 16g
(Dietary Fiber 1g)

Protein 1g

% Daily Value

Vitamin A 0%

Vitamin C 0%

Calcium 0%

Iron 0%

Diet Exchanges

1 Starch

Crunchy
Fruit Snack Mix

PREP: 15 MIN; BAKE: 15 MIN | 14 SERVINGS (1/2 CUP EACH)

4 cups Total® Raisin Bran, Total Corn Flakes or Whole Grain Total cereal

1/3 cup sliced almonds

1 package (8 ounces) mixed dried fruit, cut into 1/2-inch pieces

1/4 cup packed brown sugar

2 tablespoons margarine or butter

2 teaspoons ground cinnamon

1 teaspoon ground ginger

Heat oven to 300°. Place cereal, almonds and fruit in large bowl. Heat brown sugar and margarine in 1-quart saucepan over low heat, stirring occasionally, until margarine is melted. Stir in cinnamon and ginger.

Pour sugar mixture over cereal mixture; toss until evenly coated. Spread in ungreased jelly roll pan, 15 1/2 × 10 1/2 × 1 inch. Bake 15 minutes, stirring twice; cool. Store in airtight container at room temperature.

1 Serving

Calories 120 (Calories from Fat 30)

Fat 3g (Saturated 0g)

Cholesterol 0mg

Sodium 95mg

Carbohydrate 27g (Dietary Fiber 3g)

Protein 2g

% Daily Value

Vitamin A 16%

Vitamin C 0%

Calcium 8%

Iron 32%

Diet Exchanges

1 Starch

1 Fruit

1 **Eating Smart** • If you're trying to lose weight, dried fruit can help you feel full and give you a quick burst of energy. Combine with complex carbohydrates and protein to keep energy levels high. As with any food, the key is moderation—a handful of mixed dried fruit (about 1/4 cup) can pack as many as 120 calories.

2 **Staying Active** • Golfers can reap fitness rewards by walking instead of riding a cart. By playing an 18-hole course, you cover about 5 miles and burn about 500 calories. Carry your bag, and you could burn an additional 100 calories.

Crunchy Fruit Snack Mix

Favorite Breakfasts

2

Spring Vegetable Frittata, 44

Mediterranean Eggs, 45

Country Eggs in Tortilla Cups, 46

Cinnamon-Raisin French Toast, 48

Whole Wheat Waffles, 49

Ginger Pancakes with Lemon–Cream Cheese Topping, 50

Cocoa Crepes with Strawberry-Banana Filling, 52

Peach-Almond Coffee Cake, 54

Carrot-Pineapple Bread, 55

Fruited Bread Pudding with Eggnog Sauce, 56

Orange-Cranberry Scones, 58

Old-Fashioned Blueberry Muffins, 60

Tropical Banana Muffins, 62

Chai Tea, 63

Apple-Kiwi Smoothie, 64

Triple-Fruit Yogurt Smoothie, 66

Bagel and Cream Cheese Morning Mix, 67

Spring Vegetable Frittata (page 44)

Spring
Vegetable Frittata

PREP: 20 MIN; BAKE: 12 MIN | 6 SERVINGS

2 tablespoons margarine or
  butter

1 medium onion, chopped
  (1/2 cup)

1 clove garlic, finely chopped

1 medium green or red bell
  pepper, chopped (1 cup)

2 small zucchini, chopped
  (2 cups)

1 small tomato, chopped
  (1/2 cup)

1/4 teaspoon salt

1/4 teaspoon pepper

1 1/2 cups fat-free
  cholesterol-free egg
  product

1/4 cup grated Parmesan
  cheese

Heat oven to 375°.

Melt margarine in 10-inch ovenproof skillet over medium-
  high heat. Cook onion and garlic in margarine 3 minutes,
  stirring frequently. Stir in bell pepper; reduce heat to
  medium. Cook about 2 minutes, stirring occasionally,
  until crisp-tender. Stir in zucchini, tomato, salt and
  pepper. Cook 4 minutes, stirring occasionally. Stir in
  egg product.

Bake 10 to 12 minutes or until set in center. Sprinkle
  with cheese. Cut into wedges.

1 Serving

Calories 80
(Calories from Fat 45)

Fat 5g (Saturated 1g)

Cholesterol 5mg

Sodium 270mg

Carbohydrate 5g
(Dietary Fiber 2g)

Protein 6g

% Daily Value

Vitamin A 10%

Vitamin C 20%

Calcium 6%

Iron 6%

Diet Exchanges

1 Lean Meat

1 Vegetable

1 **Eating Smart** • Egg substitutes can replace whole
   eggs in nearly any breakfast egg dish without a loss of
   flavor or texture. Most egg substitutes are based on egg
   whites, making them low cal and fat free.

2 **Staying Active** • For best results in sticking to an
   exercise program, match your personality with your activity. If you enjoy solitude, try cycling, jogging or jumping
   rope. Competitive people might do well with basketball,
   soccer or tennis. And for those who are easily bored? Try
   aerobic dance, cross-country skiing or ice skating.

Mediterranean
Eggs

PREP: 10 MIN; COOK: 8 MIN | 2 SERVINGS

1 teaspoon olive or
   vegetable oil

4 medium green onions,
   chopped (1/4 cup)

1 medium tomato, chopped
   (3/4 cup)

1 tablespoon chopped fresh
   or 1 teaspoon dried basil
   leaves

1 cup fat-free cholesterol-
   free egg product or 2 eggs
   plus 2 egg whites

Freshly ground pepper,
   if desired

Heat oil in 8-inch nonstick skillet over medium heat.
Cook onions in oil 2 minutes, stirring occasionally. Stir
in tomato and basil. Cook about 1 minute, stirring
occasionally, until tomato is heated through.

Beat egg product thoroughly with fork or wire whisk;
pour over tomato mixture. As mixture begins to set at
bottom and side, gently lift cooked portions with spatula
so that thin, uncooked portion can flow to bottom.
Avoid constant stirring. Cook 3 to 4 minutes or until
eggs are thickened throughout but still moist. Sprinkle
with pepper.

1 Serving

Calories 90
(Calories from Fat 20)

Fat 2g (Saturated 0g)

Cholesterol 0mg

Sodium 170mg

Carbohydrate 7g
(Dietary Fiber 2g)

Protein 11g

% Daily Value

Vitamin A 10%

Vitamin C 10%

Calcium 4%

Iron 14%

Diet Exchanges

1 1/2 Lean Meat

1 Vegetable

1 **Eating Smart** • Investing in good-quality nonstick cookware is an easy way to reduce the use of fat
in your cooking. If you keep the heat low enough, you
won't need any fat to keep your food from sticking.
And reducing the oil or butter in your diet can save
mega calories. At 120 calories per tablespoon, oil has
even more calories than butter's 100 per tablespoon.

2 **Staying Active** • Bend your exercise shoes
before you buy them. If the shoe bends at mid-foot
instead of at the ball where your foot naturally bends,
it will offer little support. Also, if the shoe bends too
easily or too stiffly, you need to keep shopping.

Country Eggs in
Tortilla Cups

PREP: 10 MIN; BAKE: 10 MIN; COOK: 10 MIN | 4 SERVINGS

4 flour tortillas (6 inches in diameter)

Cooking spray

2 cups frozen fat-free Southern-style hash brown potatoes

1/4 cup chopped green bell pepper

4 medium green onions, chopped (1/4 cup)

1 cup fat-free cholesterol-free egg product or 2 eggs plus 2 egg whites

3 tablespoons water

1/4 teaspoon salt

1/4 cup shredded reduced-fat Cheddar cheese (1 ounce)

2 tablespoons fat-free sour cream

Salsa, if desired

Heat oven to 400°. Turn four 6-ounce custard cups upside down onto cookie sheet. Spray both sides of each tortilla lightly with cooking spray. Place tortilla over each cup, gently pressing edges toward cup. Bake 8 to 10 minutes or until light golden brown. Remove from cups; place upright on serving plates.

Spray 8- or 10-inch nonstick skillet with cooking spray; heat over medium heat. Cook hash browns, bell pepper and onions in skillet about 5 minutes, stirring occasionally, until hash browns are light brown. Mix egg product, water and salt; stir into hash browns. Cook about 3 minutes, stirring occasionally, until eggs are just about set.

Spoon one-fourth of the egg mixture into each tortilla cup. Top with cheese and sour cream. Serve immediately with salsa.

1 Serving

Calories 195
(Calories from Fat 20)

Fat 2g (Saturated 1g)

Cholesterol 0mg

Sodium 670mg

Carbohydrate 36g
(Dietary Fiber 3g)

Protein 11g

% Daily Value

Vitamin A 6%

Vitamin C 12%

Calcium 10%

Iron 12%

Diet Exchanges

2 Starch

1/2 Very Lean Meat

1 Vegetable

1 Eating Smart • Have your morning toast with pear or apple butter, marmalade, all-fruit jam or mashed banana. You'll enjoy the fresh, bright colors and flavors of fruit while eliminating the fat and reducing the calories found in butter and other high-fat spreads.

2 Staying Active • Use visualization to improve your workouts. Before you start exercising, picture yourself running (or biking or walking) with strength and ease. Research has shown that visualization can enhance your performance.

Country Eggs in Tortilla Cups

Cinnamon-Raisin
French Toast

PREP: 5 MIN; COOK: 16 MIN | 4 SERVINGS

3/4 cup fat-free cholesterol-free egg product or 2 eggs plus 1 egg white

3/4 cup fat-free (skim) milk

1 tablespoon sugar

1/4 teaspoon vanilla

1/8 teaspoon salt

8 slices cinnamon-raisin bread

Beat egg product, milk, sugar, vanilla and salt with hand beater until smooth.

Spray griddle or 10-inch skillet with cooking spray. Heat griddle to 375° or heat skillet over medium heat. (To test, sprinkle with a few drops of water. If bubbles jump around, heat is just right.)

Dip bread into egg mixture, coating both sides. Place on griddle. Cook about 4 minutes on each side or until golden brown.

1 **Eating Smart •** To save fat and calories, skip the butter and margarine. Top waffles, pancakes and French toast with modest amounts of syrup, molasses, apple-sauce, fruit preserves or fresh fruit slices.

2 **Staying Active •** If you're new to exercising, check with your doctor first. Checking with a physician is especially important if you're over 35; you're at least 25 pounds overweight; you have a personal or family history of high blood pressure or heart disease; and/or you haven't had a medical checkup recently.

1 Serving

Calories 180
(Calories from Fat 20)

Fat 2g (Saturated 0g)

Cholesterol 0mg

Sodium 440mg

Carbohydrate 32g
(Dietary Fiber 2g)

Protein 10g

% Daily Value

Vitamin A 4%

Vitamin C 0%

Calcium 12%

Iron 12%

Diet Exchanges

2 Starch

Whole Wheat
Waffles

PREP: 10 MIN; BAKE: 15 MIN | 12 SERVINGS

1/2 cup fat-free cholesterol-free egg product or 2 eggs

2 cups whole wheat flour

1/4 cup margarine or butter, melted

1 3/4 cups fat-free (skim) milk

1 tablespoon sugar

3 teaspoons baking powder

1/2 teaspoon salt

6 tablespoons wheat germ

Spray nonstick waffle iron with cooking spray; heat waffle iron. Beat egg product in medium bowl with hand beater until fluffy. Beat in remaining ingredients except wheat germ just until smooth.

For each waffle, pour about one-third of batter onto center of hot waffle iron; sprinkle with 2 tablespoons wheat germ. Bake about 5 minutes or until steaming stops. Carefully remove waffle.

1 Serving	
Calories 135 (Calories from Fat 45)	
Fat 5g (Saturated 1g)	
Cholesterol 0mg	
Sodium 300mg	
Carbohydrate 20g (Dietary Fiber 3g)	
Protein 6g	

% Daily Value	
Vitamin A 8%	
Vitamin C 0%	
Calcium 12%	
Iron 8%	

Diet Exchanges	
1 1/2 Starch	
1/2 Fat	

1 Eating Smart • At 25 calories per tablespoon, wheat germ is a concentrated source of vitamins, minerals and protein. Its nutty flavor enriches both sweet and savory fare. Stir wheat germ into batters for baked goods, pancakes and waffles. Or top muffins, cereal or veggies with this flavor-rich whole grain.

2 Staying Active • Do you have to be a runner to experience "runner's high"? The answer is no. But you do need to exercise aerobically. When you ask your body to do more than it's used to doing, your brain produces endorphins. Similar to morphine-like painkillers, endorphins are responsible for keeping you going without too much physical discomfort. This experience produces the "rush" enjoyed by many regular aerobic exercisers.

Ginger Pancakes with
Lemon–Cream Cheese Topping

PREP: 10 MIN; COOK: 10 MIN | 8 SERVINGS (2 PANCAKES AND 2 TEASPOONS TOPPING)

Lemon–Cream Cheese
   Topping (below)

1/4 cup fat-free cholesterol-
   free egg product or 1 egg

1 1/3 cups all-purpose flour

1 1/4 cups fat-free (skim)
   milk

1/4 cup molasses

2 tablespoons vegetable oil

1 teaspoon baking powder

1 teaspoon ground cinnamon

1/2 teaspoon ground ginger

1/4 teaspoon baking soda

1/4 teaspoon salt

Make Lemon–Cream Cheese Topping. Beat egg product in medium bowl with hand beater until fluffy. Beat in remaining ingredients just until smooth.

Spray griddle or 10-inch skillet with cooking spray. Heat griddle to 375° or heat skillet over medium heat. (To test, sprinkle with a few drops of water. If bubbles jump around, heat is just right.)

For each pancake, pour scant 1/4 cup batter onto hot griddle. Cook pancakes until puffed. Turn and cook other sides until dry around edges. Serve with topping.

Lemon–Cream Cheese Topping

3 ounces reduced-fat cream cheese (Neufchâtel), softened

1 tablespoon powdered sugar

1/2 teaspoon grated lemon peel

1 1/2 teaspoons lemon juice

Beat all ingredients with electric mixer on medium speed until fluffy.

1 Serving	
Calories 180 (Calories from Fat 55)	
Fat 6g (Saturated 2g)	
Cholesterol 10mg	
Sodium 125mg	
Carbohydrate 27g (Dietary Fiber 1g)	
Protein 5g	

% Daily Value	
Vitamin A 4%	
Vitamin C 0%	
Calcium 12%	
Iron 10%	

Diet Exchanges	
2 Starch	
1/2 Fat	

1 **Eating Smart** • Molasses, the rich, syrupy by-product of cane sugar refining, adds loads of intense flavor to baked goods. One tablespoon contains only about 50 calories and no fat. You can also use molasses as you would honey, drizzling it over cereal and toast.

2 **Staying Active** • Want to lose 25 pounds? Try this: Forty-five minutes of brisk walking (about 4 miles per hour) burns approximately 244 calories. Multiply that by 365 days per year to get 89,060 calories burned. Divide this number by 3,500 (the number of calories in a pound). You could walk off 25 pounds in one year!

Ginger Pancakes with Lemon–Cream Cheese Topping

Cocoa Crepes with
Strawberry-Banana Filling

PREP: 10 MIN; COOK: 25 MIN | 4 SERVINGS (2 CREPES EACH)

1 1/4 cups chocolate-flavored fat-free (skim) milk

1/2 cup fat-free cholesterol-free egg product or 2 eggs

1 cup all-purpose flour

1 container (8 ounces) strawberry low-fat yogurt (1 cup)

1 medium banana, sliced

8 strawberries, sliced

1 to 2 tablespoons powdered sugar

2 tablespoons chocolate-flavored syrup

Mix milk, egg product and flour in medium bowl until smooth.

Spray 8- or 10-inch nonstick skillet with cooking spray; heat over medium heat. For each crepe, pour 1/4 cup batter into skillet, and quickly rotate skillet to coat bottom with batter, forming a thin layer. Cook about 2 minutes or until edge is set; turn and cook other side about 30 seconds. Repeat with remaining batter, making 7 more crepes. Stack crepes on plate to keep warm.

To serve, spoon about 2 tablespoons yogurt down center of each crepe. Top with one-eighth of the banana slices; roll up. Place 2 filled crepes on each plate. Top with strawberries, sprinkle with powdered sugar and drizzle with chocolate syrup.

1 **Eating Smart** • Keep croissants to a minimum. These French pastries may seem light and airy, but they actually contain twelve times as much fat and 50 percent more calories than an English muffin of equal weight.

2 **Staying Active** • Walk to the gym, tennis court or kick-boxing class instead of driving. Fifteen minutes each way at a brisk pace will burn calories and serve as a great warm-up and cool-down.

1 Serving

Calories 250 (Calories from Fat 10)

Fat 1g (Saturated 1g)

Cholesterol 0mg

Sodium 150mg

Carbohydrate 53g (Dietary Fiber 3g)

Protein 11g

% Daily Value

Vitamin A 6%

Vitamin C 28%

Calcium 16%

Iron 12%

Diet Exchanges

1 Starch

2 Fruit

1/2 Skim Milk

Cocoa Crepes with Strawberry-Banana Filling

Peach-Almond
Coffee Cake

PREP: 10 MIN; BAKE: 30 MIN | 10 SERVINGS

2/3 cup fat-free (skim) milk

1/4 cup fat-free cholesterol-free egg product or 1 egg

1 tablespoon vegetable oil

1/2 teaspoon almond extract

2 cups Reduced Fat Bisquick

1/3 cup sugar

1 cup chopped fresh or frozen (thawed) peaches

1/2 cup vanilla fat-free yogurt

2 tablespoons packed brown sugar

2 tablespoons sliced almonds

Heat oven to 375°. Spray round pan, 8 × 1 1/2 inches, with cooking spray. Mix milk, egg product, oil and almond extract in large bowl until smooth. Stir in Bisquick and sugar until Bisquick is moistened (batter will be lumpy). Spread batter in pan.

Mix peaches and yogurt; spoon onto batter. Swirl lightly with knife. Sprinkle with brown sugar and almonds. Bake 25 to 30 minutes or until toothpick inserted in cake near center comes out clean. Serve warm or cool. Store covered in refrigerator.

1 Serving

Calories 170
(Calories from Fat 35)

Fat 4g (Saturated 1g)

Cholesterol 0mg

Sodium 290mg

Carbohydrate 30g
(Dietary Fiber 1g)

Protein 4g

% Daily Value

Vitamin A 2%

Vitamin C 0%

Calcium 6%

Iron 6%

Diet Exchanges

1 Starch

1 Fruit

1/2 Fat

1 **Eating Smart** • Are nuts to be banished from the table if you're trying to lose weight? Not necessarily. Studies have shown that occasionally eating a small handful of nuts (about 1/4 cup) does not cause weight gain. It may be that the satisfaction provided by the fat in the nuts makes people eat less overall.

2 **Staying Active** • Outdoor exercisers should dress in layers when cold weather comes. Heat is easily trapped between clothing layers, so you'll stay warmer. You can peel off layers as your body temperature rises.

Carrot-Pineapple
Bread

PREP: 15 MIN; BAKE: 55 MIN; COOL: 1 HR | 1 LOAF (16 SLICES)

1 can (8 ounces) crushed
    pineapple in juice, drained
    and juice reserved

2 tablespoons vegetable oil

1/4 cup fat-free cholesterol-
    free egg product or 1 egg

1 1/2 cups all-purpose flour

3/4 cup packed brown sugar

1/2 cup raisins

1 teaspoon baking powder

1/2 teaspoon baking soda

1/2 teaspoon salt

1/2 teaspoon ground
    cinnamon

1 large carrot, shredded
    (1 cup)

Heat oven to 350°. Spray loaf pan, 8 1/2 × 4 1/2 × 2 1/2 inches, with cooking spray. Discard 3 tablespoons of the pineapple juice. Mix remaining juice, pineapple, oil and egg product in medium bowl. Stir in remaining ingredients until blended. Spread batter in pan.

Bake 50 to 55 minutes or until toothpick inserted in center comes out clean. Cool 10 minutes; remove from pan to wire rack. Cool completely, about 1 hour, before slicing.

1 Slice

Calories 125
(Calories from Fat 20)

Fat 2g (Saturated 0g)

Cholesterol 0mg

Sodium 160mg

Carbohydrate 26g
(Dietary Fiber 1g)

Protein 2g

% Daily Value

Vitamin A 10%

Vitamin C 0%

Calcium 4%

Iron 6%

Diet Exchanges

1 Starch

1 Fruit

1 **Eating Smart** • Breakfast eaters have better over-all nutrition intakes than those who skip morning meals. Even when you're in a hurry, you can fuel up with a good breakfast. If you don't have time for a leisurely breakfast, grab a slice of quick bread, a carton of yogurt and a handful of berries on your way out the door.

2 **Staying Active** • Runners and walkers know the benefits of continually finding new exercise routes. If you're looking for a new route, you might want to first scope out the area by car. Not only will you make sure the area is safe, but you can also measure your mileage.

Fruited Bread
Pudding with Eggnog Sauce

PREP: 15 MIN; BAKE: 45 MIN | 8 SERVINGS

4 cups 1-inch cubes French bread

1/2 cup diced dried fruit and raisin mixture

2 cups fat-free (skim) milk

1/2 cup fat-free cholesterol-free egg product or 2 eggs

1/3 cup sugar

1/2 teaspoon vanilla

Ground nutmeg, if desired

Eggnog Sauce (below)

Heat oven to 350°. Spray pie plate, 9 × 1 1/4 inches, with cooking spray. Place bread cubes in pie plate; sprinkle with fruit mixture.

Beat milk, the egg product, sugar and vanilla with wire whisk until smooth. Pour milk mixture over bread. Press bread cubes into milk mixture. Sprinkle with nutmeg. Bake uncovered 40 to 45 minutes or until golden brown and set.

Make Eggnog Sauce. Cut bread pudding into wedges, or spoon into serving dishes. Drizzle each serving with scant tablespoon sauce. Sprinkle with additional nutmeg if desired. Store pudding and sauce covered in refrigerator.

Eggnog Sauce

1/3 cup fat-free (skim) milk

1 container (3 to 4 ounces) refrigerated vanilla fat-free pudding

1/2 teaspoon rum extract

Mix all ingredients.

1 Eating Smart • Because dried fruits have had most of their water removed, they are concentrated sources of nutrients. Raisins, for instance, are especially rich in iron and fiber. Add raisins to cereal, yogurt or low-fat granola for an on-the-run, high-energy snack, or stir them into low-fat quick bread batters or cookie dough.

2 Staying Active • When is the best time to exercise? Studies have shown that A.M. exercisers burn slightly more calories throughout the day than those who exercise later. But most experts claim it makes little difference when you work out. The best time for your workout? Whenever you'll be most likely to exercise. A word of caution—intense exercise too close to bedtime can make it harder to get to sleep.

Fruited Bread Pudding with Eggnog Sauce

1 Serving

Calories 145
(Calories from Fat 10)

Fat 1g (Saturated 0g)

Cholesterol 0mg

Sodium 180mg

Carbohydrate 29g
(Dietary Fiber 1g)

Protein 6g

% Daily Value

Vitamin A 6%

Vitamin C 0%

Calcium 12%

Iron 6%

Diet Exchanges

1 Starch

1/2 Fruit

1/2 Skim Milk

Orange-Cranberry
Scones

PREP: 20 MIN; BAKE: 9 MIN; COOL: 5 MIN | 12 SCONES

2 cups Basic 4® cereal or other whole wheat flake cereal with cranberries, slightly crushed

1 cup all-purpose flour

1/4 cup packed brown sugar

2 teaspoons baking powder

1 teaspoon grated orange peel

1/4 teaspoon salt

1/4 cup firm margarine or butter

1/2 cup dried cranberries

1/4 cup fat-free cholesterol-free egg product or 1 egg, slightly beaten

1/4 cup orange low-fat yogurt

Orange Glaze (right)

Heat oven to 400°. Slightly crush cereal; set aside.

Mix flour, brown sugar, baking powder, orange peel and salt in medium bowl. Cut in margarine, using pastry blender or crisscrossing 2 knives, until mixture looks like coarse crumbs. Stir in cereal, cranberries, egg product and yogurt until soft dough forms.

Place dough on lightly floured surface. Gently roll in flour to coat; shape into ball. Pat dough into 8-inch circle with floured hands. Cut circle into 12 wedges with sharp knife dipped in flour. Place wedges about 1 inch apart on ungreased cookie sheet.

Bake 7 to 9 minutes or until edges are light brown. Immediately remove from cookie sheet to wire rack. Cool 5 minutes; drizzle with Orange Glaze. After glaze is set, store tightly covered.

Orange Glaze

1/2 cup powdered sugar

1/4 teaspoon grated orange peel

2 to 3 teaspoons orange juice

Mix all ingredients until thin enough to drizzle.

1   **Eating Smart** • For a breakfast that stays with you through the morning, try a well-rounded meal of 300 to 400 calories that is high in complex carbohydrates and contains some protein and fat.

2   **Staying Active** • To get the most out of sit-ups, keep your knees bent, your feet flat on the floor and come up to only a 30-degree angle. Forget about the old-fashioned straight-leg sit-ups, which can make you overarch and strain your lower back.

Orange-Cranberry Scones
and Triple-Fruit Yogurt Smoothie (page 66)

1 Scone

Calories 170
(Calories from Fat 45)

Fat 5g (Saturated 3g)

Cholesterol 30mg

Sodium 220mg

Carbohydrate 31g
(Dietary Fiber 3g)

Protein 3g

% Daily Value

Vitamin A 10%

Vitamin C 6%

Calcium 12%

Iron 8%

Diet Exchanges

1 Starch

1 Fruit

1/2 Fat

Old-Fashioned
Blueberry Muffins

PREP: 10 MIN; BAKE: 25 MIN | 12 MUFFINS

1 1/2 cups plain fat-free yogurt

1 1/4 cups all-purpose flour

1 cup old-fashioned or quick-cooking oats

2/3 cup packed brown sugar

1/4 cup margarine or butter, softened

1/4 cup fat-free cholesterol-free egg product or 1 egg, slightly beaten

2 teaspoons baking powder

1 teaspoon ground cinnamon

1/2 teaspoon baking soda

1/4 teaspoon ground nutmeg

1/4 teaspoon salt

1 cup fresh or frozen (thawed and drained) blueberries

Heat oven to 400°. Place paper baking cup in each of 12 medium muffin cups, 2 1/2 × 1 1/4 inches, or grease bottoms only of muffin cups.

Mix all ingredients except blueberries in large bowl just until flour is moistened (batter will be lumpy). Fold in blueberries.

Divide batter evenly among muffin cups. Bake 20 to 25 minutes or until golden brown. Immediately remove from pan.

1 Muffin

Calories 170
(Calories from Fat 35)

Fat 4g (Saturated 1g)

Cholesterol 0mg

Sodium 220mg

Carbohydrate 31g
(Dietary Fiber 2g)

Protein 5g

% Daily Value

Vitamin A 6%

Vitamin C 0%

Calcium 12%

Iron 8%

Diet Exchanges

2 Starch

1 **Eating Smart** • Make sure you read the nutrition labels on store-bought muffins. A store-bought bran muffin may not contain whole wheat flour and may have excessive amounts of eggs, butter, oil, sugar and honey. Your best bet: Try these low-fat, mouthwatering muffins! Accompany with a glass of low-fat milk and a piece of fruit for a well-balanced breakfast.

2 **Staying Active** • Cold-weather outdoor exercisers would do well to wear mittens instead of gloves. Not only do mittens keep your hands warmer by keeping your fingers together, they also have less surface area from which heat can escape.

What Makes a Healthy Breakfast?

A good balance of fiber-rich complex carbohydrates and low-fat protein gives you the energy you'll need for the morning. Skipping the protein will leave you famished by late morning, and relying solely on protein robs you of necessary fiber and the carbohydrates your brain needs to function. Although a little fat will keep hunger at bay, high-fat breakfasts leave you sluggish long before lunchtime. Use the following chart to mix-and-match a balanced breakfast you'll enjoy.

	Calories	Fat (g)	Fiber (g)
Carbohydrates			
3/4 cup whole-grain cereal	100	1	4
1 cup oatmeal	150	3	4
1 Old-Fashioned Blueberry Muffin (p. 60)	170	4	2
1 multigrain bagel (1 1/2 ounces)	150	1	3
1 slice whole-grain toast	90	1	2
1/2 cup low-fat granola with raisins	200	3	3
1 medium banana	105	1	3
1 medium orange	65	1	4
1/2 cup fresh berries	40	0	2
1/4 cantaloupe	50	0	1
Protein			
2 tablespoons peanut butter	200	16	1
1 cup low-fat cottage cheese	160	3	0
1 cup low-fat yogurt	150	3	0
1 cup fat-free (skim) milk	80	7	0
1 ounce almonds	170	14	3
2 tablespoons low-fat cream cheese	70	5	0
1 hard-boiled egg	75	5	0

Tropical
Banana Muffins

PREP: 10 MIN; BAKE: 23 MIN | 12 MUFFINS

2 tablespoons flaked coconut

2 tablespoons chopped
pecans

1 cup mashed very ripe
bananas (2 medium)

1/2 cup packed brown sugar

1 can (8 ounces) crushed
pineapple in juice, drained
and 1/3 cup juice
reserved*

1/4 cup vegetable oil

1/4 cup fat-free cholesterol-
free egg product or 1 egg

2 cups all-purpose flour

2 1/2 teaspoons baking
powder

3/4 teaspoon salt

1/4 teaspoon ground nutmeg

Heat oven to 400°. Grease bottoms only of 12 medium
muffin cups, 2 1/2 × 1 1/4 inches, or line with paper
baking cups and spray with cooking spray.

Spread coconut and pecans in ungreased small pan. Bake
3 to 5 minutes, stirring occasionally, until golden
brown; cool.

Mix bananas, brown sugar, pineapple juice, oil and egg
product in large bowl. Stir in flour, baking powder, salt
and nutmeg just until flour is moistened. Fold in
pineapple, coconut and pecans.

Divide batter evenly among muffin cups (cups will be
very full). Bake 20 to 23 minutes or until golden
brown. Immediately remove from pan to wire rack.
Serve warm if desired.

*1/3 cup fat-free (skim) milk can be substituted for the pineapple juice.

1 Muffin

Calories 180
(Calories from Fat 45)

Fat 5g (Saturated 1g)

Cholesterol 0mg

Sodium 260mg

Carbohydrate 32g
(Dietary Fiber 1g)

Protein 3g

% Daily Value

Vitamin A 0%

Vitamin C 2%

Calcium 6%

Iron 8%

Diet Exchanges

1 Starch

1 Fruit

1 Fat

1 **Eating Smart** • Reduce calories and fat in baked
goods by partially replacing butter, margarine or oil
with bananas or applesauce. Substitute these fruit "fat
replacers" for up to one-half of the fat for the best
texture and flavor.

2 **Staying Active** • Riding a tandem bike, or bicy-
cle built for two, can be a great way to enjoy exercising
with a friend. You'll be able to share time with a loved
one and reap the benefits of a cycling workout. The best
part? You'll never get separated from one another!

Chai
Tea

2 cups water

4 tea bags black tea

2 cups milk

2 tablespoons honey

1/2 teaspoon ground ginger

1/2 teaspoon ground nutmeg

1/4 teaspoon ground
   cinnamon

Heat water to boiling. Add tea bags; reduce heat. Simmer
2 minutes. Remove tea bags.

Stir remaining ingredients into tea. Heat to boiling. Stir
with wire whisk to foam milk. Pour into cups.

1 Eating Smart • Tea has long been linked to
weight loss because of the feeling of fullness it provides.
Chai, popular in India, is black tea mixed with a sweetener,
milk and fragrant spices such as nutmeg and cinnamon.
On cool mornings, this warming tea is especially com-
forting. It's also good served iced on warm days.

2 Staying Active • When exercising in hot
weather, you can lose up to a quart of water each hour
through sweat. Make sure you replenish this lost liquid
by drinking a pint (2 cups) of fluid for each pound lost
during your workout.

1 Serving

Calories 95
(Calories from Fat 20)

Fat 2g (Saturated 1g)

Cholesterol 10mg

Sodium 65mg

Carbohydrate 15g
(Dietary Fiber 0g)

Protein 4g

% Daily Value

Vitamin A 6%

Vitamin C 0%

Calcium 14%

Iron 0%

Diet Exchanges

1/2 Fruit

1/2 Skim Milk

1/2 Fat

Apple-Kiwi
Smoothie

PREP: 10 MIN | 2 SERVINGS

1 small apple, peeled and cut
  into chunks

1 kiwifruit, peeled and cut
  into chunks

4 medium strawberries, stems
  removed

1 container (6 ounces) strawberry low-fat yogurt

1/3 cup apple juice

Place all ingredients in blender or food processor. Cover
and blend on high speed about 30 seconds or until
smooth. Pour into glasses. Serve immediately.

1 **Eating Smart** • Smoothies are quick and easy
breakfast solutions for busy mornings. This version
combines fruits and low-fat yogurt to make a flavorful,
energy-boosting drink. Enjoy it for breakfast or any
other time you need a quick, nearly fat-free pick-me-up.

2 **Staying Active** • Even if you travel a lot, you
can still fit workouts into your schedule—and suitcase.
Buy some inexpensive resistance bands and a jump rope
to accompany you on trips. Use this gear for a total body
workout without having to leave your hotel room.

1 Serving

Calories 155
(Calories from Fat 10)

Fat 1g (Saturated 1g)

Cholesterol 5mg

Sodium 55mg

Carbohydrate 36g
(Dietary Fiber 3g)

Protein 4g

% Daily Value

Vitamin A 2%

Vitamin C 90%

Calcium 14%

Iron 2%

Diet Exchanges

2 Fruit

1/2 Skim Milk

Apple-Kiwi Smoothie
and Bagel and Cream Cheese Morning Mix (page 67)

Triple-Fruit
Yogurt Smoothie

PREP: 5 MIN | 4 SERVINGS

2 cups vanilla fat-free yogurt

1 cup fresh raspberries*

1/2 cup orange juice

1 medium banana, sliced
(1 cup)

Place all ingredients in blender or food processor. Cover and blend on high speed about 30 seconds or until smooth. Pour into glasses. Serve immediately.

*1 package (10 ounces) frozen sweetened raspberries, partially thawed, can be substituted for the fresh raspberries.

1 Serving

Calories 145
(Calories from Fat 10)

Fat 1g (Saturated 0g)

Cholesterol 0mg

Sodium 50mg

Carbohydrate 31g
(Dietary Fiber 3g)

Protein 6g

% Daily Value

Vitamin A 12%

Vitamin C 18%

Calcium 16%

Iron 8%

Diet Exchanges

1 1/2 Fruit

1/2 Skim Milk

1 **Eating Smart** • Besides containing low-fat protein and calcium, yogurt—a cultured dairy product—is easy, convenient and versatile. Enjoy it as is, or use as an ingredient in breakfast smoothies, salad dressings, dips and sauces. Use low-fat and nonfat varieties to keep fat grams down without sacrificing flavor.

2 **Staying Active** • Looking for an exercise video? Before you buy, check your local library or video rental store for ones to sample. Make sure the workout is appropriate for your fitness level, and check for required equipment. Do you have enough room to do the routine safely, and is your workout surface carpeted to provide shock absorption? Research the instructor's reputation in the fitness industry. Finally, can you vary the routine as your fitness level increases?

Bagel and Cream Cheese
Morning Mix

PREP: 5 MIN; BAKE: 20 MIN; COOL: 1 HR | 15 SERVINGS (1/2 CUP EACH)

3 cups Wheat Chex® cereal

3 cups Oatmeal Crisp® Raisin cereal

1 cup cinnamon-raisin bagel chips, broken into bite-size pieces

1/2 cup raisins

2 tablespoons margarine or butter, melted

2 tablespoons packed brown sugar

3 ounces reduced-fat cream cheese (Neufchâtel)

Heat oven to 325°. Mix cereals, bagel chips and raisins in large bowl; set aside.

Place margarine, brown sugar and cream cheese in 2-cup microwavable measuring cup. Microwave uncovered on High 1 minute; stir to remove lumps. Pour over cereal mixture, stirring until evenly coated.

Spread in ungreased jelly roll pan, 15 1/2 × 10 1/2 × 1 inch. Bake uncovered 20 minutes, stirring after 10 minutes. Cool completely, about 1 hour. Store in airtight container or plastic food-storage bag.

1 Eating Smart • Even when you're in a hurry, remember to eat slowly. By taking the time to appreciate the flavors and textures of your food, you'll find that healthy eating can be incredibly satisfying. Play calming music to help set the mood.

2 Staying Active • When the sun is shining, pack a healthy lunch, grab family and friends and head for the hills. Hiking to find the perfect spot for your feast—all while carrying a picnic basket and cooler—will burn plenty of calories. And the uphill trek will strengthen and tone your lower body muscles.

1 Serving

Calories 155
(Calories from Fat 35)

Fat 4g (Saturated 1g)

Cholesterol 5mg

Sodium 220mg

Carbohydrate 29g
(Dietary Fiber 2g)

Protein 3g

% Daily Value

Vitamin A 8%

Vitamin C 0%

Calcium 2%

Iron 28%

Diet Exchanges

1 Starch

1 Fruit

1/2 Fat

Soups, Sandwiches and Main-Dish Salads

3

Italian Sausage Soup, 70

Rio Grande Turkey Soup, 71

Red Pepper–Lentil Soup, 72

Barley-Burger Stew, 73

Zesty Autumn Pork Stew, 74

Caesar Chicken Paninis, 76

Turkey Burritos, 78

Flank Steak Sandwiches, 79

Honey Ham Bagels, 80

Vegetables and Pork in Pitas, 81

Crab Tortilla Roll-Ups, 82

Veggie Focaccia Sandwiches, 85

Chicken and Strawberry–Spinach Salad, 86

Turkey–Wild Rice Salad, 88

Spinach-Shrimp Salad with Hot Bacon Dressing, 89

Gazpacho Pasta Salad with Tomato-Lime Dressing, 90

Creamy Pesto–Pasta Salad, 92

Cuban Spicy Bean Salad with Oranges and Cilantro, 93

Veggie-Foccacia Sandwiches (page 85)

Italian
Sausage Soup

PREP: 10 MIN; COOK: 20 MIN | 6 SERVINGS

1 pound turkey Italian
  sausage links, cut into
  1-inch pieces

2 cups broccoli flowerets

1 cup uncooked mostaccioli
  pasta (3 ounces)

2 1/2 cups water

1/2 teaspoon dried basil
  leaves

1/4 teaspoon fennel seed,
  crushed

1/4 teaspoon pepper

1 medium onion, chopped
  (1/2 cup)

1 clove garlic, finely chopped

1 can (28 ounces) whole
  Italian-style tomatoes,
  undrained

1 can (10 1/2 ounces)
  condensed beef broth

Cook sausage in 4-quart Dutch oven over medium-high
  heat, stirring occasionally, until brown; drain.

Stir in remaining ingredients, breaking up tomatoes. Heat
  to boiling; reduce heat to medium-low. Cover and cook
  about 15 minutes, stirring occasionally, until pasta is
  tender.

1 Serving	
Calories 240 (Calories from Fat 90)	
Fat 10g (Saturated 3g)	
Cholesterol 45mg	
Sodium 820mg	
Carbohydrate 22g (Dietary Fiber 3g)	
Protein 18g	

% Daily Value	
Vitamin A 16%	
Vitamin C 38%	
Calcium 6%	
Iron 12%	

Diet Exchanges	
1 Starch	
1 1/2 Medium-Fat Meat	
2 Vegetable	

1 Eating Smart • Filling up on soup can help you
lose weight. Low-fat, broth-based soups that are loaded
with veggies will fill you faster, leaving less room for
higher-calorie foods.

2 Staying Active • Make exercise a family affair.
An afternoon game of tag or hide-and-seek works well
for families with younger kids. Older children might
enjoy a game of Frisbee®, or a few hours of shooting
hoops. Not only will you get a good workout and spend
quality time with your family, you'll also be teaching
your children that fitness can be fun.

Rio Grande
Turkey Soup

PREP: 5 MIN; COOK: 15 MIN | 6 SERVINGS

1 can (14 1/2 ounces) fat-free chicken broth

1 can (28 ounces) whole tomatoes, undrained

1 jar (16 ounces) thick-and-chunky salsa

2 to 3 teaspoons chili powder

1/2 bag (16-ounce size) frozen corn, broccoli and red peppers

1 cup uncooked cavatappi pasta (3 ounces)

2 cups cut-up cooked turkey or chicken

1/4 cup chopped fresh parsley

Heat broth, tomatoes, salsa and chili powder to boiling in 4-quart Dutch oven, breaking up tomatoes. Stir in vegetables and pasta. Heat to boiling; reduce heat.

Simmer uncovered about 12 minutes, stirring occasionally, until pasta and vegetables are tender. Stir in turkey and parsley; cook until hot.

(photo on page 4)

1 Serving

Calories 220
(Calories from Fat 45)

Fat 5g (Saturated 1g)

Cholesterol 40mg

Sodium 760mg

Carbohydrate 29g
(Dietary Fiber 5g)

Protein 20g

% Daily Value

Vitamin A 24%

Vitamin C 48%

Calcium 10%

Iron 16%

Diet Exchanges

1 Starch

1 1/2 Lean Meat

3 Vegetable

Eating Smart • Skinless turkey breast is just about the leanest of all meats. Three ounces contain less than a gram of fat, contributing a small percentage of its 80 calories.

Staying Active • It's happened to us all—after lunch, you find yourself losing concentration and starting to nod off. A quick solution is to stand up and walk around, or do a couple of quick, simple stretches. Your energy and concentration should return, and you'll be ready to face the rest of the afternoon.

Red Pepper–Lentil
Soup

PREP: 10 MIN; COOK: 50 MIN | 4 SERVINGS

3/4 cup dried lentils, sorted and rinsed

2 cloves garlic, finely chopped

1 can (14 1/2 ounces) fat-free chicken broth

2 cups water

3 ounces fully cooked low-fat turkey kielbasa, cut lengthwise in half and cut crosswise into slices (1 cup)

1/2 cup sliced drained roasted red bell peppers

2 tablespoons chopped fresh basil leaves

1/8 teaspoon pepper

Heat lentils, garlic, broth and water to boiling in 3-quart saucepan; reduce heat. Cover and simmer 30 minutes.

Stir in remaining ingredients. Heat to boiling; reduce heat. Cover and simmer 10 to 15 minutes or until lentils are tender.

1 Serving

Calories 145
(Calories from Fat 25)

Fat 3g (Saturated 1g)

Cholesterol 10mg

Sodium 690mg

Carbohydrate 22g
(Dietary Fiber 8g)

Protein 15g

% Daily Value

Vitamin A 8%

Vitamin C 26%

Calcium 2%

Iron 20%

Diet Exchanges

1 Starch

1 1/2 Very Lean Meat

1 Vegetable

1 Eating Smart • Lentils are great for time-pressed cooks, as they cook faster than other dried beans and are high in fiber, B vitamins and minerals and low in calories, fat and cholesterol. They also provide protein and complex carbohydrates.

2 Staying Active • Anyone can run. Short, tall, big or small, body size makes no difference in this popular sport. Advice for novice runners: Start slowly to prevent injuries, wear good running shoes, increase mileage gradually, stretch, hydrate and get plenty of rest.

Barley-Burger
Stew

1 pound diet-lean or extra-
lean ground beef

2 medium onions, chopped
(1 cup)

1/2 cup uncooked barley

1 cup water

2 to 3 teaspoons chili powder

1 1/2 teaspoons salt

1/2 teaspoon pepper

1 medium stalk celery,
chopped (1/2 cup)

4 cups tomato juice

Cook beef and onions in 4-quart Dutch oven over medium heat, stirring occasionally, until beef is brown; drain.

Stir in remaining ingredients. Heat to boiling; reduce heat. Cover and simmer about 1 hour or until barley is tender and stew is desired consistency.

1 Serving

Calories 320
(Calories from Fat 80)

Fat 9g (Saturated 5g)

Cholesterol 70mg

Sodium 1,950mg

Carbohydrate 37g
(Dietary Fiber 7g)

Protein 30g

% Daily Value

Vitamin A 20%

Vitamin C 46%

Calcium 6%

Iron 28%

Diet Exchanges

2 Starch

3 Lean Meat

1 Vegetable

1 Eating Smart • Just 1 cup of cooked barley packs about 6 grams of fiber. This virtually fat-free whole grain also contains complex carbohydrates, B vitamins and protein.

2 Staying Active • Exercise with encouraging friends to increase your confidence in your workout. Researchers have found that regardless of actual performance, women who were told they had done well felt better about their workouts than those who had been told they had performed poorly.

Zesty
Autumn Pork Stew

PREP: 10 MIN; COOK: 20 MIN | 4 SERVINGS

1 pound pork tenderloin

2 cloves garlic, finely
   chopped

2 medium sweet potatoes,
   peeled and cubed (2 cups)

1 cup coarsely chopped
   cabbage

1 medium green bell pepper,
   chopped (1 cup)

1 can (14 1/2 ounces) fat-free
   chicken broth

1 teaspoon Cajun seasoning

Remove fat from pork. Cut pork into 1-inch cubes. Spray 4-quart Dutch oven with cooking spray; heat over medium-high heat. Cook pork in Dutch oven, stirring occasionally, until brown.

Stir in remaining ingredients. Heat to boiling; reduce heat. Cover and simmer about 15 minutes, stirring once, until sweet potatoes are tender.

1 Eating Smart • Comfort foods, like stew, are really satisfying. Savor hearty stews, creamy mashed potatoes or any other food that brings you comfort. Enjoy every moment of your meal. You may just find yourself eating less than if you had forced yourself to eat food you don't enjoy.

2 Staying Active • Subscribing to a fitness-themed magazine or newsletter is a great motivator. Reading about the latest fitness research and trends can be very informative. And the regular delivery of an exercise-based publication to your doorstep will serve as an ongoing reminder of your fitness goals.

1 Serving

Calories 240
(Calories from Fat 45)

Fat 5g (Saturated 2g)

Cholesterol 70mg

Sodium 530mg

Carbohydrate 22g
(Dietary Fiber 3g)

Protein 30g

% Daily Value

Vitamin A 100%

Vitamin C 44%

Calcium 4%

Iron 12%

Diet Exchanges

1 Starch

3 Very Lean Meat

1 Vegetable

1 Fat

Zesty Autumn Pork Stew

Caesar
Chicken Paninis

4 boneless, skinless chicken breast halves (about 1 1/4 pounds)

4 hard rolls (about 5 × 3 inches), split

4 slices red onion

1 large tomato, sliced

1/3 cup fat-free Caesar dressing

2 tablespoons grated fat-free Parmesan cheese topping

4 leaves romaine

Remove fat from chicken. Flatten each chicken breast half to 1/4-inch thickness between sheets of waxed paper or plastic wrap. Spray 8- or 10-inch skillet with cooking spray; heat over medium-high heat. Cook chicken in skillet 10 to 15 minutes, turning once, until juice of chicken is no longer pink when center of thickest pieces are cut. Remove chicken from skillet; keep warm.

Place rolls, cut sides down, in skillet. Cook over medium heat about 2 minutes or until toasted.

Place chicken on bottom halves of rolls. Top with onion, tomato, dressing, cheese, romaine and top half of roll.

1 Serving

Calories 320
(Calories from Fat 65)

Fat 7g (Saturated 2g)

Cholesterol 75mg

Sodium 660mg

Carbohydrate 34g
(Dietary Fiber 3g)

Protein 33g

% Daily Value

Vitamin A 6%

Vitamin C 20%

Calcium 8%

Iron 16%

Diet Exchanges

2 Starch

4 Very Lean Meat

1 Vegetable

1 **Eating Smart** • Panini, or "little breads," are small Italian sandwiches. Here, panini takes on a new identity by combining low-fat chicken with the savory flavors of traditional Caesar salad. The protein-carbohydrate mix in this sandwich will keep you going well into the afternoon.

2 **Staying Active** • Proper form is essential when running down steep hills. Instead of running straight down, run in a zigzag pattern. Running downhill puts extra stress on joints and muscles in your feet and legs. As you run downhill, your speed increases, putting even more stress on your lower body. Zigzagging keeps your speed under control, which means less impact on your feet and legs.

Caesar Chicken Paninis

Honey
Ham Bagels

PREP: 5 MIN; BAKE: 5 MIN | 4 SERVINGS

2 pumpernickel bagels, split and toasted

4 teaspoons honey mustard

4 slices (1 ounce each) fully cooked honey ham

4 thin slices (1/2 ounce each) reduced-fat mozzarella cheese

Chili pepper rings, if desired

Heat oven to 400°. Spread each bagel half with 1 teaspoon mustard. Top each with ham and cheese. Place on cookie sheet.

Bake 3 to 5 minutes or until cheese is melted. Top with chili pepper rings.

1 **Eating Smart** • Smart shoppers will compare labels on packaged deli meats. One ounce of lean deli ham contains about 1 1/2 grams of fat. One ounce of regular ham contains about four grams of fat.

2 **Staying Active** • Post-workout snacks are essential for repairing, maintaining and building muscle tissue. Within 2 hours of exercising, refuel with a low-calorie snack that contains carbohydrates and protein. Good post-workout snacks include low-fat cottage cheese with fruit or fat-free tuna salad and whole-grain, low-fat crackers.

1 Serving

Calories 160
(Calories from Fat 35)

Fat 4g (Saturated 2g)

Cholesterol 20mg

Sodium 450mg

Carbohydrate 21g
(Dietary Fiber 1g)

Protein 11g

% Daily Value

Vitamin A 2%

Vitamin C 0%

Calcium 10%

Iron 6%

Diet Exchanges

1 Starch

1 Lean Meat

1/2 Fat

Honey
Ham Bagels

PREP: 5 MIN; BAKE: 5 MIN | 4 SERVINGS

2 pumpernickel bagels, split and toasted

4 teaspoons honey mustard

4 slices (1 ounce each) fully cooked honey ham

4 thin slices (1/2 ounce each) reduced-fat mozzarella cheese

Chili pepper rings, if desired

Heat oven to 400°. Spread each bagel half with 1 teaspoon mustard. Top each with ham and cheese. Place on cookie sheet.

Bake 3 to 5 minutes or until cheese is melted. Top with chili pepper rings.

1 Eating Smart • Smart shoppers will compare labels on packaged deli meats. One ounce of lean deli ham contains about 1 1/2 grams of fat. One ounce of regular ham contains about four grams of fat.

2 Staying Active • Post-workout snacks are essential for repairing, maintaining and building muscle tissue. Within 2 hours of exercising, refuel with a low-calorie snack that contains carbohydrates and protein. Good post-workout snacks include low-fat cottage cheese with fruit or fat-free tuna salad and whole-grain, low-fat crackers.

1 Serving	
Calories 160 (Calories from Fat 35)	
Fat 4g (Saturated 2g)	
Cholesterol 20mg	
Sodium 450mg	
Carbohydrate 21g (Dietary Fiber 1g)	
Protein 11g	

% Daily Value	
Vitamin A 2%	
Vitamin C 0%	
Calcium 10%	
Iron 6%	

Diet Exchanges	
1 Starch	
1 Lean Meat	
1/2 Fat	

Flank Steak
Sandwiches

PREP: 10 MIN; MARINATE: 4 HR; GRILL: 12 MIN | 8 SERVINGS

2 beef flank steaks (1 pound each)

1/4 cup honey

2 tablespoons soy sauce

1 tablespoon grated gingerroot

1 can or bottle (12 ounces) regular or nonalcoholic beer

8 pita breads (6 inches in diameter), cut in half to form pockets

Sliced tomato, if desired

Grilled sliced onion, if desired

Remove fat from beef. Make cuts about 1/2 inch apart and 1/8 inch deep in diamond pattern on both sides of beef. Place in shallow glass dish. Mix honey, soy sauce, gingerroot and beer; pour over beef. Cover and refrigerate, turning occasionally, at least 4 hours but no longer than 24 hours.

Brush grill rack with vegetable oil. Heat coals or gas grill for direct heat. Remove beef from marinade; reserve marinade. Cover and grill beef 6 inches from medium heat about 12 minutes for medium doneness, turning after 6 minutes and brushing frequently with marinade. Discard any remaining marinade.

Cut beef diagonally into thin slices. Serve beef in pita bread halves with tomato and onion.

1 Serving

Calories 320
(Calories from Fat 70)

Fat 8g (Saturated 3g)

Cholesterol 60mg

Sodium 530mg

Carbohydrate 36g
(Dietary Fiber 1g)

Protein 27g

% Daily Value

Vitamin A 0%

Vitamin C 0%

Calcium 4%

Iron 18%

Diet Exchanges

2 Starch

3 Lean Meat

1 Eating Smart • Lunching on an oversized deli sandwich can cost you anywhere from 600 to 800 calories. Instead, bring a healthy lunch from home. Pack sandwiches that feature lean meats or cheeses for a midday protein punch. Also include raw vegetable sticks and fresh fruit for fiber and nutrients.

2 Staying Active • Contrary to popular belief, drinking cold beverages during exercise doesn't cause cramps. Cold drinks are actually better choices than warm—they leave the stomach more rapidly and quickly supply the body with the fluid it needs.

Turkey
Burritos

PREP: 10 MIN; COOK: 7 MIN | 6 SERVINGS

1/2 pound ground turkey
    breast

2 cloves garlic, finely
    chopped

1 jalapeño chili, seeded and
    chopped

1/2 cup fat-free refried beans

2 tablespoons lime juice

6 fat-free flour tortillas (6 to
    8 inches in diameter)

6 tablespoons fat-free sour
    cream

1 large tomato, chopped
    (1 cup)

1/4 cup chopped fresh
    cilantro

Salsa, if desired

Spray 8- to 10-inch skillet with cooking spray; heat over medium-high heat. Cook turkey, garlic and chili in skillet about 5 minutes, stirring constantly, until turkey is no longer pink. Stir in beans and lime juice. Cook about 2 minutes, stirring occasionally, until heated.

Place one-fourth of the turkey mixture on center of each tortilla. Top with sour cream, tomato and cilantro. Fold one end of tortilla up about 1 inch over filling; fold right and left sides over folded end, overlapping. Fold remaining end down. Place seam side down on serving platter or plate. Serve with salsa.

1 Serving

Calories 185
(Calories from Fat 20)

Fat 2g (Saturated 1g)

Cholesterol 25mg

Sodium 460mg

Carbohydrate 31g
(Dietary Fiber 3g)

Protein 14g

% Daily Value

Vitamin A 12%

Vitamin C 18%

Calcium 4%

Iron 10%

Diet Exchanges

2 Starch

1 Very Lean Meat

1 Eating Smart • Jazzing up your diet by serving a variety of fun, ethnic foods can actually help you lose weight. Variety is key for a couple of reasons. First, more variety means more types of food and, as a result, more types of nutrients. Treating yourself with a wide variety of many different foods is also more satisfying and encourages smaller portions of each single food.

2 Staying Active • The latest fitness craze, pilates is a series of non-impact conditioning exercises to strengthen and stretch muscles and properly align the body. This technique, developed by Joseph Pilates in the 1920s, is used to develop the deep muscles of the trunk, abdomen and spine, and has long been practiced by professional dancers.

Vegetables and
Pork in Pitas

PREP: 15 MIN; BROIL: 8 MIN | 4 SERVINGS

3 medium zucchini (1 1/2 pounds), cut into 3 × 1/2-inch strips

2 medium red bell peppers, cut into 1/4-inch strips

2 pork boneless loin chops (about 1/2 pound), cut into 1/4-inch strips

1/4 cup fat-free Italian dressing

1/2 teaspoon pepper

2 tablespoons grated fat-free Parmesan cheese topping

2 tablespoons chopped fresh parsley or 2 teaspoons parsley flakes

4 whole wheat pita breads (6 inches in diameter), cut in half to form pockets

Set oven control to broil. Spray jelly roll pan, 15 1/2 × 10 1/2 × 1 inch, with cooking spray.

Place zucchini, bell peppers and pork in heavy-duty resealable plastic food-storage bag. Add dressing and pepper. Seal bag; shake bag to coat ingredients. Pour mixture into pan; spread evenly.

Broil with tops 2 to 3 inches from heat 6 to 8 minutes, stirring once, until pork is no longer pink. Sprinkle with cheese and parsley. Spoon into pita bread halves.

1 Serving

Calories 270 (Calories from Fat 55)

Fat 6g (Saturated 2g)

Cholesterol 35mg

Sodium 510mg

Carbohydrate 42g (Dietary Fiber 7g)

Protein 19g

% Daily Value

Vitamin A 40%

Vitamin C 100%

Calcium 4%

Iron 16%

Diet Exchanges

2 Starch

1 Lean Meat

2 Vegetable

1 **Eating Smart** • Whether dark or light, most breads contain about 65 calories per slice. Because whole-grain breads contain more fiber and more minerals than white breads, they're the better nutritional choice.

2 **Staying Active** • Ever wonder how much fat your workout burns? Exercising for 45 to 60 minutes at a heart rate of 55 to 65 percent of your maximum burns 60 percent fat and 40 percent carbohydrates. Increasing your heart rate to 75 to 80 percent of your maximum burns 30 percent fat and 70 percent carbs, but you burn more calories and fat overall.

Crab
Tortilla Roll-Ups

PREP: 15 MIN; COOK: 5 MIN | 4 SERVINGS

Yogurt Salsa (below)

12 imitation crabmeat sticks
(about 1 ounce each),
chopped*

1 cup finely shredded cabbage

1/2 cup finely shredded red
bell pepper

2 medium green onions,
sliced (2 tablespoons)

1/4 teaspoon red pepper
sauce

1/4 teaspoon salt

1/8 teaspoon pepper

4 flour tortillas (10 inches in
diameter)

Make Yogurt Salsa. Mix remaining ingredients except tortillas in 12-inch nonstick skillet. Cook over medium-high heat 3 to 5 minutes, stirring frequently, until hot.

Spread 3 to 4 tablespoons salsa on each tortilla; top with about 2/3 cup crabmeat mixture. Roll up each tortilla; cut diagonally into thirds.

Yogurt Salsa

1/2 cup plain fat-free yogurt

1 tablespoon chopped fresh cilantro

1/4 teaspoon ground cumin

1 small tomato, chopped (1/2 cup)

2 medium green onions, chopped (2 tablespoons)

Mix all ingredients.

12 ounces shredded cooked crabmeat (2 1/2 cups) can be substituted for the imitation crabmeat sticks.

1 Serving	
Calories 320 (Calories from Fat 55)	
Fat 6g (Saturated 1g)	
Cholesterol 25mg	
Sodium 1,240mg	
Carbohydrate 49g (Dietary Fiber 4g)	
Protein 21g	

% Daily Value	
Vitamin A 14%	
Vitamin C 40%	
Calcium 16%	
Iron 16%	

Diet Exchanges	
3 Starch	
1 1/2 Very Lean Meat	
1 Vegetable	

1 **Eating Smart** • Flour tortillas make great "wrappers" for sandwich fillings of all kinds. Low in fat (some brands are fat free), flour tortillas can also be cut into triangles and baked, giving you a healthier alternative to fried tortilla chips.

2 **Staying Active** • Fueling up properly can help power your workout. Pre-workout snacks should be carbohydrate based, low in calories (about 200 max), and easy to digest. For the best workout, enjoy your pre-workout snack about an hour before exercise. Good pre-exercise snacks include calcium-enriched orange juice or a banana.

Crab Tortilla Roll-Ups

The Deli Dilemma

Stopping by the deli for a sandwich or salad is often a quick lunchtime solution. But beware: Some deli selections are better than others when watching calories and fat. Check the chart below to see how your favorite sandwich or salad stacks up.

	Calories	Fat (g)	Fiber (g)
Sandwiches			
Turkey club on white bread	485	23	1
Tuna salad on white bread	400	13	2
Ham and cheese on white bread	385	20	1
Roast beef on whole wheat bread	345	14	3
Grilled chicken breast on whole wheat bun	265	8	4
Salads			
Taco salad	1,420	86	17
Chicken Caesar salad	580	40	7
Chef's salad	330	22	4
Garden salad (with 1/4 cup each bell peppers, carrots, tomatoes and garbanzo beans, and 1 tablespoon dressing)	235	12	9

Veggie
Focaccia Sandwiches

PREP: 15 MIN; COOK: 5 MIN | 4 SERVINGS

1 round focaccia bread
(8 inches in diameter)

1/2 yellow bell pepper, cut
into strips

1/2 green bell pepper, cut
into strips

1 small onion, sliced

2 tablespoons fat-free Italian
dressing

2 roma (plum) tomatoes,
sliced

2 tablespoons chopped fresh
basil leaves

1/2 cup shredded reduced-
fat mozzarella cheese
(2 ounces)

Heat oven to 350°. Place focaccia on oven rack. Bake 5 to
7 minutes or until warm.

Spray 8- or 10-inch skillet with cooking spray; heat over
medium-high heat. Cook bell peppers, onion and dressing in skillet 4 to 5 minutes, stirring occasionally, until
peppers are crisp-tender. Stir in remaining ingredients;
remove from heat.

Cut focaccia into 4 wedges; split each wedge horizontally.
Spoon one-fourth of vegetable mixture onto each bottom half; top with other half of bread wedge.

1 Serving

Calories 240
(Calories from Fat 70)

Fat 8g (Saturated 2g)

Cholesterol 5mg

Sodium 670mg

Carbohydrate 35g
(Dietary Fiber 2g)

Protein 9g

% Daily Value

Vitamin A 6%

Vitamin C 54%

Calcium 12%

Iron 12%

Diet Exchanges

2 Starch

1 Vegetable

1 Fat

1 **Eating Smart** • If you're a fast-food fanatic,
you might want to think about replacing some of those
high-calorie meals with easy-to-make, low-fat, tasty
sandwiches. Compared with a quarter-pound burger
(430 calories and 21 fat grams), this sandwich wins
hands down in nutrition, appearance and taste!

2 **Staying Active** • Making a gym date with
a friend can strengthen your commitment to exercise.
Schedule your workout dates like you'd schedule any
other meeting or appointment. Write it down on
your calendar to reinforce the importance of your
new lifestyle.

Chicken and
Strawberry–Spinach Salad

PREP: 10 MIN; COOK: 20 MIN | 4 SERVINGS

Strawberry Dressing (below)

1 pound boneless, skinless chicken breast halves

8 cups bite-size pieces spinach

1 cup strawberries, stems removed and cut in half

1/4 cup crumbled Gorgonzola cheese (1 ounce)

1/4 cup chopped walnuts

Make Strawberry Dressing. Remove fat from chicken. Spray 8- or 10-inch skillet with cooking spray; heat over medium high heat. Cook chicken in skillet about 15 to 20 minutes, turning once, until juice of chicken is no longer pink when centers of thickest pieces are cut. Remove chicken to cutting board.

Add dressing to skillet; stir to loosen any pan drippings. Cut chicken into slices. Arrange spinach on individual serving plates. Top with chicken, strawberries and cheese. Drizzle with dressing. Sprinkle with walnuts.

Strawberry Dressing

3 tablespoons apple juice

2 tablespoons strawberry spreadable fruit

2 tablespoons balsamic vinegar

Mix all ingredients until blended.

1 **Eating Smart •** An exquisite Italian ingredient, balsamic vinegar is made from white Trebbiano grape juice. This vinegar's dark color and pungent flavor develops while it ages in wooden barrels. Balsamic vinegar is fat free and imparts an intense, sweet flavor to food. Use it to jazz up low-fat recipes.

2 **Staying Active •** You may already have what you need in your kitchen cupboard to start weight training! Canned vegetables and jugs of milk are unlikely dumbbells, but they work. When you're ready to move on to heavier weights, look for inexpensive free weights at sporting goods stores.

1 Serving

Calories 225
(Calories from Fat 90)

Fat 10g (Saturated 3g)

Cholesterol 55mg

Sodium 210mg

Carbohydrate 14g
(Dietary Fiber 3g)

Protein 23g

% Daily Value

Vitamin A 52%

Vitamin C 64%

Calcium 12%

Iron 14%

Diet Exchanges

3 Very Lean Meat

1 Vegetable

1/2 Fruit

1 1/2 Fat

Chicken and Strawberry–Spinach Salad

Turkey–Wild Rice
Salad

PREP: 20 MIN; COOK: 6 MIN | 4 SERVINGS

1 pound uncooked turkey
breast slices, about
1/4 inch thick

1/4 teaspoon seasoned salt

1/4 teaspoon dried marjoram
leaves

3 cups cold cooked wild rice

1/4 cup chopped walnuts

1/4 cup dried cranberries

4 medium green onions,
chopped (1/4 cup)

1/4 teaspoon salt

1/2 cup raspberries

Leaf lettuce leaves

1/2 cup fat-free raspberry
vinaigrette dressing

Sprinkle turkey with seasoned salt and marjoram. Spray skillet with cooking spray; heat over medium-high heat. Cook turkey in skillet 4 to 6 minutes, turning once, until no longer pink in center. Cut into 2-inch pieces.

Mix wild rice, walnuts, cranberries, onions and salt. Carefully stir in raspberries.

Arrange rice mixture on lettuce leaves on 4 plates. Arrange warm turkey on rice mixture. Drizzle with dressing.

1 Serving

Calories 345
(Calories from Fat 45)

Fat 5g (Saturated 1g)

Cholesterol 75mg

Sodium 440mg

Carbohydrate 50g
(Dietary Fiber 7g)

Protein 32g

% Daily Value

Vitamin A 6%

Vitamin C 32%

Calcium 4%

Iron 16%

Diet Exchanges

2 Starch

3 Very Lean Meat

1 Vegetable

1 Fruit

1

Eating Smart • On average, nuts weigh in at about 275 calories and 28 grams of fat per 1/3 cup, chopped. Sounds like a lot. But by sprinkling a small handful of nuts on a salad, stir-fry or veggie side dish, you balance out other low-fat, low-calorie ingredients with protein and a bit of heart-healthy fat.

2

Staying Active • If you're able to walk to work, make this a part of your daily exercise plan. For a more intense workout, give yourself less time than you know you'll need. For instance, if it takes you 15 minutes to walk to work, give yourself only 10. Unless you don't mind being late, you'll pick up your pace and burn more calories.

Spinach-Shrimp Salad with
Hot Bacon Dressing

PREP: 10 MIN; COOK: 10 MIN | 4 SERVINGS

3 slices bacon, cut into 1-inch
   pieces

1/4 cup white vinegar

1 tablespoon sugar

1/4 teaspoon ground mustard

6 cups bite-size pieces
   spinach leaves

1 cup sliced mushrooms
   (3 ounces)

1/4 cup crumbled feta cheese
   (1 ounce)

1/2 pound cooked peeled
   deveined medium shrimp,
   thawed if frozen

Cook bacon in 10-inch skillet over medium-high heat, stirring occasionally, until crisp. Stir in vinegar, sugar and mustard; continue stirring until sugar is dissolved.

Toss spinach, mushrooms, cheese and shrimp in large bowl. Drizzle hot bacon dressing over spinach mixture; toss to coat. Serve immediately.

1 Serving

Calories 130
(Calories from Fat 45)

Fat 5g (Saturated 2g)

Cholesterol 120mg

Sodium 310mg

Carbohydrate 6g
(Dietary Fiber 1g)

Protein 16g

% Daily Value

Vitamin A 30%

Vitamin C 16%

Calcium 8%

Iron 16%

Diet Exchanges

2 Lean Meat

1 Vegetable

1 **Eating Smart** • Popeye's addiction to fat-free, nutrient-rich spinach makes sense when you learn that this veggie is a top-notch source of iron, calcium and vitamins A and C. Be sure to enjoy spinach with a glass of orange juice. The vitamin C in the juice helps your body absorb iron.

2 **Staying Active** • Keeping a workout diary provides you with concrete evidence that you're improving. Use a notebook in which to record your activity, workout length, heart rate before and after, and a brief description of how you felt during and after your workout. You'll be inspired when you see yourself improving over time.

Gazpacho Pasta Salad with
Tomato-Lime Dressing

PREP: 20 MIN | 4 SERVINGS

Tomato-Lime Dressing (below)

1 package (8 ounces) farfalle (bow-tie) pasta

1 large tomato, seeded and coarsely chopped (1 cup)

1 small cucumber, coarsely chopped (3/4 cup)

1 small bell pepper, coarsely chopped (1/2 cup)

4 medium green onions, sliced (1/4 cup)

1/2 green Anaheim chili, seeded and chopped

1 can (2 1/4 ounces) sliced ripe olives, drained

1/4 cup chopped fresh cilantro

Make Tomato-Lime Dressing. Cook and drain pasta as directed on package.

Mix pasta and remaining ingredients in large bowl. Pour dressing over mixture; toss. Serve immediately, or cover and refrigerate until serving.

Tomato-Lime Dressing

1/4 cup tomato juice

2 tablespoons olive or vegetable oil

2 tablespoons lime juice

1/4 teaspoon salt

1/8 teaspoon pepper

1 clove garlic, finely chopped

Shake all ingredients in tightly covered container.

1 Serving
Calories 320 (Calories from Fat 90)
Fat 10g (Saturated 2g)
Cholesterol 0mg
Sodium 350mg
Carbohydrate 62g (Dietary Fiber 4g)
Protein 5g

% Daily Value
Vitamin A 18%
Vitamin C 44%
Calcium 4%
Iron 20%

Diet Exchanges
1/3 Starch
2 Vegetable
1 Fat

1 **Eating Smart** • Gazpacho, a cold, nearly fat-free soup that originated in southern Spain, is usually made from a pureed mixture of fresh tomatoes, bell peppers, onions, celery, cucumber, bread crumbs, garlic, olive oil, vinegar and lemon juice. This low-cal salad borrows from traditional gazpacho to bring you a salad bursting with nutrient-rich veggies.

2 **Staying Active** • Ways to get more from your swimming workout include kicking from your hips instead of your knees and only just breaking the surface of the water with the heel of your kicking foot. Kicking your feet out of the water slows you down.

Gazpacho Pasta Salad with Tomato-Lime Dressing

Pesto-Pasta Salad

PREP: 15 MIN; CHILL: 2 HR | 4 SERVINGS

2 cups uncooked rotini pasta (6 ounces)

3/4 cup plain fat-free yogurt

1/4 cup pesto

1/4 teaspoon salt

2 cups sliced cauliflower

1/2 cup sliced quartered cucumber

1 medium red or yellow bell pepper, chopped (1 cup)

Cook and drain pasta as directed on package. Rinse with cold water; drain.

Mix yogurt, pesto and salt in serving bowl. Stir in pasta and remaining ingredients. Cover and refrigerate 2 to 4 hours to blend flavors.

1 Serving

Calories 335 (Calories from Fat 80)

Fat 9g (Saturated 2g)

Cholesterol 5mg

Sodium 180mg

Carbohydrate 55g (Dietary Fiber 4g)

Protein 13g

% Daily Value

Vitamin A 10%

Vitamin C 100%

Calcium 16%

Iron 16%

Diet Exchanges

3 Starch

2 Vegetable

1 Fat

1 **Eating Smart** • Don't listen to the "pasta bashers" who tell you that pasta makes you fat. Pasta contains about 200 nearly fat-free calories per 1 cup cooked serving and contributes B vitamins, fiber and some protein to your diet. To keep fat grams low, serve your pasta with low-fat sauce.

2 **Staying Active** • Do you want to exercise in the morning but aren't always ready to jump out of bed when the alarm goes off? Try laying out your exercise clothes before you go to sleep. Seeing them first thing when you wake up will help get you up and at 'em!

Cuban Spicy Bean Salad with
Oranges and Cilantro

PREP: 10 MIN; STAND: 30 MIN | 4 SERVINGS

2 oranges, peeled and sliced, or 1 can (11 ounces) mandarin orange segments in light syrup, drained

2 cans (15 ounces each) black beans, rinsed and drained

3 medium carrots, shredded (2 cups)

2/3 cup chopped fresh cilantro

1/2 cup balsamic or red wine vinegar

2 tablespoons sugar

2 teaspoons chopped fresh or canned jalapeňo chilies

4 cups bite-size pieces curly endive or lettuce

Mix all ingredients except endive in glass or plastic bowl. Cover and let stand 30 minutes.

Divide endive among 4 salad plates. Top with bean mixture.

1 Serving

Calories 330
(Calories from Fat 10)

Fat 1g (Saturated 0g)

Cholesterol 0mg

Sodium 840mg

Carbohydrate 78g
(Dietary Fiber 18g)

Protein 20g

% Daily Value

Vitamin A 94%

Vitamin C 38%

Calcium 20%

Iron 34%

Diet Exchanges

2 Starch

3 Vegetable

2 Fruit

1 **Eating Smart •** With only about 65 calories, one orange supplies you with 100 percent of the RDA for vitamin C. Oranges are also good sources of fiber, containing nearly 7 grams. Studies have shown that oranges outrank other fruits, including bananas, in providing a feeling of fullness.

2 **Staying Active •** Want to add variety to your workout? Crank up the tunes, and dance around your house. An hour of fast dancing can burn more than 400 calories. The harder you dance, the more calories you burn. No partner? No problem. This is your chance to claim the dance floor as your own!

Sensational
Poultry, Fish and
Seafood

4

Chicken with Couscous and Chili Sauce, 96

Herbed Baked Chicken Breasts, 98

Sichuan Cashew Chicken, 100

Chicken Niçoise, 102

Garlic-Ginger Chicken with Fettuccine, 104

Chicken and Pasta Stir-Fry, 105

Chicken Chili with Cheese, 106

Mediterranean Chicken with Rosemary Orzo, 107

Spicy Turkey Burgers, 108

Cheesy Turkey, Rice and Broccoli, 109

Honey-Mustard Turkey with Snap Peas, 110

Red Snapper with Mango Relish, 112

Crispy Baked Catfish, 113

Glazed Salmon with Apples, 114

Spinach-Filled Fish Rolls, 116

Marinated Tuna Steaks with Cucumber Sauce, 118

Grilled Fish with Jicama Salsa, 120

Parmesan Perch, 121

Garlic Shrimp, 122

Seafood and Vegetables with Rice, 124

Sea Scallop Stir-Fry, 126

Savory Scallops and Shrimp, 128

Grilled Shrimp Kabobs, 129

Mediterranean Chicken with Rosemary Orzo (page 107)

Chicken with
Couscous and Chili Sauce

PREP: 20 MIN; COOK: 30 MIN; STAND: 5 MIN | 8 SERVINGS

Green Chili Sauce (below)

8 boneless, skinless chicken breast halves (about 2 1/2 pounds)

1/4 teaspoon salt

1/4 teaspoon pepper

1 can (15 to 16 ounces) garbanzo beans, undrained

1 can (8 ounces) stewed tomatoes, undrained

1 cup fat-free chicken broth

1/3 cup raisins

1 tablespoon margarine or butter

1/2 teaspoon chili powder

1/2 teaspoon ground ginger

1/2 teaspoon ground cumin

1 cup uncooked couscous

Make Green Chili Sauce. Remove fat from chicken. Sprinkle salt and pepper over chicken. Spray 12-inch nonstick skillet with cooking spray; heat over medium heat. Cook chicken in skillet 15 to 20 minutes, turning once, until brown.

Add remaining ingredients except couscous to skillet. Heat to boiling; reduce heat. Cover and simmer about 10 minutes. Stir in couscous; remove from heat. Cover and let stand about 5 minutes or until liquid is absorbed. Serve chicken and couscous mixture with sauce.

Green Chili Sauce

1 can (8 ounces) stewed tomatoes, undrained

1 small onion, coarsely chopped (1/4 cup)

1/4 cup parsley sprigs

1 to 2 tablespoons coarsely chopped canned jalapeño chilies

1 tablespoon lemon juice

1 teaspoon ground cumin

1 teaspoon ground coriander

Place all ingredients in blender or food processor. Cover and blend on low speed just until chunky. Cover and refrigerate until serving.

1 Serving
Calories 335 (Calories from Fat 65)
Fat 7g (Saturated 2g)
Cholesterol 75mg
Sodium 530mg
Carbohydrate 40g (Dietary Fiber 6g)
Protein 35g

% Daily Value
Vitamin A 6%
Vitamin C 10%
Calcium 6%
Iron 18%

Diet Exchanges
2 Starch
2 Lean Meat
2 Vegetable

1 **Eating Smart** • Eat what you like. Nothing makes a diet more difficult than forcing yourself to eat foods you dislike. Also, slow down and sit down when you eat. Overeating is too easy when meals are grabbed on the run. Train yourself to eat seated at a table.

2 **Staying Active** • As your fitness level increases, you'll want to boost the intensity of your workouts. To prevent injury and keep yourself motivated, follow the 10 percent rule—try not to increase your mileage, pace or weight lifted by more than 10 percent each week.

Chicken with Couscous and Chili Sauce

Herbed Baked
Chicken Breasts

PREP: 15 MIN; BAKE: 35 MIN | 6 SERVINGS

6 boneless, skinless chicken breast halves (about 1 3/4 pounds)

1/2 cup fat-free mayonnaise or salad dressing

1 teaspoon garlic salt

1 tablespoon chopped fresh or 1 teaspoon dried marjoram leaves

2 teaspoons chopped fresh or 1/2 teaspoon dried rosemary leaves

2 teaspoons chopped fresh or 1/2 teaspoon dried thyme leaves

1 cup cornflakes cereal, crushed (1/2 cup)

1/2 teaspoon paprika

Heat oven to 375°. Spray rectangular pan, 13 × 9 × 2 inches, with cooking spray. Remove fat from chicken.

Mix mayonnaise, garlic salt, marjoram, rosemary and thyme; set aside. Mix cereal and paprika. Spread rounded tablespoon of mayonnaise mixture over both sides of each chicken breast half; coat evenly with cereal mixture. Place chicken in pan.

Bake uncovered 30 to 35 minutes or until juice of chicken is no longer pink when centers of thickest pieces are cut.

1 Serving

Calories 175
(Calories from Fat 35)

Fat 4g (Saturated 1g)

Cholesterol 5mg

Sodium 650mg

Carbohydrate 8g
(Dietary Fiber 0g)

Protein 27g

% Daily Value

Vitamin A 4%

Vitamin C 2%

Calcium 2%

Iron 14%

Diet Exchanges

1/2 Starch

4 Very Lean Meat

Eating Smart • By relying on flavor-intense herb coatings instead of fat-laden batters, you maximize flavor and minimize fat and calories. After you get the hang of it, experiment with your own herb combinations. You may never have the same dish twice!

Staying Active • Several brief bouts of exercise may burn more calories than one long exercise session. Some studies have shown that short-session exercisers drop a few more pounds than their longer-session counterparts. Short bursts of exercise boost metabolism regularly throughout the day, meaning calories are burned at a steady rate over a longer period of time.

The Particulars on Poultry

Chicken and turkey can be a boon or a bust to a low-fat diet, depending on how they are prepared. Take a look at the big differences among some popular poultry picks.

	Calories	Total Fat (g)	Saturated Fat (g)
Chicken (3 ounces, cooked)			
Breast, no skin, baked	150	4	1
Breast, with skin, baked	190	9	2
Thigh, no skin, baked	175	8	2
Thigh, with skin, baked	215	14	5
Drumstick, with skin, fried	200	11	3
Wings, with skin, fried	300	21	6
Nuggets, battered, fried	285	18	4
Turkey (3 ounces, cooked)			
Light meat, no skin, baked	145	4	<1
Light meat, with skin, baked	160	6	2
Dark meat, no skin, baked	160	6	2
Dark meat, with skin, baked	180	9	3
Ground, breast	160	6	2
Ground, dark meat	200	12	3

Sichuan
Cashew Chicken

PREP: 5 MIN; COOK: 23 MIN | 4 SERVINGS

4 boneless, skinless chicken breast halves (about 1 1/4 pounds)

1 tablespoon chili or vegetable oil

1 bag (1 pound) frozen broccoli, carrots and water chestnuts (or other combination)

1/3 cup stir-fry sauce

Hot cooked noodles or rice, if desired

1/4 cup cashew halves, if desired

Remove fat from chicken. Heat oil in 12-inch skillet over medium-high heat. Cook chicken in oil 15 to 20 minutes, turning once, until juice of chicken is no longer pink when centers of thickest pieces are cut. Remove chicken from skillet; keep warm.

Add vegetables to skillet; stir-fry about 2 minutes or until crisp-tender. Stir in stir-fry sauce; cook and stir about 30 seconds or until heated through.

Cut chicken into 1-inch diagonal slices. Serve chicken with vegetables and noodles. Sprinkle with cashews.

1 Serving

Calories 310
(Calories from Fat 70)

Fat 8g (Saturated 2g)

Cholesterol 95mg

Sodium 1,020mg

Carbohydrate 30g
(Dietary Fiber 4g)

Protein 32g

% Daily Value

Vitamin A 88%

Vitamin C 16%

Calcium 4%

Iron 16%

Diet Exchanges

1 1/2 Starch

3 1/2 Very Lean Meat

1 Vegetable

1 Fat

1 **Eating Smart** • Don't assume that dry-roasted nuts are significantly lower in fat and calories than regular roasted nuts. Nuts absorb little oil during roasting. All nuts, whether roasted in oil or not, are high-calorie foods and should be enjoyed in moderation.

2 **Staying Active** • We all struggle to find time to exercise. By limiting TV to a half hour a night (most of us watch far more than that), you free up more time for exercise. You can even stay active while you watch by doing crunches, push-ups and leg lifts.

Sichuan Cashew Chicken

Niçoise

4 boneless, skinless chicken breasts or thighs (about 1 1/4 pounds)

1 1/4 cups dry white wine or fat-free chicken broth

3 cloves garlic, finely chopped

1/2 cup frozen small whole onions

1 tablespoon Italian seasoning

2 medium bell peppers, sliced

6 Kalamata olives (2 ounces), pitted and chopped

2 cups hot cooked rice

Remove fat from chicken. Heat 1/4 cup of the wine to boiling in 10-inch nonstick skillet. Cook chicken in wine, turning once, until brown. Remove chicken from skillet; keep warm.

Add garlic, onions, Italian seasoning, bell peppers, olives and remaining 1 cup wine to skillet. Heat to boiling; boil 5 minutes.

Add chicken; reduce heat to medium. Cook 10 to 15 minutes or until juice of chicken is no longer pink when centers of thickest pieces are cut. Serve over rice.

1 Serving

Calories 265
(Calories from Fat 65)

Fat 7g (Saturated 2g)

Cholesterol 40mg

Sodium 290mg

Carbohydrate 30g
(Dietary Fiber 2g)

Protein 18g

% Daily Value

Vitamin A 4%

Vitamin C 46%

Calcium 6%

Iron 18%

Diet Exchanges

1 1/2 Starch

2 Lean Meat

1 Vegetable

1 Eating Smart • Research suggests that eating with soft music in the background, especially classical, encourages you to eat more slowly. Savoring your food will help prevent you from overeating and can ease digestion.

2 Staying Active • Push-ups tend to put most people off—especially women. But they can actually be a great addition to any workout. When done correctly, push-ups work muscles in the shoulders, upper arms, chest, abdomen, hips and back.

Chicken Niçoise

Garlic-Ginger Chicken with
Fettuccine

PREP: 10 MIN; COOK: 18 MIN | 4 SERVINGS

1 package (8 ounces)
   fettuccine (dry)

4 small boneless, skinless
   chicken breast halves
   (about 1 pound)

3 cloves garlic, finely
   chopped

1 tablespoon grated
   gingerroot

1/2 teaspoon salt

2 tablespoons dry sherry or
   apple juice

1 tablespoon apple jelly

2 tablespoons chopped fresh
   cilantro

Remove fat from chicken. Cook and drain fettuccine as directed on package.

While fettuccine is cooking, spray 10-inch nonstick skillet with cooking spray; heat over medium-high heat. Cook chicken in skillet about 5 minutes, turning once, until brown. Stir in garlic, gingerroot, salt, sherry and jelly. Turn chicken to glaze with sauce; reduce heat. Cover and simmer about 7 minutes or until juice of chicken is no longer pink when centers of thickest pieces are cut. Remove chicken from skillet.

Add fettuccine to sauce in skillet; toss lightly to coat. Serve chicken on fettuccine. Sprinkle with cilantro.

1 Serving

Calories 335
(Calories from Fat 55)

Fat 6g (Saturated 1g)

Cholesterol 110mg

Sodium 370mg

Carbohydrate 42g
(Dietary Fiber 2g)

Protein 30g

% Daily Value

Vitamin A 0%

Vitamin C 0%

Calcium 4%

Iron 18%

Diet Exchanges

2 Starch

3 Very Lean Meat

1 Fruit

1 **Eating Smart** • Does pasta make you fat? It depends on your serving size. Eating more pasta than your body needs will cause you to gain weight (which is true for all foods). Keep your serving size—one serving of pasta is usually about 1/2 cup—and number of daily servings in line with the Food Guide Pyramid, and pasta won't cause weight gain.

2 **Staying Active** • Keep your workouts fresh by changing the scenery. If you usually walk on an indoor treadmill, take your walk to a nearby park. If you always run outside, switch to the stationary bike. Try varying your workout with the seasons. Cold winter weather might mean you bring exercise indoors; when summer heats things up, take it outside again.

Chicken and Pasta
Stir-Fry

PREP: 10 MIN; COOK: 14 MIN | 4 SERVINGS

1 pound boneless, skinless chicken breast halves

2 cups uncooked farfalle (bow-tie) pasta (4 ounces)

1 pound asparagus, cut into 2-inch pieces (3 cups)

2 medium onions, sliced

1 1/2 cups fat-free chicken broth

3 tablespoons chopped fresh or 1 tablespoon dried basil leaves

3 tablespoons chopped sun-dried tomatoes (not oil-packed)

1/4 teaspoon pepper

Freshly grated Parmesan cheese, if desired

Remove fat from chicken. Cut chicken into 1-inch pieces.

Cook and drain pasta as directed on package. While pasta is cooking, spray 12-inch skillet with cooking spray; heat over medium heat. Cook asparagus, onions and 1 cup of the broth in skillet 5 to 7 minutes, stirring occasionally, until liquid has evaporated. Remove mixture from skillet.

Spray skillet with cooking spray; heat over medium-high heat. Add chicken; stir-fry about 5 minutes or until no longer pink in center.

Return asparagus mixture to skillet. Stir in remaining 1/2 cup broth, basil, tomatoes, pepper and pasta. Cook about 2 minutes, stirring frequently, until mixture is hot. Sprinkle with cheese.

1 Serving

Calories 250 (Calories from Fat 35)

Fat 4g (Saturated 1g)

Cholesterol 50mg

Sodium 490mg

Carbohydrate 31g (Dietary Fiber 3g)

Protein 26g

% Daily Value

Vitamin A 4%

Vitamin C 14%

Calcium 4%

Iron 14%

Diet Exchanges

1 1/2 Starch

3 Very Lean Meat

1 Vegetable

1 Eating Smart • The stir-fry originated in northern China. To make a little food go a long way, thrifty cooks would supplement small amounts of meat with a large quantity of inexpensive vegetables. This dish would then be cooked quickly over high heat to conserve fuel. Today, stir-fries are enjoyed for much the same reason— low-fat fare that cooks up quickly!

2 Staying Active • Instead of doing one 30-minute treadmill session, try doing 10 minutes on the treadmill followed by 10 minutes on a stationary bike and 10 minutes of jumping rope. Surprising the body with new activities keeps your workout fresh and actually burns more calories than doing one activity during the length of your workout.

Chicken
Chili with Cheese

PREP: 5 MIN; COOK: 15 MIN | 4 SERVINGS

1 pound skinless, boneless chicken breast halves

1 can (14 1/2 ounces) salsa-style chunky tomatoes, undrained

1 can (15 ounces) chili beans, undrained

1/2 cup shredded reduced-fat Cheddar cheese (2 ounces)

Remove fat from chicken. Cut chicken into 3/4-inch pieces. Spray 12-inch nonstick skillet with cooking spray; heat over medium-high heat. Cook chicken in skillet 3 to 5 minutes, stirring frequently, until light brown.

Stir in tomatoes and beans; reduce heat to medium-low. Cook uncovered 8 to 10 minutes, stirring frequently, until chicken is no longer pink in center. Sprinkle each serving with 2 tablespoons cheese.

1 Serving

Calories 260
(Calories from Fat 45)

Fat 5g (Saturated 2g)

Cholesterol 70mg

Sodium 1,200mg

Carbohydrate 24g
(Dietary Fiber 5g)

Protein 35g

% Daily Value

Vitamin A 10%

Vitamin C 18%

Calcium 12%

Iron 18%

Diet Exchanges

1 Starch

4 Very Lean Meat

2 Vegetable

1 **Eating Smart** • Including fresh or cooked tomatoes or salsas adds Vitamin C to dishes containing meat. The iron in the meat is more readily absorbed when eaten with a source of Vitamin C.

2 **Staying Active** • Remember to breathe deeply and maintain correct posture with a straight back and tight abdominal muscles as you exercise. This opens your rib cage so your lungs can fill to capacity. You can inhale to capacity by expanding your stomach as you fill your lungs. Called belly breathing, this helps get the oxygen pumped through the bloodstream to the muscles, where it is needed during exercise.

Mediterranean Chicken with
Rosemary Orzo

PREP: 10 MIN; COOK: 20 MIN | 4 SERVINGS

1 pound chicken breast
    tenders

2 cloves garlic, finely
    chopped

1 1/3 cups uncooked rosa-
    marina (orzo) pasta

1 can (14 1/2 ounces) fat-
    free chicken broth

1/2 cup water

1 tablespoon chopped fresh
    or 1 teaspoon dried rose-
    mary leaves

1/2 teaspoon salt

2 medium zucchini, cut
    lengthwise into fourths,
    then cut crosswise into
    slices (1 1/2 cups)

3 roma (plum) tomatoes, cut
    into fourths and sliced
    (1 1/2 cups)

1 medium green bell pepper,
    chopped (1 cup)

Spray 10-inch skillet with cooking spray; heat over
    medium-high heat. Add chicken; stir-fry about 5 min-
    utes or until brown. Stir in garlic, pasta and broth.
    Heat to boiling; reduce heat. Cover and simmer about
    8 minutes or until most of the liquid is absorbed.

Stir in remaining ingredients. Heat to boiling; reduce
    heat. Cover and simmer about 5 minutes, stirring once,
    until bell pepper is crisp-tender and pasta is tender.

1 Serving

Calories 300
(Calories from Fat 35)

Fat 4g (Saturated 1g)

Cholesterol 50mg

Sodium 820mg

Carbohydrate 42g
(Dietary Fiber 4g)

Protein 28g

% Daily Value

Vitamin A 8%

Vitamin C 42%

Calcium 4%

Iron 18%

Diet Exchanges

2 Starch

3 Very Lean Meat

2 Vegetable

Eating Smart • Although people in the
Mediterranean region consume as much as 40 percent of
their calories from fat, they have nowhere near the health
and weight problems that exist in the United States.
Researchers say this may be due, in part, to the plentiful
supply of fresh vegetables in the Mediterranean diet.

Staying Active • Metabolism is the term for how
our bodies convert food into energy. These rates vary
from person to person. Someone with a fast metabolism
burns more fat at rest than someone with a slow metabolism. Heredity is partially responsible for metabolism,
but you can counteract an inherited slow metabolism
with regular aerobic exercise and weight lifting.

Spicy
Turkey Burgers

Chili-Cheese Spread (below)

1 pound ground turkey breast

1 small onion, chopped
(1/4 cup)

1 clove garlic, finely chopped

2 to 3 tablespoons canned
chopped green chilies

1/8 teaspoon salt

1/8 teaspoon pepper

4 hamburger buns, split

Make Chili-Cheese Spread. Mix remaining ingredients except buns. Shape turkey mixture into 4 patties, each about 1/2 inch thick.

Set oven control to broil. Place patties on rack in broiler pan. Broil with tops 3 to 4 inches from heat about 14 minutes, turning once, until no longer pink in center. Serve on buns with Chili-Cheese spread.

Chili-Cheese Spread

1/2 cup shredded reduced-fat Cheddar cheese (2 ounces)

2 tablespoons fat-free sour cream

2 tablespoons canned chopped green chilies

Mix all ingredients.

1 Serving	
Calories 280 (Calories from Fat 80)	
Fat 9g (Saturated 2g)	
Cholesterol 75mg	
Sodium 400mg	
Carbohydrate 23g (Dietary Fiber 1g)	
Protein 28g	

% Daily Value	
Vitamin A 2%	
Vitamin C 2%	
Calcium 8%	
Iron 14%	

Diet Exchanges
1 Starch
3 Lean Meat
1 Vegetable

1 Eating Smart • Read labels when buying ground turkey. If the package doesn't say that it's ground turkey breast (96 to 98 percent fat-free by weight), your best bet is to ask the butcher to grind some breast meat for you.

2 Staying Active • Fitness goals are best achieved by starting small. Instead of trying to run a mile, begin by running or walking 2 blocks. When you've mastered that, add another few blocks. Keep adding distance, and before you know it, you'll have run your mile and will be ready to set another fitness goal!

Cheesy
Turkey, Rice and Broccoli

PREP: 10 MIN; COOK: 17 MIN; STAND: 5 MIN | 4 SERVINGS

1 pound turkey breast tenderloins, cut into 1-inch pieces

1 package (10 ounces) frozen broccoli with low-fat cheese-flavored sauce

1 2/3 cups uncooked instant brown rice

1 cup sliced mushrooms (3 ounces)

1/2 cup sliced water chestnuts

1 1/2 cups fat-free chicken broth

1 teaspoon chopped fresh or 1/2 teaspoon dried thyme leaves

1/2 teaspoon salt

5 medium green onions, sliced (1/3 cup)

Spray 12-inch skillet with cooking spray; heat over medium heat. Cook turkey in skillet about 5 minutes, stirring occasionally, until no longer pink in center.

Meanwhile, microwave broccoli in pouch on High 1 minute to easily remove from package. Add broccoli mixture to turkey. Stir in remaining ingredients. Heat to boiling; reduce heat. Cover and simmer about 10 minutes, stirring occasionally, until most of liquid is absorbed. Let stand 5 minutes before serving.

1 Serving
Calories 305 (Calories from Fat 25)
Fat 3g (Saturated 1g)
Cholesterol 60mg
Sodium 660mg
Carbohydrate 43g (Dietary Fiber 5g)
Protein 31g

% Daily Value
Vitamin A 8%
Vitamin C 14%
Calcium 12%
Iron 4%

Diet Exchanges
2 Starch
3 Very Lean Meat
2 Vegetable

1 **Eating Smart** • Vegetables that are deep green, red, orange, yellow or purple offer the most nutrients per calorie. Consider broccoli: One-half cup of chopped broccoli provides 90 percent of your RDA for Vitamin A and 100 percent of Vitamin C. No matter their color, most veggies are practically fat free and extremely low in calories.

2 **Staying Active** • Jumping rope isn't just for little girls anymore. With an inexpensive rope, room to jump and a good pair of shoes, you can design a great workout. Not only is jumping rope fun, but it also burns calories, boosts cardio endurance and improves balance, coordination and timing.

Honey-Mustard Turkey with
Snap Peas

PREP: 5 MIN; MARINATE: 20 MIN; COOK: 12 MIN | 4 SERVINGS

1 pound uncooked turkey
   breast slices, about
   1/4 inch thick

1/2 cup Dijon and honey
   poultry and meat marinade

1 cup baby carrots, cut
   lengthwise in half

2 cups frozen snap pea pods

Place turkey in shallow glass or plastic dish. Pour marinade over turkey; turn slices to coat evenly. Cover dish and let stand 20 minutes at room temperature.

Spray 10-inch skillet with cooking spray; heat over medium heat. Drain most of marinade from turkey. Cook turkey in skillet about 5 minutes, turning once, until brown.

Add carrots, lifting turkey to place carrots on bottom of skillet. Top turkey and carrots with pea pods. Cover and simmer about 7 minutes or until carrots are tender and turkey is no longer pink in center.

1 **Eating Smart** • Turkey brings a versatile, low-fat source of protein to your table, but not all turkey meat is created equal. White meat contains about 175 calories and less than 4 fat grams per 4-ounce serving. Compare this to 4 ounces of dark meat, which contains about 210 calories and 8 grams of fat.

2 **Staying Active** • How much should you drink during exercise? You can't rely on thirst alone for the answer. By the time you feel thirsty, you're already slightly dehydrated. Be sure to drink 16 ounces of water *before* exercise, plus 5 to 10 ounces every 15 minutes *during*, and 16 ounces per pound of lost weight *after* your workout.

1 Serving

Calories 150
(Calories from Fat 10)

Fat 1g (Saturated 0g)

Cholesterol 75mg

Sodium 65mg

Carbohydrate 9g
(Dietary Fiber 3g)

Protein 29g

% Daily Value

Vitamin A 60%

Vitamin C 28%

Calcium 4%

Iron 16%

Diet Exchanges

3 Very Lean Meat

2 Vegetable

Honey-Mustard Turkey with Snap Peas

Red Snapper with
Mango Relish

PREP: 10 MIN; STAND: 30 MIN; BROIL: 8 MIN | 4 SERVINGS

Mango Relish (below)

1 pound red snapper, orange roughy or walleye fillets

Cooking spray

1/2 teaspoon salt

Make Mango Relish.

Set oven control to broil. Place fish on rack in broiler pan. Spray fish with cooking spray; sprinkle with salt. Broil with tops 4 to 6 inches from heat 5 to 8 minutes or until fish is light brown and flakes easily with fork. Serve with relish.

Mango Relish

1 large mango, cut lengthwise in half, pitted and diced (3/4 cup)

1 small tomato, diced (1/2 cup)

2 tablespoons finely chopped red onion

1/2 cup chopped fresh cilantro

1/4 cup lime juice

Mix all ingredients in glass or plastic bowl. Cover and let stand 30 minutes.

1 **Eating Smart** • Low-fat relishes, salsas and chutneys can turn humble, low-fat foods into taste sensations. Featuring the intense flavor of tropical fruit, this relish is only one of many you could use to top red snapper. Use this same sauce to top other lean cuts of fish, chicken or turkey breast, lean hamburgers or thinly sliced pork tenderloin.

2 **Staying Active** • You don't have to run up and down stairs to burn calories. Ten minutes of slow and steady stair climbing will burn about 65 calories.

1 Serving

Calories 125
(Calories from Fat 10)

Fat 1g (Saturated 0g)

Cholesterol 50mg

Sodium 380mg

Carbohydrate 11g
(Dietary Fiber 1g)

Protein 19g

% Daily Value

Vitamin A 22%

Vitamin C 18%

Calcium 2%

Iron 2%

Diet Exchanges

2 1/2 Very Lean Meat

1 Vegetable

1/2 Fruit

Crispy
Baked Catfish

PREP: 10 MIN; BAKE: 18 MIN | 4 SERVINGS

1/4 cup yellow cornmeal

1/4 cup dry bread crumbs

1 teaspoon chili powder

1/2 teaspoon paprika

1/2 teaspoon garlic salt

1/4 teaspoon pepper

1 pound catfish fillets

1/4 cup fat-free French or
   ranch dressing

Heat oven to 450°. Spray broiler pan rack with cooking
   spray. Mix cornmeal, bread crumbs, chili powder,
   paprika, garlic salt and pepper.

If fish fillets are large, cut into 4 serving pieces. Lightly
   brush dressing on all sides of fish. Coat fish with cornmeal mixture. Place fish on rack in broiler pan. Bake
   uncovered 15 to 18 minutes or until fish flakes easily
   with fork.

1 **Eating Smart** • Instead of adding fat to otherwise
lean fish, coat it with crumbs and bake it to crisp perfec-
tion. Use this same method to "fry" a batch of chicken.
Oven-frying allows you to eliminate excess fat, without
sacrificing flavor and texture.

2 **Staying Active** • Q: If I'm not sore after a workout, does that mean I didn't work hard enough?

A: Soreness, which usually means that you've made your
muscles do something new, is a sign that your muscles
are repairing themselves. If you're already in good shape,
you may not experience soreness after exercise. Sharp
pain that lingers can indicate an injury. Get it checked
out right away.

1 Serving

Calories 175
(Calories from Fat 20)

Fat 2g (Saturated 0g)

Cholesterol 60mg

Sodium 430mg

Carbohydrate 17g
(Dietary Fiber 1g)

Protein 23g

% Daily Value

Vitamin A 4%

Vitamin C 0%

Calcium 4%

Iron 6%

Diet Exchanges

1 Starch

3 Very Lean Meat

Glazed
Salmon with Apples

PREP: 10 MIN; BAKE: 25 MIN | 6 SERVINGS

2 large apples, sliced

1 small onion, sliced

1 1/2-pound salmon fillet

2 tablespoons Dijon mustard

1 tablespoon honey

1/4 teaspoon garlic salt

Heat oven to 400°. Mix apples and onion in ungreased rectangular baking dish, 11 × 7 × 1 1/2 inches. Place fish, skin side down, on apple mixture. Mix mustard, honey and garlic salt. Spoon onto fish; spread evenly.

Bake uncovered 20 to 25 minutes or until fish flakes easily with fork. Serve apple mixture with fish.

1 **Eating Smart** • Apples are ideal snacks. One medium apple contains about 80 calories. Like other fruit, apples are fat, cholesterol and sodium free. And if you eat the peel, you'll get nearly 4 grams of fiber, compared to a peeled medium apple, which contains about 2 grams of fiber.

2 **Staying Active** • If your office building is located in or near a skyway system, you have a built-in fitness opportunity. Break up your day with brisk walks around the skyway. You can even fit in errands—dry cleaner, supermarket, bank—that you'd have to do anyway. Skyways work especially well in colder climates because you can walk "outdoors" year-round!

1 Serving

Calories 190
(Calories from Fat 55)

Fat 6g (Saturated 2g)

Cholesterol 65mg

Sodium 160mg

Carbohydrate 15g
(Dietary Fiber 2g)

Protein 21g

% Daily Value

Vitamin A 2%

Vitamin C 4%

Calcium 2%

Iron 4%

Diet Exchanges

3 Very Lean Meat

1 Fruit

1/2 Fat

Glazed Salmon with Apples

Spinach-Filled
Fish Rolls

PREP: 10 MIN; BAKE: 20 MIN | 4 SERVINGS

1 pound sole, orange roughy or flounder fillets

1 1/2 cups firmly packed spinach leaves

1/4 teaspoon garlic salt

1/3 cup fat-free mayonnaise or salad dressing

1/2 teaspoon Dijon mustard

1/4 cup garlic-flavored croutons, crushed

Lemon wedges, if desired

Heat oven to 400°. Spray square baking dish, 8 × 8 × 2 inches, with cooking spray. If fish fillets are large, cut into 4 serving pieces. Place spinach on fish; sprinkle with garlic salt. Roll up each fillet, beginning at narrow end. Place rolls, with points underneath, in baking dish. Mix mayonnaise and mustard; spoon onto each roll. Sprinkle with crushed croutons.

Bake uncovered 15 to 20 minutes or until fish flakes easily with fork. Serve with lemon wedges.

1 Serving

Calories 95 (Calories from Fat 10)

Fat 1g (Saturated 0g)

Cholesterol 45mg

Sodium 300mg

Carbohydrate 5g (Dietary Fiber 0g)

Protein 17g

% Daily Value

Vitamin A 10%

Vitamin C 2%

Calcium 2%

Iron 4%

Diet Exchanges

2 Very Lean Meat

1 Vegetable

1 Eating Smart • Want to replace some of the meat in your diet with fish? Try lean white fish such as orange roughy, halibut, cod, haddock or sole. With a subtle yet distinct flavor, these fish lend themselves to countless menu options. Low in fat and calories, they are also a good source of protein, plus the heart smart omega-3 fats.

2 Staying Active • Knowing yourself is key to creating a fitness program you can stick with. Do you live by your day planner? Then be sure to schedule exercise "appointments" with yourself. If you tend to be more flexible, commit to a weekly exercise goal, such as three 30-minute sessions per week, and make it up as you go along.

Spinach-Filled Fish Rolls

Marinated Tuna Steaks with
Cucumber Sauce

PREP: 10 MIN; MARINATE: 1 HR; BROIL: 10 MIN | 4 SERVINGS

3 tablespoons lime juice

2 tablespoons chopped fresh cilantro

1 clove garlic, finely chopped

1/4 teaspoon salt

1 pound tuna steaks

Cucumber Sauce (below)

Mix lime juice, cilantro, garlic and salt in pie plate, 9 × 1 1/4 inches. Cut fish steaks into 4 serving pieces. Add fish to lime mixture, turning several times to coat with marinade. Cover and refrigerate 1 hour, turning once.

Set oven control to boil. Spray broiler pan rack with cooking spray. Remove fish from marinade; discard marinade. Place fish on rack in broiler pan. Broil with tops 4 inches from heat 7 to 10 minutes, turning once, until fish flakes easily with fork. Serve with Cucumber Sauce.

Cucumber Sauce

1/2 cup chopped cucumber

1/4 cup plain yogurt

2 tablespoons chopped fresh cilantro

1 tablespoon fat-free mayonnaise or salad dressing

Mix all ingredients.

1 **Eating Smart** • Studies show that eating fatty fish, such as tuna and salmon, once or twice a week is good for the heart and waistline. The omega-3 fatty acids found in fish oil may protect against heart disease. Eating fatty fish will also help you feel full faster, meaning you'll eat less overall.

2 **Staying Active** • Warm-ups and cool-downs are important parts of any exercise program. By gently stretching before you work out, you tell your muscles that they'll soon be needed. Cooling down with light calisthenics and more gentle stretching will help return your heart rate to normal, and help reduce post-workout soreness.

Marinated Tuna Steaks with Cucumber Sauce

1 Serving

Calories 140
(Calories from Fat 45)

Fat 5g (Saturated 2g)

Cholesterol 60mg

Sodium 240mg

Carbohydrate 3g
(Dietary Fiber 0g)

Protein 20g

% Daily Value

Vitamin A 2%

Vitamin C 4%

Calcium 4%

Iron 4%

Diet Exchanges

3 Very Lean Meat

1 Fat

Grilled Fish with
Jicama Salsa

PREP: 15 MIN; CHILL: 2 HR; MARINATE 30 MIN; GRILL: 10 MIN | 6 SERVINGS

Jicama Salsa (below)

1 1/2 pounds swordfish, tuna or marlin steaks, 3/4 to 1 inch thick

3 tablespoons olive or vegetable oil

1 tablespoon lime juice

1/4 teaspoon salt

1/8 teaspoon crushed red pepper

Make Jicama Salsa.

If fish steaks are large, cut into 6 serving pieces. Mix oil, lime juice, salt and red pepper in shallow glass or plastic dish or heavy-duty resealable plastic bag. Add fish; turn to coat with marinade. Cover dish or seal bag and refrigerate 30 minutes.

Heat coals or gas grill for direct heat. Remove fish from marinade; reserve marinade. Cover and grill fish 5 to 6 inches from medium heat about 10 minutes, brushing 2 or 3 times with marinade and turning once, until fish flakes easily with fork. Discard any remaining marinade. Serve fish with salsa.

Jicama Salsa

2 cups chopped peeled jicama (3/4 pound)

1 tablespoon chopped fresh cilantro or parsley

1 tablespoon lime juice

1/2 teaspoon chili powder

1/4 teaspoon salt

1 medium cucumber, peeled and chopped (1 cup)

1 medium orange, peeled and chopped (3/4 cup)

Mix all ingredients in glass or plastic bowl. Cover and refrigerate at least 2 hours to blend flavors.

1 **Eating Smart** • What's jicama? Also referred to as a "Mexican potato," this large, bulbous root vegetable has a thin brown skin and white crunchy flesh. Its sweet, nutty flavor is good both raw and cooked. Like most other veggies, jicama is low calorie, contains negligible fat and is cholesterol and sodium free.

2 **Staying Active** • Joining a softball, volleyball or basketball team can be a good exercise motivator. You'll enjoy the camaraderie of your teammates, and the practices and games will give you plenty of time to get fit.

1 Serving

Calories 165
(Calories from Fat 70)

Fat 8g (Saturated 2g)

Cholesterol 55mg

Sodium 250mg

Carbohydrate 8g
(Dietary Fiber 3g)

Protein 18g

% Daily Value

Vitamin A 4%

Vitamin C 20%

Calcium 2%

Iron 4%

Diet Exchanges

2 Lean Meat

2 Vegetable

Parmesan
Perch

PREP: 10 MIN; BAKE: 10 MIN | 4 SERVINGS

1 pound ocean perch, cod or haddock fillets

2 tablespoons dry bread crumbs

1 tablespoon grated Parmesan cheese

1 teaspoon dried basil leaves

1/2 teaspoon paprika

Dash of pepper

1 tablespoon reduced-calorie margarine, melted

2 tablespoons chopped fresh parsley

Move oven rack to position slightly above middle of oven. Heat oven to 500°. Spray rectangular pan, 13 × 9 × 2 inches, with cooking spray.

If fish fillets are large, cut into 4 serving pieces. Mix remaining ingredients except margarine and parsley.

Brush one side of fish with margarine; dip into crumb mixture. Place fish, coated sides up, in pan. Bake uncovered about 10 minutes or until fish flakes easily with fork. Sprinkle with parsley.

1 Serving

Calories 120
(Calories from Fat 25)

Fat 3g (Saturated 1g)

Cholesterol 55mg

Sodium 150mg

Carbohydrate 3g
(Dietary Fiber 0g)

Protein 20g

% Daily Value

Vitamin A 6%

Vitamin C 2%

Calcium 4%

Iron 4%

Diet Exchanges

3 Very Lean Meat

1 **Eating Smart** • Fish is a top-notch option for those trying to get the most satisfaction from the fewest calories. Per calorie, fish has been found to be more satisfying than lean beef or chicken.

2 **Staying Active** • How's this for an exercise quickie? Just 4 minutes of jumping jacks and 4 minutes of jumping rope burns about 80 calories in 8 minutes! Be sure to include a couple of minutes to warm up and a couple of minutes to cool down and stretch properly.

Garlic
Shrimp

PREP: 15 MIN; COOK: 5 MIN | 4 SERVINGS

1 tablespoon vegetable oil

3 large cloves garlic, finely chopped

1 pound uncooked peeled deveined medium shrimp, thawed if frozen

1 large carrot, shredded (2/3 cup)

2 tablespoons chopped fresh cilantro

Hot cooked noodles or rice, if desired

Heat wok or 12-inch skillet over medium-high heat. Add oil; rotate wok to coat side. Add garlic; stir-fry 1 minute. Add shrimp; stir-fry 1 minute.

Add carrot; stir-fry about 3 minutes or until shrimp are pink and firm. Stir in cilantro. Serve with noodles.

1 Serving

Calories 90
(Calories from Fat 35)

Fat 4g (Saturated 1g)

Cholesterol 105mg

Sodium 130mg

Carbohydrate 3g
(Dietary Fiber 1g)

Protein 12g

% Daily Value

Vitamin A 30%

Vitamin C 2%

Calcium 2%

Iron 10%

Diet Exchanges

2 Very Lean Meat

1/2 Vegetable

1 **Eating Smart** • Garlic has many health benefits. This pungent herb supports the immune system and kills viruses and may help reduce blood cholesterol levels. It may even help protect against certain cancers. What's more, the intense flavor garlic brings to low-fat foods means that you won't miss the fat!

2 **Staying Active** • Inspirational words can make a big difference when your spirit flags. Find a couple of meaningful quotes, and post them where they'll motivate you most—on your mirror, on the refrigerator, in your gym bag or on the door of your gym locker.

Garlic Shrimp

Seafood and
Vegetables with Rice

PREP: 15 MIN; COOK: 10 MIN | 6 SERVINGS

1 package (8 ounces) sliced mushrooms

1 can (14 1/2 ounces) fat-free chicken broth

3 roma (plum) tomatoes, cut into fourths and sliced (1 1/2 cups)

1/2 cup sliced drained roasted red bell peppers

1/2 pound uncooked peeled deveined small shrimp, thawed if frozen

1/2 pound cod fillets, cubed

6 ounces bay scallops

1/2 cup white wine or chicken broth

1/2 teaspoon salt

1/4 to 1/2 teaspoon red pepper sauce

1/4 cup chopped fresh cilantro

4 cups hot cooked rice

Heat mushrooms and broth to boiling in 3-quart saucepan. Stir in remaining ingredients except cilantro or rice. Heat to boiling; reduce heat. Cover and simmer 5 to 7 minutes or until shrimp are pink and firm. Stir in cilantro. Serve in bowls over rice.

1 Serving

Calories 225
(Calories from Fat 20)

Fat 2g (Saturated 0g)

Cholesterol 55mg

Sodium 710mg

Carbohydrate 31g
(Dietary Fiber 1g)

Protein 19g

% Daily Value

Vitamin A 8%

Vitamin C 22%

Calcium 4%

Iron 18%

Diet Exchanges

2 Starch

1 1/2 Very Lean Meat

1 Vegetable

1 **Eating Smart** • Enliven sauces, sandwiches, soups and salads by adding a handful of chopped roasted red bell peppers. These nutrient-rich gems are also rich in fat-free flavor. One-half cup contains less than 10 calories.

2 **Staying Active** • Varying the intensity of your workouts keeps them interesting and may even help burn calories. Your metabolism idles when you repeatedly do the same activities at the same intensity. By working at a higher target heart rate, cutting back during your next session and revving up again later, you increase your calorie burn.

Seafood and Vegetables with Rice

Sea Scallop
Stir-Fry

PREP: 20 MIN; COOK: 8 MIN | 4 SERVINGS

1 package (3 ounces)
    Oriental-flavor ramen
    noodle soup mix

1 tablespoon olive or
    vegetable oil

3/4 pound asparagus,
    cut into 1-inch pieces
    (2 1/2 cups)

1 large red bell pepper, cut
    into thin strips

1 small onion, chopped
    (1/4 cup)

2 cloves garlic, finely
    chopped

3/4 pound sea scallops, cut
    in half

1 tablespoon soy sauce

2 tablespoons lemon juice

1 teaspoon sesame oil

1/4 teaspoon red pepper
    sauce

Reserve seasoning packet from noodles. Cook and drain noodles as directed on package.

While noodles are cooking, heat olive oil in wok or 12-inch skillet over high heat. Add asparagus, bell pepper, onion and garlic; stir-fry 2 to 3 minutes or until vegetables are crisp-tender. Add scallops; stir-fry until white.

Mix contents of reserved seasoning packet, the soy sauce, lemon juice, sesame oil and pepper sauce; stir into scallop mixture. Stir in noodles; heat through.

1 Serving

Calories 200
(Calories from Fat 80)

Fat 9g (Saturated 1g)

Cholesterol 15mg

Sodium 620mg

Carbohydrate 19g
(Dietary Fiber 2g)

Protein 13g

% Daily Value

Vitamin A 30%

Vitamin C 76%

Calcium 6%

Iron 12%

Diet Exchanges

1 Starch

1 Very Lean Meat

1 Vegetable

1 1/2 Fat

1 Eating Smart • Scallops have slightly less cholesterol than chicken or beef. These shellfish are also significantly lower in fat than meat and poultry. Better yet, the fat found in shellfish is largely unsaturated and includes heart-healthy omega-3 fatty acids.

2 Staying Active • Outdoor, upright, recumbent and mountain. So many bikes, so little time! Which type of bike burns the most calories? The mountain bike comes in on top, burning about 700 calories during a vigorous, uphill, 45-minute workout. In the same time period on flat terrain, outdoor bikes burn about 410 calories. Both the recumbent and upright stationary bikes burn about 360 calories in 45 minutes.

Sea Scallop Stir-Fry

Savory
Scallops and Shrimp

PREP: 15 MIN; COOK: 10 MIN | 4 SERVINGS

2 tablespoons olive or
vegetable oil

1 clove garlic, finely chopped

1 medium green onion,
chopped (1 tablespoon)

1 medium green bell pepper,
diced (1 cup)

1 tablespoon chopped fresh
parsley or 1 teaspoon
parsley flakes

1 pound sea scallops, cut in
half

1 pound peeled deveined
medium shrimp, thawed if
frozen

1/2 cup dry white wine or
fat-free chicken broth

1 tablespoon lemon juice

1/4 to 1/2 teaspoon crushed
red pepper

Heat oil in 10-inch skillet over medium heat. Cook garlic,
onion, bell pepper and parsley in oil about 5 minutes,
stirring occasionally, until bell pepper is crisp-tender.

Stir in remaining ingredients. Cook 4 to 5 minutes, stirring frequently, until shrimp are pink and firm and
scallops are white.

1 Serving

Calories 220
(Calories from Fat 80)

Fat 9g (Saturated 1g)

Cholesterol 180mg

Sodium 400mg

Carbohydrate 5g
(Dietary Fiber 1g)

Protein 31g

% Daily Value

Vitamin A 10%

Vitamin C 26%

Calcium 10%

Iron 26%

Diet Exchanges

4 Very Lean Meat

1 Vegetable

1 Fat

1 **Eating Smart** • Rather than eliminating fat from
our diets, experts recommend that we simply reduce the
amount we consume. Cooking low-fat foods such as pasta,
veggies, or seafood in a tablespoon or so of olive oil provides a flavor boost and makes for a more filling meal.

2 **Staying Active** • At least two days a week, pre-
tend your car is in for repairs. Without your car, you'll
need to walk and ride your bike to work, pick up groceries, visit the bank . . . you get the idea. Use the bus if
you have to. Running to catch public transportation still
burns more calories than sitting in traffic.

Grilled
Shrimp Kabobs

PREP: 10 MIN; MARINATE: 30 MIN; GRILL: 8 MIN | 4 SERVINGS

1 pound uncooked peeled deveined large shrimp, thawed if frozen

1 cup fat-free Italian dressing

1 medium red onion, cut into 8 pieces

1 medium green bell pepper, cut into 8 pieces

16 medium cherry tomatoes

16 small whole mushrooms

4 cups hot cooked rosamarina (orzo) pasta

Place shrimp and dressing in shallow glass or plastic dish or heavy-duty resealable plastic food-storage bag. Cover dish or seal bag and refrigerate 30 minutes.

Heat coals or gas grill for direct heat. Remove shrimp from marinade; reserve marinade. Thread shrimp, onion, bell pepper, tomatoes and mushrooms alternately on each of four 15-inch metal skewers, leaving space between each piece.

Grill kabobs uncovered 4 to 6 inches from medium heat 6 to 8 minutes, turning frequently and brushing several times with marinade, until shrimp are pink and firm. Discard any remaining marinade. Serve kabobs with pasta.

1 Eating Smart • By planning weekly menus and shopping lists, you eliminate the "what's for dinner?" dilemma that can spoil the best healthy-eating intentions. But remain flexible to leave room for improvisation. Shopping, especially for fresh produce, can depend on what's available—and what looks good—at the market.

2 Staying Active • Want to try power-walking? Tips to make the most of your workout include carrying a weighted backpack, walking up hills, bending your arms at the waist and pumping hard during the walk. If you find a speed at which you're sweating but still able to talk, you're on your way to a great workout. Power-walking for 45 minutes 5 days a week can burn as many as 1,600 calories.

1 Serving

Calories 340
(Calories from Fat 25)

Fat 3g (Saturated 0g)

Cholesterol 160mg

Sodium 740mg

Carbohydrate 56g
(Dietary Fiber 5g)

Protein 27g

% Daily Value

Vitamin A 10%

Vitamin C 38%

Calcium 6%

Iron 34%

Diet Exchanges

3 Starch

2 Very Lean Meat

2 Vegetable

Great Beef, Pork and Lamb

5

Beef Medallions with Pear–Cranberry Chutney, 132

Saucy Italian Steak, 134

Orange-Teriyaki Beef with Noodles, 136

Philly Cheese Steak Casserole, 138

Spicy Pepper Steak, 139

Pizza Casserole, 140

Garlic Shepherds Pie, 142

Giant Oven Burger, 143

Veal and Potato Strata with Roasted Peppers, 144

Caribbean Pork Roast, 146

Italian Roasted Pork Tenderloin, 147

Roasted Pork Chops and Vegetables, 148

Grilled Southwestern Pork Chops, 150

Skillet Ham and Vegetables au Gratin, 151

Creamy Ham and Pasta, 152

Spanish Lamb and Couscous, 154

Mustard Lamb Chops, 155

Spanish Lamb and Couscous (page 154)

Beef Medallions with
Pear-Cranberry Chutney

PREP: 15 MIN; COOK: 23 MIN | 4 SERVINGS

4 beef tenderloin steaks, about 1 inch thick (1 pound)

1/2 large red onion, thinly sliced

2 cloves garlic, finely chopped

2 tablespoons dry red wine or grape juice

2 firm ripe pears, peeled and diced

1/2 cup fresh or frozen cranberries

2 tablespoons packed brown sugar

1/2 teaspoon pumpkin pie spice

Remove fat from beef. Spray 12-inch skillet with cooking spray; heat over medium-high heat. Cook onion, garlic and wine in skillet about 5 minutes, stirring frequently, until onion is tender but not brown.

Stir in remaining ingredients except beef; reduce heat. Simmer uncovered about 10 minutes, stirring frequently, until cranberries burst. Place chutney in small bowl; set aside.

Wipe out skillet; spray with cooking spray. Cook beef in skillet over medium heat about 8 minutes for medium doneness, turning once. Serve with chutney.

1 Serving

Calories 250 (Calories from Fat 70)

Fat 8g (Saturated 3g)

Cholesterol 65mg

Sodium 60mg

Carbohydrate 23g (Dietary Fiber 3g)

Protein 25g

% Daily Value

Vitamin A 0%

Vitamin C 4%

Calcium 2%

Iron 14%

Diet Exchanges

3 Lean Meat

1 1/2 Fruit

1 **Eating Smart** • You don't have to avoid all red meat if you're trying to lose weight. By selecting lean cuts (round tip, eye of round, top round, top loin, tenderloin and sirloin), trimming all visible fat and eating small portions, you can enjoy meat as part of a healthy diet.

2 **Staying Active** • Skip the drive-through next time you're at the bank or a fast-food restaurant. Also bypass book and video slots at the library and video rental store. The short walk in and out burns more calories than just sitting in your car. These trips, though brief, add up over time.

Beef Medallions with Pear-Cranberry Chutney

Saucy
Italian Steak

PREP: 10 MIN; BAKE: 1 1/2 HR | 6 SERVINGS

1 1/2-pound beef round
    steak, about 1 inch thick

2 tablespoons all-purpose
    flour

1/4 teaspoon pepper

1 tablespoon olive or
    vegetable oil

2 cups fat-free tomato pasta
    sauce (any variety)

1 package (9 ounces) frozen
    Italian or regular cut
    green beans

1/4 cup sliced ripe olives

Heat oven to 375°. Remove fat from beef. Mix flour and
    pepper; rub over both sides of beef, shaking off excess.
    Cut beef into 6 serving pieces.

Heat oil in 12-inch nonstick skillet over medium heat.
    Cook beef in oil about 5 minutes, turning once, until
    brown. Place beef in ungreased rectangular baking
    dish, 11 × 7 × 1 1/2 inches. Pour pasta sauce over beef.

Cover and bake 1 hour. Add frozen green beans to sauce
    around beef. Cover and bake about 30 minutes longer
    or until beef is tender. Sprinkle with olives.

1 Serving

Calories 230
(Calories from Fat 70)

Fat 8g (Saturated 2g)

Cholesterol 55mg

Sodium 450mg

Carbohydrate 18g
(Dietary Fiber 2g)

Protein 23g

% Daily Value

Vitamin A 8%

Vitamin C 10%

Calcium 4%

Iron 6%

Diet Exchanges

1 Starch

2 1/2 Lean Meat

1 Vegetable

1 Eating Smart • Depending on the season, frozen
vegetables can be better nutritional choices than fresh.
Packaged almost immediately after harvest, frozen veggies retain more of their nutrients than do fresh veggies
that are shipped cross-country only to sit in grocery bins
until purchase.

2 Staying Active • Work out in a traffic jam? You
can make good use of time spent in gridlock by taking a
couple of deep breaths and stretching your neck and
shoulders. Besides increasing flexibility, stretching will
keep your blood pressure down in an otherwise stressful
situation.

The Skinniest Seven Cuts of Beef

Beef may have gotten a bad rap for being high in fat and saturated fat, but if you choose the right cut, it can be a healthy addition to your diet. Searching the meat case for the leanest cuts? They're easy to find if you look for "loin" or "round" in the name.

	Calories	Total Fat(g)	Saturated Fat(g)
Cut (3 ounces, cooked)			
Top round	155	4	1
Eye of round	155	4	1
Round tip	165	6	2
Bottom Round	165	6	2
Top Sirloin	165	6	2
Top Loin	175	8	3
Tenderloin	180	9	3

The Top Three Picks of Pork

Pork fits in perfectly with a low-fat diet. Just be sure to trim off all the visible fat before cooking.

	Calories	Total Fat(g)	Saturated Fat(g)
Cut (3 ounces, cooked)			
Tenderloin	140	4	1
Chop, loin	180	8	3
Roast, loin	180	9	3

Orange-Teriyaki
Beef with Noodles

PREP: 10 MIN; COOK: 15 MIN | 4 SERVINGS

1 pound beef boneless sirloin

1 can (14 1/2 ounces) fat-free beef broth

1/4 cup teriyaki stir-fry cooking sauce

2 tablespoons orange marmalade

Dash of ground red pepper (cayenne)

1 1/2 cups frozen snap pea pods

1 1/2 cups uncooked fine egg noodles (3 ounces)

Remove fat from beef. Cut beef into thin strips. Spray 12-inch skillet with cooking spray; heat over medium-high heat. Cook beef in skillet 2 to 4 minutes, stirring occasionally, until brown. Remove beef from skillet; keep warm.

Add broth, cooking sauce, marmalade and red pepper to skillet. Heat to boiling. Stir in pea pods and noodles; reduce heat to medium. Cover and cook about 5 minutes or until noodles are tender. Stir in beef. Cook uncovered 2 to 3 minutes or until sauce is slightly thickened.

1 **Eating Smart** • Remember when peas were found only in gardens and cans? Now we find a handful of varieties throughout the grocery store. Produce sections usually carry snow peas and snap pea pods. These peas are also available, along with traditional shelled peas, in your grocer's freezer. Regardless of variety, peas are fat-free sources of vitamin C and fiber.

2 **Staying Active** • Next time you order in lunch at work, volunteer to be the one to pick it up. You'll get in a mini workout and have an excuse to get out of the office. Plus, the change of scenery just may put a spring in your step.

1 Serving

Calories 265
(Calories from Fat 45)

Fat 5g (Saturated 2g)

Cholesterol 80mg

Sodium 1,210mg

Carbohydrate 28g
(Dietary Fiber 2g)

Protein 29g

% Daily Value

Vitamin A 0%

Vitamin C 20%

Calcium 4%

Iron 24%

Diet Exchanges

1 1/2 Starch

2 1/2 Lean Meat

1 Vegetable

Orange-Teriyaki Beef with Noodles

Philly

Cheese Steak Casserole

3 cups uncooked wide egg
noodles (6 ounces)

1 pound beef boneless sirloin
steak, about 3/4 inch thick

1/4 teaspoon pepper

2 medium onions, chopped
(1 cup)

1 small green bell pepper,
chopped (1/2 cup)

1 can (14 1/2 ounces) fat-
free beef broth

1/4 cup all-purpose flour

1/2 cup fat-free half-and-
half

1 tablespoon Dijon mustard

3/4 cup shredded reduced-fat
Cheddar cheese (3 ounces)

Heat oven to 350°. Spray rectangular baking dish, 11 × 7
× 1 1/2 inches, with cooking spray. Cook and drain egg
noodles as directed on package.

Remove fat from beef. Cut beef into 3/4-inch pieces.
Spray 12-inch nonstick skillet with cooking spray; heat
over medium heat. Cook beef and pepper in skillet 2 to
3 minutes, stirring occasionally, until beef is brown.
Stir in onions and bell pepper. Cook 2 minutes, stirring
occasionally. Spoon into baking dish.

Beat broth and flour with wire whisk until smooth. Add
to skillet; heat to boiling. Cook, stirring constantly,
until mixture thickens; remove from heat. Stir in
half-and-half and mustard. Spoon over beef. Stir in
cooked noodles.

Cover and bake 30 minutes. Sprinkle with cheese. Bake
uncovered about 10 minutes or until cheese is melted
and casserole is bubbly.

1 Serving

Calories 245
(Calories from Fat 45)

Fat 5g (Saturated 2g)

Cholesterol 65mg

Sodium 470mg

Carbohydrate 28g
(Dietary Fiber 2g)

Protein 24g

% Daily Value

Vitamin A 2%

Vitamin C 10%

Calcium 8%

Iron 16%

Diet Exchanges

1 1/2 Starch

3 Very Lean Meat

1 Vegetable

1 **Eating Smart** • The trick to eating meat when
watching your waistline is to watch the portion size.
Figure on 3 to 4 ounces (about the size of a deck of
cards) of lean cuts of meat per person rather than enor-
mous restaurant-size portions.

2 **Staying Active** • Talk and tone! Use the time you
spend on the telephone for arm curls, knee bends and other
simple muscle exercises as you chat. It's easy to sneak in
some exercise during normally sedentary activities.

Spicy
Pepper Steak

PREP: 10 MIN; COOK: 4 MIN | 4 SERVINGS

1 tablespoon chili oil or
vegetable oil

1 pound cut-up beef for
stir-fry

1 large bell pepper, cut into
3/4-inch squares

1 medium onion, sliced

1/4 cup hoisin sauce

Heat oil in 12-inch nonstick skillet over medium-high
heat. Add beef; stir-fry about 2 minutes or until brown.

Add bell pepper and onion; stir-fry about 1 minute or
until vegetables are crisp-tender. Stir in hoisin sauce;
cook and stir about 30 seconds or until hot.

1 Eating Smart • A mixture of soybeans, garlic
and chili peppers, hoisin sauce is one of several fat-free
Asian seasonings that enhances meat and vegetables.
Other low-fat sauce varieties to try include duck, sweet-
and-sour, tamari (wheat-free soy sauce), plum, hot chili
and bean sauce.

2 Staying Active • Make the most of your holi-
days by encouraging family members to accompany you
on a long walk after the big meal. You'll be able to
spend time chatting with loved ones and avoid the sluggish feeling that follows big meals. The best part? You
burn calories and avoid the guilt that can lead to holiday
eating binges.

1 Serving

Calories 205
(Calories from Fat 70)

Fat 8g (Saturated 2g)

Cholesterol 60mg

Sodium 300mg

Carbohydrate 11g
(Dietary Fiber 2g)

Protein 24g

% Daily Value

Vitamin A 4%

Vitamin C 32%

Calcium 2%

Iron 14%

Diet Exchanges

3 Lean Meat

2 Vegetable

Pizza

Casserole

PREP: 20 MIN; BAKE: 30 MIN; STAND: 5 MIN | 6 SERVINGS

4 cups uncooked wagon
   wheel pasta (8 ounces)

1/2 pound diet-lean or extra-
   lean ground beef

1/4 cup sliced ripe olives

1 can (4 ounces) mushroom
   pieces and stems, drained

1 jar (26 to 28 ounces) fat-
   free tomato pasta sauce

1 cup shredded reduced-fat
   mozzarella cheese
   (4 ounces)

Heat oven to 350°. Cook and drain pasta as directed on package. While pasta is cooking, cook beef in 10-inch skillet over medium-high heat, stirring frequently, until brown; drain. Mix pasta, beef and remaining ingredients except cheese in ungreased 2 1/2-quart casserole.

Cover and bake about 30 minutes or until hot. Sprinkle with cheese. Cover and let stand about 5 minutes or until cheese is melted.

1 **Eating Smart** • Move over, macaroni! Using different pasta shapes and colors brings variety to your meals. Wagon wheel, radiatore, penne, farfalle and rigatoni are only a few of many fun pasta shapes available. Or treat yourself to spinach, lemon pepper or sun-dried tomato pasta. These pasta varieties add fat-free fun to your meal.

2 **Staying Active** • When you visit the grocery store or mall, walk around the periphery two or three times before you start shopping. You'll get an especially good workout at the mall. You might even feel less guilty about exercising your credit card if you've gotten *your* exercise first!

1 Serving

Calories 310
(Calories from Fat 80)

Fat 9g (Saturated 4g)

Cholesterol 30mg

Sodium 630mg

Carbohydrate 41g
(Dietary Fiber 3g)

Protein 19g

% Daily Value

Vitamin A 8%

Vitamin C 4%

Calcium 16%

Iron 16%

Diet Exchanges

2 Starch

1 Lean Meat

2 Vegetable

1 Fat

Pizza Casserole

Garlic
Shepherds Pie

PREP: 25 MIN; BAKE: 30 MIN | 6 SERVINGS

1 pound diet-lean or extra-lean ground beef

1 medium onion, chopped (1/2 cup)

2 cups frozen baby beans and carrots

1 cup sliced mushrooms (3 ounces)

1 can (14 1/2 ounces) diced tomatoes, undrained

1 jar (12 ounces) fat-free beef gravy

2 tablespoons chili sauce

1/2 teaspoon dried basil leaves

1/8 teaspoon pepper

1/2 package (7.6-ounce size) mashed potatoes with roasted garlic or 2 cups warm mashed potatoes

1 1/2 cups hot water

1/2 cup fat-free (skim) milk

2 teaspoons margarine or butter

2 teaspoons shredded Parmesan cheese

Heat oven to 350°. Cook beef and onion in 12-inch non-stick skillet over medium heat, stirring occasionally, until beef is brown; drain well. Stir in frozen vegetables, mushrooms, tomatoes, gravy, chili sauce, basil and pepper. Heat to boiling; reduce heat. Cover and simmer about 10 minutes or until vegetables are tender.

Cook potatoes as directed on package for 4 servings, using 1 packet potatoes and seasoning, hot water, fat-free milk and margarine. Let stand 5 minutes.

Spoon beef mixture into ungreased square baking dish, 8 × 8 × 2 inches, or 2-quart casserole. Spoon potatoes onto beef mixture around edge of dish. Sprinkle with cheese. Bake uncovered 25 to 30 minutes or until potatoes are firm and beef mixture is bubbly.

1 Serving

Calories 240 (Calories from Fat 100)

Fat 11g (Saturated 4g)

Cholesterol 45mg

Sodium 660mg

Carbohydrate 18g (Dietary Fiber 2g)

Protein 19g

% Daily Value

Vitamin A 8%

Vitamin C 12%

Calcium 6%

Iron 14%

Diet Exchanges

1 Starch

1 Lean Meat

1 Vegetable

1 Fat

1 Eating Smart • Your supermarket has probably four types of ground beef: regular, lean, extra-lean and diet-lean. At about 27 percent fat, regular ground beef cooks up the greasiest of the three. Lean weighs in at 15 to 20 percent fat, and diet-lean goes as low as 8 percent.

2 Staying Active • America loves to walk, and it's easy to see why. It's a great solo activity but can also be enjoyed with others. Other walking pluses include picking your own pace and the fact that no clothing changes are needed. Also, by changing routes, you add endless variety to your routine.

Giant
Oven Burger

PREP: 10 MIN; BAKE: 50 MIN; STAND: 5 MIN | 6 SERVINGS

1 pound diet-lean or extra-lean ground beef

1 small bell pepper, finely chopped (1/2 cup)

1 small onion, finely chopped (1/4 cup)

1 tablespoon prepared horseradish

1 tablespoon yellow mustard

1/2 teaspoon salt

1/3 cup chili sauce or ketchup

1 unsliced round loaf Italian or sourdough bread (8 inches in diameter)

Heat oven to 350°. Mix all ingredients except chili sauce and bread. Press beef mixture in ungreased pie plate, 9 × 1 1/4 inches. Spread chili sauce over top.

Bake uncovered 45 to 50 minutes or until no longer pink in center and juice is clear (meat thermometer should reach at least 160°); drain. Let stand 5 minutes. Cut bread horizontally in half. Carefully place burger between halves. Cut into wedges.

1 Serving

Calories 195 (Calories from Fat 80)

Fat 9g (Saturated 3g)

Cholesterol 45mg

Sodium 500mg

Carbohydrate 12g (Dietary Fiber 1g)

Protein 17g

% Daily Value

Vitamin A 2%

Vitamin C 12%

Calcium 2%

Iron 12%

Diet Exchanges

1 Starch

2 Lean Meat

1 **Eating Smart** • Choose your condiments wisely. Ketchup, mustard and salsa are all low-calorie, low-fat flavor boosters. Fresh veggies such as tomato slices, onion rings, bell pepper strips and lettuce leaves are also good burger toppers. Steer clear of higher-fat toppings such as full-fat cheese, mayonnaise and creamy "special sauce."

2 **Staying Active** • Next time you head out to your mailbox, take a walk around the block first. Little trips like this add up. With 12 blocks in a mile, you'll walk a mile simply by circling your block three times!

Veal and Potato Strata with
Roasted Peppers

PREP: 20 MIN; BAKE: 40 MIN | 6 SERVINGS

1 1/2 pounds tenderized
boneless veal cutlets

1 bag (1 pound 4 ounces)
refrigerated shredded hash
brown potatoes

1 jar (12 ounces) roasted red
bell peppers, drained

1/2 teaspoon salt

3 medium onions, cut lengthwise in half, then cut
crosswise into thin slices

3 cloves garlic, finely
chopped

1 teaspoon chopped fresh or
1/2 teaspoon dried
oregano leaves

1/2 teaspoon cracked black
pepper

4 ounces feta cheese,
crumbled (1 cup)

Heat oven to 350°. Spray rectangular baking dish, 13 × 9 × 2 inches, with cooking spray. Remove fat from veal. Cut veal into 6 serving pieces.

Spread potatoes in baking dish. Spread bell peppers over potatoes. Sprinkle with salt. Cover and bake 15 minutes.

While potatoes are baking, spray 12-inch nonstick skillet with cooking spray; heat over medium-high heat. Cook veal in skillet about 5 minutes, turning once, until slightly pink in center. Remove veal from skillet.

Cook onions and garlic in same skillet over medium heat about 5 minutes, stirring frequently, until onions are tender.

Place veal on potato mixture. Spread onion mixture over veal. Sprinkle with oregano and pepper. Sprinkle with cheese. Cover and bake 20 to 25 minutes or until heated through.

1 Serving

Calories 340
(Calories from Fat 90)

Fat 10g (Saturated 5g)

Cholesterol 95mg

Sodium 850mg

Carbohydrate 43g
(Dietary Fiber 5g)

Protein 25g

% Daily Value

Vitamin A 24%

Vitamin C 94%

Calcium 18%

Iron 10%

Diet Exchanges

3 Starch

2 Lean Meat

1 **Eating Smart** • Tender veal brings sophistication to low-fat dining, plus an abundance of vitamins and minerals. One 3-ounce portion of veal contains about 165 calories and less than 6 grams of fat.

2 **Staying Active** • Attention, all bus riders: Getting off the bus a few stops before your destination gives you the perfect opportunity to squeeze a short walk into a busy day.

Veal and Potato Strata with Roasted Peppers

Caribbean
Pork Roast

2- to 2 1/2-pound pork
boneless center loin roast

1 cup orange juice

1/2 cup lime juice

1 1/2 teaspoons ground
cumin

1 1/2 teaspoons red pepper
sauce

3/4 teaspoon ground allspice

1 medium green bell pepper,
cut into eighths

1 medium onion, cut into
fourths

4 cloves garlic, finely
chopped

Salt and pepper, if desired

1 1/2 teaspoons sugar

1/2 teaspoon salt

Remove fat from pork. Pierce pork deeply in several places with meat fork or skewer. Place pork in heavy resealable plastic food-storage bag. Place remaining ingredients except salt and pepper, sugar and 1/2 teaspoon salt in blender or food processor. Cover and blend on medium speed until smooth. Pour blended mixture over pork. Seal bag; place in dish. Refrigerate, turning bag occasionally, at least 4 hours but no longer than 24 hours.

Heat oven to 325°. Remove pork from marinade; refrigerate marinade. Sprinkle pork with salt and pepper. Place pork on rack in shallow roasting pan. Insert meat thermometer so tip is in center of thickest part of pork. Roast uncovered 1 to 1 1/2 hours for medium doneness (160°). Remove pork from pan. Cover and let stand about 15 minutes before slicing.

Pour marinade into 1 1/2-quart saucepan. Stir in sugar and 1/2 teaspoon salt. Heat to boiling; reduce heat. Simmer uncovered about 5 minutes, stirring occasionally, until mixture is slightly thickened. Serve sauce with pork.

1 Serving

Calories 215
(Calories from Fat 80)

Fat 9g (Saturated 3g)

Cholesterol 75mg

Sodium 290mg

Carbohydrate 8g
(Dietary Fiber 1g)

Protein 26g

% Daily Value

Vitamin A 2%

Vitamin C 24%

Calcium 2%

Iron 8%

Diet Exchanges

3 Lean Meat

2 Vegetable

1 **Eating Smart** • Like other fruit juices, orange juice is virtually fat, cholesterol and sodium free. Orange juice also offers some folic acid, a B vitamin that's vital to women of childbearing age. Extremely flavorful, orange juice also makes a great stand-in for oil in sautés, sauces and salad dressings.

2 **Staying Active** • Here's a wake-up call: The American Heart Association considers exercise at least as important to good health as not smoking. Some studies have shown that inactivity can be as harmful to heart health as smoking two packs of cigarettes a day.

Italian

Roasted Pork Tenderloin

PREP: 10 MIN; ROAST: 35 MIN | 6 SERVINGS

2 pork tenderloins, about
    3/4 pound each

1 teaspoon olive or
    vegetable oil

1/2 teaspoon salt

1/2 teaspoon fennel seed,
    crushed

1/4 teaspoon pepper

1 clove garlic, finely chopped

Heat oven to 375°. Spray rack of roasting pan with cooking spray. Remove fat from pork. Mash remaining ingredients into a paste. Rub paste on pork.

Place pork on rack in shallow roasting pan. Insert meat thermometer so tip is in center of thickest part of pork. Roast uncovered about 35 minutes for medium doneness (160°).

1 **Eating Smart** • Today's pork is considerably leaner than the pork of 10 or 20 years ago; many cuts are as much as one-third leaner. The leanest cut, pork tenderloin, has just 5 grams of fat and about 160 calories per 3-ounce serving.

2 **Staying Active** • Who says exercise has to be boring? Nature hikes rejuvenate the mind and spirit, burn calories and tone leg muscles. You can up the intensity of your hike by finding hilly terrain to trek.

1 Serving

Calories 150
(Calories from Fat 45)

Fat 5g (Saturated 2g)

Cholesterol 70mg

Sodium 250mg

Carbohydrate 0g
(Dietary Fiber 0g)

Protein 26g

% Daily Value

Vitamin A 0%

Vitamin C 0%

Calcium 0%

Iron 6%

Diet Exchanges

4 Very Lean Meat

Roasted
Pork Chops and Vegetables

PREP: 20 MIN; BAKE: 1 HR | 4 SERVINGS

4 pork rib chops, 1/2 inch thick (1 pound)

2 teaspoons parsley flakes

1/2 teaspoon dried marjoram leaves

1/2 teaspoon dried thyme leaves

1/2 teaspoon garlic salt

1/4 teaspoon coarsely ground pepper

Olive oil-flavored cooking spray

6 new potatoes, cut into fourths (3 cups)

4 ounces mushrooms, cut in half (1 1/2 cups)

1 medium green bell pepper, cut into 1-inch pieces

1 medium onion, cut into thin wedges

1 medium tomato, cut into 8 wedges

Heat oven to 425°. Spray jelly roll pan, 15 1/2 × 10 1/2 × 1 inch, with cooking spray. Remove fat from pork. Mix parsley, marjoram, thyme, garlic salt and pepper. Spray both sides of pork chops with cooking spray. Sprinkle with 1 to 1 1/2 teaspoons herb mixture. Place in corners of pan.

Mix potatoes, mushrooms, bell pepper and onion in large bowl. Spray vegetables 2 or 3 times with cooking spray; stir. Sprinkle with remaining herb mixture; toss to coat. Spread evenly in center of pan between pork chops.

Bake uncovered 45 minutes. Turn pork; stir vegetables. Place tomato wedges over vegetables. Bake uncovered 10 to 15 minutes or until pork is slightly pink when cut near bone and vegetables are tender.

1 Serving

Calories 265
(Calories from Fat 65)

Fat 7g (Saturated 2g)

Cholesterol 55mg

Sodium 170mg

Carbohydrate 31g
(Dietary Fiber 4g)

Protein 23g

% Daily Value

Vitamin A 4%

Vitamin C 40%

Calcium 2%

Iron 16%

Diet Exchanges

1 1/2 Starch

2 Lean Meat

1 Vegetable

Eating Smart • Love veggies? Add sliced carrots, zucchini and a variety of bell peppers to the vegetable mixture for a jolt of color, texture and flavor.

Staying Active • Even if you have a desk job, you can stay active at work. Try visiting office mates in person instead of telephoning them. Use rest rooms or break rooms on other floors so you can use the stairs.

Roasted Pork Chops and Vegetables

Grilled
Southwestern Pork Chops

PREP: 10 MIN; MARINATE: 1 HR; GRILL: 12 MIN | 8 SERVINGS

8 pork loin or rib chops,
about 1/2 inch thick
(2 pounds)

1 tablespoon chili powder

1 teaspoon ground cumin

1/4 teaspoon ground red
pepper (cayenne)

1/4 teaspoon salt

1 large clove garlic, finely
chopped

Remove fat from pork. Mix remaining ingredients. Rub chili powder mixture evenly on both sides of pork. Cover and refrigerate 1 hour to blend flavors.

Heat coals or gas grill for direct heat. Cover and grill pork 4 to 6 inches from medium heat 10 to 12 minutes, turning frequently, until slightly pink when cut near bone.

1 **Eating Smart** • Grilling is one of many cooking techniques you can use to reduce fat. Other low-fat cooking methods include steaming, baking, stir-frying, microwaving, stewing and broiling.

2 **Staying Active** • Bagging and carrying your own groceries may seem like a small contribution to overall fitness. But when combined with similar activities throughout the day, it brings you one step closer to your fitness goals.

1 Serving

Calories 130
(Calories from Fat 55)

Fat 6g (Saturated 2g)

Cholesterol 50mg

Sodium 115mg

Carbohydrate 1g
(Dietary Fiber 0g)

Protein 18g

% Daily Value

Vitamin A 2%

Vitamin C 0%

Calcium 0%

Iron 4%

Diet Exchanges

3 1/2 Lean Meat

Skillet Ham and
Vegetables au Gratin

PREP: 10 MIN; COOK: 30 MIN | 6 SERVINGS

1 1/2 cups cut-up fully
   cooked lean ham

1 large onion, chopped
   (1 cup)

1 package (5.25 ounces)
   au gratin potato mix

2 1/2 cups hot water

1/4 teaspoon pepper

1 bag (1 pound) frozen
   broccoli, cauliflower and
   carrots (or other combination), thawed

1 cup shredded reduced-fat
   Cheddar cheese (4 ounces)

Spray 10-inch nonstick skillet with cooking spray; heat over medium-high heat. Cook ham and onion in skillet about 5 minutes, stirring frequently, until onion is tender.

Stir in potatoes and sauce mix from potato mix, the hot water and pepper. Heat to boiling; reduce heat. Cover and simmer 10 minutes, stirring occasionally. Stir in vegetables. Cover and simmer about 10 minutes or until potatoes are tender. Sprinkle with cheese.

1 Serving

Calories 270
(Calories from Fat 90)

Fat 10g (Saturated 4g)

Cholesterol 60mg

Sodium 1,590mg

Carbohydrate 20g
(Dietary Fiber 3g)

Protein 28g

% Daily Value

Vitamin A 62%

Vitamin C 18%

Calcium 10%

Iron 10%

Diet Exchanges

1 Starch

3 Lean Meat

1 Vegetable

1

Eating Smart • *Au gratin* usually refers to dishes topped with a crunchy crust of bread or cracker crumbs mixed with a liberal amount of butter. Many gratins also contain high-fat ingredients such as whole milk and cheese. To lighten the load and cut the fat in au gratin dishes, use low-fat cheese and fat-free milk, and leave out the margarine or butter.

2

Staying Active • Combine exercise with good deeds by offering to run errands for those who can't get out. Walk to the supermarket to pick up their groceries, or pick up their packages at the post office. Helping to maintain a neighbor's yard or shoveling snow are also ways to burn calories while lending a helping hand.

Creamy
Ham and Pasta

PREP: 15 MIN; COOK: 20 MIN | 4 SERVINGS

1 cup uncooked penne pasta
(3 ounces)

1 cup baby-cut carrots, cut
lengthwise in half

8 medium green onions,
sliced (1/2 cup)

12 ounces fully cooked lean
ham, cut into thin strips
(1 1/2 cups)

3/4 cup fat-free half-and-
half

2 ounces fat-free cream
cheese

1 teaspoon Dijon mustard

1/4 teaspoon dried tarragon
leaves

1/8 teaspoon white pepper

Cook pasta as directed on package, adding carrots during last 4 minutes of cooking. Cook until carrots are crisp-tender; drain.

Spray 12-inch nonstick skillet with cooking spray; heat over medium heat. Cook onions in skillet 1 minute. Stir in ham. Cook 2 to 3 minutes, stirring frequently, until thoroughly heated. Stir in remaining ingredients until cheese is melted and mixture is smooth. Stir in pasta and carrots.

1 Serving

Calories 265
(Calories from Fat 55)

Fat 6g (Saturated 2g)

Cholesterol 45mg

Sodium 1,170mg

Carbohydrate 30g
(Dietary Fiber 2g)

Protein 25g

% Daily Value

Vitamin A 58%

Vitamin C 6%

Calcium 10%

Iron 14%

Diet Exchanges

2 Starch

3 Very Lean Meat

1 Eating Smart • Not all low-fat dairy products are created equal. One cup of 2 percent milk has 5 grams of fat and gets 25 percent of its calories from fat. Better bets include 1 percent milk (less than 3 grams of fat per cup) or fat-free (skim) milk. Other fat-free dairy products to try include fat-free half-and-half and evaporated fat-free milk.

2 Staying Active • Don't have 10 minutes to exercise? Take 2! Briskly walk around the block (or in your office building or at the store) for 2 minutes. You'll be surprised at how quickly time passes and by the distance you cover. Fit as many 2-minute walks in your day as possible. It's amazing how quickly the time will add up.

Creamy Ham and Pasta

Spanish Lamb and
Couscous

PREP: 10 MIN; COOK: 20 MIN | 4 SERVINGS

4 lamb sirloin chops, 1/2 inch thick (about 2 pounds)

1 medium green bell pepper, chopped (1 cup)

1 can (14 1/2 ounces) diced tomatoes, undrained

1/4 cup chili sauce

1/2 teaspoon ground cumin

1/2 teaspoon dried marjoram leaves

1/4 teaspoon garlic powder

1/4 teaspoon salt

1/4 cup pitted ripe olives, cut in half

2 tablespoons chopped fresh parsley

2 cups hot cooked couscous

Spray 12-inch nonstick skillet with cooking spray; heat over medium heat. Cook lamb in skillet, turning once, until brown on both sides.

Stir in bell pepper, tomatoes, chili sauce, cumin, marjoram, garlic powder and salt; reduce heat to medium-low. Cover and simmer about 10 minutes or until lamb is light pink in center. Stir in olives; sprinkle with parsley. Serve with couscous.

1 Serving

Calories 310
(Calories from Fat 80)

Fat 9g (Saturated 3g)

Cholesterol 70mg

Sodium 840mg

Carbohydrate 33g
(Dietary Fiber 3g)

Protein 27g

% Daily Value

Vitamin A 10%

Vitamin C 38%

Calcium 6%

Iron 18%

Diet Exchanges

2 Starch

3 Very Lean Meat

1 Vegetable

1/2 Fat

1 **Eating Smart** • Couscous may sound exotic, but it's simply a tiny pasta. This complex carbohydrate takes only minutes to cook, is low in calories (about 100 per cooked 1/2 cup), is practically fat free and has plenty of fiber to fill you up.

2 **Staying Active** • Remind yourself of your fitness goals by writing them on sticky notes and putting them where they'll help you most. For instance, your goal of riding the exercise bike in the morning can be placed on your alarm clock. Stick a note reminding yourself to take the stairs instead of the elevator on your desk.

Mustard
Lamb Chops

PREP: 10 MIN; BROIL: 11 MIN | 6 SERVINGS

6 lamb sirloin or shoulder
   chops, about 3/4 inch
   thick (about 2 pounds)

1 tablespoon chopped fresh
   or 1 teaspoon dried thyme
   leaves

2 tablespoons Dijon mustard

1/4 teaspoon salt

Set oven control to broil. Remove fat from lamb. Place lamb on rack in broiler pan. Mix remaining ingredients. Brush half of the mustard mixture evenly over lamb.

Broil lamb with tops 3 to 4 inches from heat about 4 minutes or until brown. Turn lamb; brush with remaining mustard mixture. Broil 5 to 7 minutes longer for medium doneness (160°).

1 **Eating Smart** • Lamb, usually reserved for special occasions, can help you break out of a tired dinner routine. Note that lamb can be a lean source of protein with about 8 grams of fat per 3-ounce serving. It's also rich in B vitamins, zinc and magnesium.

2 **Staying Active** • Are you a new mom who's too busy to exercise? Take your little one out for a walk. Pushing a stroller for 30 minutes 4 days a week can burn nearly 5 pounds a year. Think of the pounds you could drop by combining this with a healthy weight-loss eating regimen!

1 Serving

Calories 150
(Calories from Fat 65)

Fat 7g (Saturated 3g)

Cholesterol 70mg

Sodium 200mg

Carbohydrate 0g
(Dietary Fiber 0g)

Protein 22g

% Daily Value

Vitamin A 0%

Vitamin C 0%

Calcium 0%

Iron 10%

Diet Exchanges

3 Lean Meat

Easy Meatless Meals

6

Tabbouleh with Garbanzo Beans, 158

Curried Lentil and Barley Casserole, 160

Creamy Corn and Garlic Risotto, 161

Ratatouille Polenta Bake, 162

Vegetarian Paella, 164

Five-Spice Tofu Stir-Fry, 166

Creole Soy Beans and Rice, 168

Confetti Beans and Rice, 169

Butter Bean Patties with Southwestern Sauce, 170

Chipotle–Black Bean Burritos, 171

Vegetarian Cannellini Bean Lasagna, 172

Tuscan Pasta and Beans, 174

Asian Noodle Bowl, 175

Southwest Fettuccine Bowl, 176

Whole Wheat Spaghetti with Spicy Eggplant Sauce, 178

Easy Mac 'n Cheese, 179

Ravioli with Tomato-Alfredo Sauce, 180

Pizza Primavera, 182

Potato and Tomato Pizza, 183

White Bean and Spinach Pizza, 184

Creamy Mushroom–Topped Baked Potatoes, 187

Potato and Tomato Pizza (page 183)

Tabbouleh with
Garbanzo Beans

PREP: 15 MIN; STAND: 1 HR | 4 SERVINGS

1 1/2 cups boiling water

3/4 cup uncooked bulgur

Lemon-Garlic Dressing
(below)

3 medium tomatoes, chopped
(about 2 1/4 cups)

8 medium green onions,
chopped (1/2 cup)

1 medium green bell pepper,
chopped (1 cup)

1 cup chopped cucumber

3/4 cup chopped fresh
parsley

3 tablespoons chopped fresh
or 1 tablespoon dried mint
leaves, crumbled

1 can (15 to 16 ounces)
garbanzo beans, drained

Pour boiling water over bulgur in medium bowl. Let
stand 1 hour.

Make Lemon-Garlic Dressing. Drain any remaining water
from bulgur. Stir remaining ingredients into bulgur.
Toss with dressing.

Lemon-Garlic Dressing

1/4 cup lemon juice

1 tablespoon olive or vegetable oil

3/4 teaspoon salt

1/4 teaspoon pepper

3 cloves garlic, finely chopped

Shake all ingredients in tightly covered container.

1 Serving

Calories 305
(Calories from Fat 65)

Fat 7g (Saturated 1g)

Cholesterol 0mg

Sodium 1,350mg

Carbohydrate 60g
(Dietary Fiber 15g)

Protein 15g

% Daily Value

Vitamin A 16%

Vitamin C 100%

Calcium 10%

Iron 30%

Diet Exchanges

3 Starch

2 Vegetable

1 **Eating Smart** • Middle Eastern cuisine gives
us many foods that are low in fat and high in fiber,
complex carbohydrates, vitamins, minerals and—most
important—flavor. A favorite from this region is tabbouleh, which features bulgur—wheat kernels that have
been steamed, dried and crushed.

2 **Staying Active** • Make time pass on the treadmill, stationary bike or stair climber by reading a book,
watching TV or listening to a favorite tape. But remember
to pay attention enough to your workout to keep your
heart rate up—and keep from falling off the machine.

Tabbouleh with Garbanzo Beans

Curried
Lentil and Barley Casserole

PREP: 10 MIN; COOK: 50 MIN | 4 SERVINGS

1/4 cup dried lentils, sorted and rinsed

2 cups fat-free vegetable or chicken broth

1 teaspoon curry powder

3 cloves garlic, finely chopped

3/4 cup uncooked quick-cooking barley

1 bag (1 pound) frozen corn, green peas and carrots (or other combination)

1 cup crumbled feta cheese (4 ounces)

Heat lentils, broth, curry powder and garlic to boiling in 3-quart saucepan; reduce heat. Cover and simmer 30 minutes, stirring occasionally.

Stir in barley and vegetables. Heat to boiling; reduce heat. Cover and simmer 10 to 15 minutes, stirring occasionally, until lentils and barley are tender and liquid is absorbed. Sprinkle with cheese.

1 Serving

Calories 320 (Calories from Fat 80)

Fat 9g (Saturated 6g)

Cholesterol 35mg

Sodium 970mg

Carbohydrate 56g (Dietary Fiber 13g)

Protein 15g

% Daily Value

Vitamin A 100%

Vitamin C 6%

Calcium 22%

Iron 18%

Diet Exchanges

3 Starch

2 Vegetable

1 Fat

1 **Eating Smart** • If you're new to meatless dining, you might want to gradually increase the amount of high-fiber foods you eat. Introducing too much fiber too quickly can cause bloating and gas. Also, try a variety of fiber-rich fare until you find foods that don't cause digestive problems.

2 **Staying Active** • Start using the "two-for-one" mentality with your daily activities. Instead of taking a coffee break with your neighbor, make this a "two-for-one" by catching up on conversation during a walk. Encourage your children to help you "two-for-one" by sharing the events of their day on an after-school walk instead of over snacks at the kitchen table.

Creamy Corn and
Garlic Risotto

PREP: 10 MIN; COOK: 25 MIN | 4 SERVINGS

3 3/4 cups fat-free vegetable or chicken broth

4 cloves garlic, finely chopped

1 cup uncooked Arborio or regular long-grain rice

2 cups frozen whole kernel corn

1/3 cup grated fat-free Parmesan cheese topping

1/4 cup shredded reduced-fat mozzarella cheese

1/4 cup chopped fresh parsley

Heat 1/3 cup of the broth to boiling in 10-inch skillet. Cook garlic in broth 1 minute, stirring occasionally. Stir in rice and corn. Cook 1 minute, stirring occasionally.

Stir in remaining broth. Heat to boiling; reduce heat to medium. Cook uncovered 15 to 20 minutes, stirring occasionally, until rice is tender and creamy; remove from heat. Stir in cheeses and parsley.

1 Serving

Calories 340
(Calories from Fat 35)

Fat 4g (Saturated 2g)

Cholesterol 10mg

Sodium 1,200mg

Carbohydrate 69g
(Dietary Fiber 4g)

Protein 11g

% Daily Value

Vitamin A 20%

Vitamin C 8%

Calcium 16%

Iron 12%

Diet Exchanges

4 Starch

1 Vegetable

1 Eating Smart • Traditional risotto often includes high-fat dairy products such as butter, half-and-half and cream. This low-fat version relies on frozen corn and fat-free broth and cheeses for its rich texture and sweet flavor.

2 Staying Active • Set a timer on your computer or watch to remind yourself to get up and move around every hour. A quiet alarm clock or kitchen timer also works. Even if you're not able to get up every hour, the alarm reminds you of your commitment to an active lifestyle.

Ratatouille
Polenta Bake

PREP: 25 MIN; BAKE: 45 MIN; STAND: 5 MIN | 6 SERVINGS

1 medium onion, coarsely
chopped (1/2 cup)

1 medium bell pepper,
coarsely chopped (1 cup)

1 small unpeeled eggplant
(1 pound), diced (2 cups)

1 medium zucchini, diced
(1 cup)

1/2 teaspoon salt

1/4 teaspoon pepper

1 can (14 1/2 ounces)
Italian-style stewed
tomatoes, undrained

1 tube (16 ounces) refrigerated
plain polenta (or any flavor)

2 tablespoons shredded
Parmesan cheese

3/4 cup finely shredded
reduced-fat mozzarella
cheese (3 ounces)

1/4 cup chopped fresh parsley

Heat oven to 375°. Spray 12-inch nonstick skillet with
cooking spray; heat over medium-high heat. Cook
onion and bell pepper in skillet 2 minutes, stirring
occasionally. Stir in eggplant, zucchini, salt and pepper.
Cook 3 to 4 minutes, stirring occasionally, until vegetables are tender. Stir in tomatoes, breaking up with
spoon; reduce heat to low. Cook 3 minutes, stirring
occasionally.

Spray rectangular baking dish, 11 × 7 × 1 1/2 inches,
with cooking spray. Cut polenta into 1/4-inch slices.
Arrange over bottom of dish, overlapping and cutting
to fit where necessary. Sprinkle with Parmesan cheese.
Spoon vegetable mixture evenly over top.

Cover and bake 30 minutes. Sprinkle with mozzarella
cheese and parsley. Bake uncovered about 15 minutes
or until cheese is melted and casserole is bubbly. Let
stand 5 minutes before serving.

1 Serving

Calories 205
(Calories from Fat 35)

Fat 4g (Saturated 2g)

Cholesterol 10mg

Sodium 500mg

Carbohydrate 39g
(Dietary Fiber 6g)

Protein 9g

% Daily Value

Vitamin A 10%

Vitamin C 28%

Calcium 16%

Iron 12%

Diet Exchanges

2 Starch

2 Vegetable

1 Eating Smart • With a mere 20 calories per
1/2 cup, eggplant is an exceptional choice for a low-fat
eating plan. Keep in mind that a pound of uncooked
eggplant will yield about half a pound cooked.

2 Staying Active • Next time you find yourself
waiting at the doctor's office, or for any appointment,
find out how long your wait will be. Let whoever's in
charge know that you'll be out for a bit, and enjoy a
short walk around the block.

Ratatouille Polenta Bake

Vegetarian
Paella

PREP: 10 MIN; COOK: 25 MIN | 4 SERVINGS

2 large onions, chopped (2 cups)

5 cloves garlic, finely chopped

1 cup uncooked basmati or regular long-grain rice

1 can (14 ounces) quartered artichoke hearts, drained

2 cups dry white wine or fat-free vegetable broth

1 teaspoon salt

1 bag (1 pound) cauliflower, carrots and snow pea pods (or other combination), thawed

1 cup frozen sliced bell peppers (from 16-ounce bag)

Spray 10-inch nonstick skillet with cooking spray; heat over medium-high heat. Cook onions and garlic in skillet about 5 minutes, stirring occasionally, until onions are tender.

Stir in rice and artichoke hearts. Cook 3 minutes, stirring occasionally. Stir in wine and salt. Heat to boiling; reduce heat. Cover and simmer about 10 minutes. Stir in vegetables. Cover and cook about 5 minutes or until liquid is absorbed.

1 Serving

Calories 285 (Calories from Fat 10)

Fat 1g (Saturated 0g)

Cholesterol 0mg

Sodium 640mg

Carbohydrate 68g (Dietary Fiber 11g)

Protein 12g

% Daily Value

Vitamin A 40%

Vitamin C 72%

Calcium 12%

Iron 24%

Diet Exchanges

3 Starch

4 Vegetable

1 Eating Smart • A Spanish dish of rice, meat, shellfish and vegetables, paella can be high in saturated fat and calories. By eliminating the meat and relying on fiber-rich complex carbohydrates such as rice and fresh veggies, our adaptation of paella becomes a flavorful, low-fat feast.

2 Staying Active • Ask your coworkers to join you for a walking business meeting. Besides the exercise and fresh air you'll both be getting, you'll also boost your creative powers with the feel-good chemicals that come from exercise.

Vegetarian Paella

fu Stir-Fry

PREP: 15 MIN; STAND: 10 MIN; COOK: 18 MIN | 4 SERVINGS

1/4 cup stir-fry sauce

2 tablespoons orange juice

1 tablespoon honey

3/4 teaspoon five-spice
    powder

1 package (14 ounces) firm
    tofu, cut into 3/4-inch
    cubes

1 small red onion, cut into
    thin wedges

1 bag (1 pound) frozen baby
    beans and carrots

1/4 cup water

4 cups hot cooked rice,
    if desired

Mix stir-fry sauce, orange juice, honey and five-spice
    powder in medium bowl. Press tofu between paper
    towels to absorb excess moisture. Stir into sauce mix-
    ture. Let stand 10 minutes to marinate.

Spray 12-inch nonstick skillet with cooking spray; heat
    over medium heat. Remove tofu from sauce mixture;
    reserve sauce mixture. Cook tofu in skillet 3 to 4 min-
    utes, stirring occasionally, just until light golden
    brown; remove from skillet.

Add onion to skillet. Cook 2 minutes, stirring constantly.
    Add vegetables and water. Heat to boiling; reduce heat
    to medium. Cover and cook 6 to 8 minutes, stirring
    occasionally, until vegetables are crisp-tender.

Stir in reserved sauce mixture and tofu. Cook 2 to 3 min-
    utes, stirring occasionally, until mixture is slightly
    thickened and hot. Serve over rice.

1 **Eating Smart** • A first-rate addition to healthy
weight-loss diets, soy foods contain complex carbohydrates, protein and heart-healthy fat. The soybean has
been linked to diets that may prevent against cancer,
heart disease and diabetes. Soy foods may also reduce
symptoms associated with menopause.

2 **Staying Active** • True or false? The more you
sweat, the more fat you lose. False. Those who perspire
more are not necessarily burning more fat than those
who perspire less. Sweating is influenced by many
factors, including heredity, fitness level, temperature
and humidity.

1 Serving

Calories 105
(Calories from Fat 10)

Fat 1g (Saturated 0g)

Cholesterol 0mg

Sodium 730mg

Carbohydrate 20g
(Dietary Fiber 5g)

Protein 9g

% Daily Value

Vitamin A 100%

Vitamin C 6%

Calcium 6%

Iron 14%

Diet Exchanges

4 Vegetable

Five-Spice Tofu Stir-Fry

Creole
Soy Beans and Rice

PREP: 10 MIN; COOK: 30 MIN | 4 SERVINGS

1 cup frozen stir-fry bell peppers and onions

1 medium stalk celery, sliced (1/2 cup)

1 can (14 1/2 ounces) fat-free vegetable broth

3/4 cup uncooked regular long-grain rice

1 teaspoon Creole seasoning or chili powder

1/4 teaspoon dried thyme leaves

1 can (15 ounces) regular or black soy beans, rinsed and drained

1 can (14 1/2 ounces) stewed tomatoes, undrained

Spray 12-inch nonstick skillet with cooking spray; heat over medium-high heat. Cook stir-fry vegetables and celery in skillet 2 to 3 minutes, stirring occasionally, until vegetables are crisp-tender.

Stir in broth, rice, Creole seasoning and thyme. Heat to boiling; reduce heat. Cover and simmer 15 minutes, stirring occasionally.

Stir in remaining ingredients. Cover and cook 5 to 10 minutes, stirring occasionally, until almost all liquid has been absorbed and rice is tender.

1 Serving

Calories 330
(Calories from Fat 70)

Fat 8g (Saturated 1g)

Cholesterol 0mg

Sodium 890mg

Carbohydrate 53g
(Dietary Fiber 5g)

Protein 17g

% Daily Value

Vitamin A 12%

Vitamin C 28%

Calcium 14%

Iron 40%

Diet Exchanges

3 Starch

1 Lean Meat

1 Vegetable

1 **Eating Smart** • It may seem surprising, but soybeans contain more fat than other dried beans (8 grams of fat per cup). This fat is mainly unsaturated and is a source of essential fatty acids. As well, the fat in soybeans provides satiety. Combining these beans with low-fat foods such as rice and pasta reduces the overall fat content of the dish.

2 **Staying Active** • Still think taking the stairs instead of the elevator is a waste of time? Consider that you would have to ride the elevator 299 floors to burn the same amount of calories you'd burn if you simply walked two flights of stairs.

Confetti
Beans and Rice

PREP: 10 MIN; COOK: 25 MIN | 4 SERVINGS

1/2 cup uncooked regular
   long-grain rice

1/4 cup chopped green bell
   pepper

1/2 cup water

1/4 teaspoon salt

1/8 teaspoon pepper

1 small zucchini, sliced
   (1 cup)

1 can (15 to 16 ounces)
   kidney beans, rinsed and
   drained

1 can (14 1/2 ounces) stewed
   tomatoes, undrained

Heat all ingredients to boiling in 2-quart saucepan; reduce heat. Cover and simmer 20 minutes, stirring occasionally.

1 Serving

Calories 240
(Calories from Fat 10)

Fat 1g (Saturated 0g)

Cholesterol 0mg

Sodium 720mg

Carbohydrate 54g
(Dietary Fiber 9g)

Protein 13g

% Daily Value

Vitamin A 6%

Vitamin C 22%

Calcium 6%

Iron 26%

Diet Exchanges

3 Starch

1 Vegetable

1 Eating Smart • Make sure you get your fiber from foods, not supplements. Most fiber pills actually have little fiber; some contain only half a gram each. Considering we should consume 25 to 35 grams of fiber each day, it makes sense to get fiber from beans (about 8 grams per 1/2 cup) and other fiber-rich foods.

2 Staying Active • If swimming bores you but you like being in the water, try water aerobics. Enjoyed by people of all ages and sizes, water aerobics can be a challenging workout. Better yet, it's gentler on your joints than most land exercises.

Butter Bean Patties with
Southwestern Sauce

PREP: 15 MIN; COOK: 18 MIN | 4 SERVINGS

1 can (15 to 16 ounces) butter beans, rinsed and drained

10 round buttery crackers, crushed (1/3 cup)

1/4 cup fat-free cholesterol-free egg product or 1 egg

2 tablespoons chili sauce

2 tablespoons finely chopped onion

1 cup frozen mixed peas and carrots

1/4 cup raisins

1/4 teaspoon ground cumin

1 can (14 1/2 ounces) Mexican-style stewed tomatoes, undrained

Mash beans in medium bowl. Stir in crackers, egg product, chili sauce and onion. Shape mixture into 4 patties, each about 1/2 inch thick.

Spray 10-inch skillet with cooking spray. Cook patties in skillet 8 to 10 minutes, turning once, until golden brown. Remove from skillet; keep warm.

Add remaining ingredients to skillet. Cook over medium-low heat 5 to 8 minutes, stirring occasionally, until vegetables are tender. Serve sauce over patties.

1 Serving

Calories 215 (Calories from Fat 20)

Fat 2g (Saturated 1g)

Cholesterol 0mg

Sodium 720mg

Carbohydrate 48g (Dietary Fiber 11g)

Protein 12g

% Daily Value

Vitamin A 52%

Vitamin C 12%

Calcium 6%

Iron 22%

Diet Exchanges

2 1/2 Starch

1 Vegetable

1 **Eating Smart** • In the South, dried lima beans are often referred to as *butter beans*. These beans contain plenty of protein, fiber, phosphorus, potassium and iron. Like other legumes, butter beans contain complex carbohydrates that provide a filling, long-lasting energy source.

2 **Staying Active** • How do you know when you're ready to lift more weight? When you can easily do the maximum number of reps you're aiming for—ten to twelve is the standard—you should increase the weight by the smallest increment possible and drop down to the minimum number of reps in your range until you adjust to the new weight.

Chipotle–Black Bean
Burritos

PREP: 10 MIN; COOK: 7 MIN | 4 SERVINGS

1 large onion, chopped
(1 cup)

6 cloves garlic, finely
chopped

1 can (15 ounces) black
beans, rinsed, drained and
mashed

1 to 2 teaspoons finely
chopped chipotle chilies in
adobo sauce, drained

4 fat-free flour tortillas (6 to
8 inches in diameter)

1/2 cup shredded reduced-fat
mozzarella cheese (2
ounces)

1 large tomato, chopped
(1 cup)

Spray 10-inch nonstick skillet with cooking spray; heat over medium-high heat. Cook onion and garlic in skillet about 5 minutes, stirring occasionally, until onion is tender. Stir in beans and chilies; cook until hot.

Place one-fourth of the bean mixture on center of each tortilla. Top with cheese and tomato. Fold one end of tortilla up about 1 inch over filling; fold right and left sides over folded end, overlapping. Fold remaining end down. Place seam side down on serving platter or plate.

1 **Eating Smart** • One-half cup of most cooked beans contains 6 to 9 grams of protein and less than 1 gram of fat. Other essential nutrients abundant in beans include calcium, iron, phosphorus, potassium and B vitamins.

2 **Staying Active** • Many people are successful at designing exercise programs that revolve around going to the gym, but this is not the only way to be active. What some experts call "lifestyle fitness" can also increase your fitness level. You can stay active by consciously working at moving. Gardening, running errands and doing housework all fill the bill.

1 Serving

Calories 255
(Calories from Fat 25)

Fat 3g (Saturated 2g)

Cholesterol 8mg

Sodium 600mg

Carbohydrate 49g
(Dietary Fiber 9g)

Protein 16g

% Daily Value

Vitamin A 4%

Vitamin C 12%

Calcium 22%

Iron 20%

Diet Exchanges

3 Starch

1 Vegetable

Vegetarian
Cannellini Bean Lasagna

PREP: 40 MIN; BAKE: 1 HR; STAND: 10 MIN | 12 SERVINGS

9 uncooked lasagna noodles
(9 ounces)

1 medium onion, chopped
(1/2 cup)

1/2 cup chopped green bell
pepper

2 cloves garlic, finely chopped

2 cans (15 ounces each)
chunky Italian-style
tomato sauce

1 can (19 ounces) cannellini
beans, rinsed and drained

3/4 teaspoon fennel seed

1/2 teaspoon sugar

1 container (15 ounces) fat-
free ricotta cheese

1/4 cup shredded Parmesan
cheese

3 cups frozen cut leaf
spinach, thawed and
squeezed to drain

1 1/2 cups finely shredded
mozzarella cheese
(6 ounces)

Heat oven to 350°. Spray rectangular baking dish, 13 × 9 × 2 inches, with cooking spray. Cook and drain lasagna noodles as directed on package.

Spray 12-inch nonstick skillet with cooking spray; heat over medium-high heat. Cook onion, bell pepper and garlic in skillet about 3 minutes, stirring occasionally, until vegetables are crisp-tender. Stir in tomato sauce, beans, fennel seed and sugar; reduce heat to medium. Cook 5 to 10 minutes, stirring occasionally, until sauce is slightly thickened.

Mix ricotta cheese, 2 tablespoons of the Parmesan cheese and the spinach. Spread about 1 cup tomato sauce mixture in baking dish. Top with 3 noodles. Spread with half of the ricotta mixture. Top with about 1 1/2 cups tomato sauce mixture, 1/2 cup of the mozzarella cheese, 3 noodles, remaining ricotta mixture, remaining tomato sauce mixture and remaining 3 noodles. Sprinkle with remaining 1 cup mozzarella cheese and remaining 2 tablespoons Parmesan cheese.

Cover and bake 45 minutes. Bake uncovered 10 to 15 minutes or until top is light golden brown and mixture is bubbly. Let stand 5 to 10 minutes before serving.

1 Serving

Calories 260
(Calories from Fat 55)

Fat 6g (Saturated 2g)

Cholesterol 10mg

Sodium 610mg

Carbohydrate 40g
(Dietary Fiber 6g)

Protein 17g

% Daily Value

Vitamin A 30%

Vitamin C 16%

Calcium 26%

Iron 14%

Diet Exchanges

2 Starch

1 Lean Meat

2 Vegetable

1 **Eating Smart** • No need to give up favorite comfort foods such as lasagna when trying to lose weight. You can reduce fat and calories by replacing meat with a variety of low-cal beans and vegetables.

2 **Staying Active** • Start a walking club at work, in your neighborhood, at church or anywhere you find others who want to walk. Commit to regular sessions so it becomes a weekly habit. Make the last stop on your walk at a member's house, and enjoy a tasty, low-fat snack or a glass of ice water with a fresh lemon twist.

Vegetarian Cannellini Bean Lasagna

Tuscan
Pasta and Beans

PREP: 20 MIN; COOK: 15 MIN | 6 SERVINGS

3 cups uncooked gemelli
(twist) pasta (12 ounces)

2 medium bell peppers,
chopped (2 cups)

1/2 pound green beans, cut
into 1-inch pieces (1 cup)

1 medium onion, chopped
(1/2 cup)

2 cloves garlic, finely
chopped

1 can (14 1/2 ounces) diced
tomatoes with Italian
herbs, undrained

1/2 cup fat-free vegetable or
chicken broth

1 tablespoon chopped fresh
or 1/2 teaspoon dried
rosemary leaves, crumbled

2 cups lightly packed
chopped escarole or
spinach leaves

1 can (15 to 16 ounces) great
northern beans, rinsed and
drained

2 tablespoons red wine
vinegar

Shredded Parmesan cheese,
if desired

Cook and drain pasta as directed on package.

While pasta is cooking, spray 4-quart Dutch oven with
cooking spray; heat over medium-high heat. Cook bell
peppers, green beans, onion and garlic in Dutch oven
about 7 minutes, stirring occasionally, until vegetables
are crisp-tender.

Stir tomatoes, broth and rosemary into vegetable mixture;
reduce heat. Simmer uncovered about 3 minutes or
until vegetables are tender. Stir in escarole and great
northern beans. Simmer uncovered about 3 minutes or
until escarole is wilted. Toss vegetable mixture and
pasta. Sprinkle with vinegar and cheese.

1 Serving

Calories 340
(Calories from Fat 20)

Fat 2g (Saturated 0g)

Cholesterol 0mg

Sodium 200mg

Carbohydrate 74g
(Dietary Fiber 10g)

Protein 17g

% Daily Value

Vitamin A 18%

Vitamin C 42%

Calcium 12%

Iron 34%

Diet Exchanges

4 Starch

2 Vegetable

1 **Eating Smart** • Foods that work best in healthy
weight-loss plans are also often low in cost. Pasta, dried
beans, rice, bread and fresh produce are easy on the
pocketbook and on the waistline.

2 **Staying Active** • When you exercise at home,
remember that this is *your* time. Don't answer the phone
or start other household tasks. And ask your family for
some quiet time while you exercise. Unless, of course,
they decide to join you!

Asian
Noodle Bowl

PREP: 15 MIN; COOK: 15 MIN | 4 SERVINGS

1/4 cup barbecue sauce

2 tablespoons hoisin sauce

1 tablespoon peanut butter

Dash of ground red pepper (cayenne), if desired

1 small onion, cut into thin wedges

1/2 cup coarsely chopped red bell pepper

2 cups fresh broccoli flowerets or 1 package (14 ounces) frozen broccoli flowerets

3/4 cup water

1 can (14 ounces) baby corn cob nuggets, drained

1 package (10 ounces) Chinese curly noodles

1 tablespoon chopped peanuts

Mix barbecue sauce, hoisin sauce, peanut butter and ground red pepper in medium bowl; set aside.

Spray 12-inch nonstick skillet with cooking spray; heat over medium heat. Cook onion and bell pepper in skillet 2 minutes, stirring occasionally. Stir in broccoli and water. Cover and cook 4 to 6 minutes, stirring occasionally, until broccoli is crisp-tender. Stir in corn and reserved sauce mixture. Cook 3 to 4 minutes, stirring occasionally, until mixture is hot.

Cook and drain noodles as directed on package. Spoon noodles into 4 individual serving bowls. Top with vegetable mixture. Sprinkle with peanuts.

1 Serving

Calories 325 (Calories from Fat 45)

Fat 5g (Saturated 1g)

Cholesterol 0mg

Sodium 510mg

Carbohydrate 67g (Dietary Fiber 6g)

Protein 9g

% Daily Value

Vitamin A 20%

Vitamin C 72%

Calcium 6%

Iron 16%

Diet Exchanges

2 Starch

4 Vegetable

1 Fruit

1 **Eating Smart** • Do you love the noodles with peanut sauce served in Chinese and Thai restaurants? Make your own lower-fat version: add fat-free, flavor-rich hoisin and barbecue sauces to a small amount of peanut butter. Toss this mixture with Asian noodles and lots of fat-free veggies for a filling vegetarian main dish.

2 **Staying Active** • Outdoor and treadmill walking at the same pace burn approximately the same number of calories. Walking outdoors may burn slightly more calories because your body adjusts to different road and weather conditions. You can make up for this difference by changing the treadmill settings during your workout.

Southwest
Fettuccine Bowl

PREP: 15 MIN; COOK: 25 MIN | 4 SERVINGS

8 ounces uncooked fettuccine

Olive oil–flavored cooking
spray

1 cup salsa

1/3 cup frozen whole kernel
corn

1/4 cup water

2 tablespoons chili sauce

1/2 teaspoon ground cumin

1 can (15 ounces) black
beans, rinsed and drained

1/4 cup chopped fresh
cilantro

Cook and drain fettuccine as directed on package. Spray
fettuccine 2 or 3 times with cooking spray, tossing
after each spray. Cover to keep warm.

Mix remaining ingredients except cilantro in same
saucepan used to cook fettuccine. Cook over medium
heat 4 to 6 minutes, stirring occasionally, until corn
is tender.

Divide fettuccine among 4 individual bowls. Top each with
about 3/4 cup sauce mixture. Sprinkle with cilantro.

1 Serving
Calories 350 (Calories from Fat 25)
Fat 3g (Saturated 1g)
Cholesterol 50mg
Sodium 690mg
Carbohydrate 73g (Dietary Fiber 10g)
Protein 17g

% Daily Value
Vitamin A 6%
Vitamin C 12%
Calcium 12%
Iron 30%

Diet Exchanges

4 1/2 Starch

1 **Eating Smart** • No need to add oil to the water
you boil for pasta. By using enough water—4 cups water
for every 4 ounces of pasta—adding pasta slowly and
stirring frequently, you can keep the noodles from sticking together without having to add fat.

2 **Staying Active** • Exercise can be an education.
A visit to an art museum, state park, historic monument,
arboretum or zoo provides miles of ground to be covered. Make it a family activity, or enjoy learning at your
own pace by going solo.

Southwest Fettuccine Bowl

Whole Wheat Spaghetti with
Spicy Eggplant Sauce

PREP: 10 MIN; COOK: 20 MIN | 4 SERVINGS

8 ounces uncooked whole wheat or regular spaghetti

1 small eggplant (1 pound), peeled and cubed (3 cups)

1 can (14 1/2 ounces) Italian-style stewed tomatoes, undrained

1 can (8 ounces) tomato sauce

1/2 teaspoon crushed red pepper

2 tablespoons chopped fresh parsley or 2 teaspoons parsley flakes

Cook and drain spaghetti as directed on package.

While spaghetti is cooking, heat eggplant, tomatoes, tomato sauce and red pepper to boiling in 10-inch skillet, stirring occasionally; reduce heat. Simmer uncovered about 15 minutes or until eggplant is tender. Stir in parsley. Serve over spaghetti.

1 Serving

Calories 255 (Calories from Fat 10)

Fat 1g (Saturated 0g)

Cholesterol 0mg

Sodium 630mg

Carbohydrate 62g (Dietary Fiber 9g)

Protein 11g

% Daily Value

Vitamin A 10%

Vitamin C 18%

Calcium 6%

Iron 16%

Diet Exchanges

2 Starch

2 Vegetable

1 Fruit

1 Eating Smart • Although full of vitamins and minerals, eggplant can become a fat trap when fried. The spongelike texture of eggplant means it soaks up oil quickly—even quicker than French fries! Fortunately, there are plenty of alternatives to frying eggplant. Try grilling, broiling, baking or steaming.

2 Staying Active • Staying active is essential to good heath. But to maintain a lifetime of fitness, you need to balance physical activity with rest. Enjoy activities such as stretching and *tai chi*, a moving meditation that combines breathing exercises with gentle stretches. Also, make sure you get enough sleep.

Easy
Mac 'n Cheese

PREP: 10 MIN; COOK: 12 MIN | 4 SERVINGS

1 package (7 ounces) macaroni shells (2 cups)

1 tablespoon margarine or
butter

2 tablespoons all-purpose
flour

1/4 teaspoon salt

1/4 teaspoon ground mustard

1/8 teaspoon pepper

1 cup fat-free (skim) milk

1 cup shredded reduced-fat
Cheddar cheese (4 ounces)

2 tablespoons chopped red
bell pepper

1 medium green onion, sliced
(1 tablespoon)

Cook and drain macaroni as directed on package. While macaroni is cooking, melt margarine in 3-quart nonstick saucepan over low heat. Stir in flour, salt, mustard and pepper. Cook over low heat, stirring constantly, until margarine is absorbed; remove from heat.

Gradually stir milk into flour mixture. Heat to boiling, stirring constantly. Boil and stir 1 minute. Stir in cheese until melted.

Stir macaroni, bell pepper and onion into sauce. Cook, stirring constantly, until hot.

1 Serving

Calories 295
(Calories from Fat 55)

Fat 6g (Saturated 2g)

Cholesterol 5mg

Sodium 390mg

Carbohydrate 46g
(Dietary Fiber 2g)

Protein 16g

% Daily Value

Vitamin A 12%

Vitamin C 8%

Calcium 20%

Iron 12%

Diet Exchanges

3 Starch

1 Lean Meat

Eating Smart • Kid-pleasing meals like good ol' macaroni and cheese don't have to be high in fat to be delicious. By replacing whole milk with fat-free (skim) milk and using reduced-fat cheese, the youngsters at your house will never miss the added calories and fat.

Staying Active • When shopping for exercise shoes, be sure to wear the same type of socks that you wear during exercise. You'll also get the best fit by shoe shopping after you've been on your feet all day because this is when feet are at their largest.

Ravioli with
Tomato-Alfredo Sauce

PREP: 10 MIN; COOK: 10 MIN | 6 SERVINGS

2 packages (9 ounces each) refrigerated tomato- or cheese-filled ravioli

1 package (8 ounces) sliced mushrooms (3 cups)

1 large onion, coarsely chopped (1 cup)

1 jar (24 to 28 ounces) fat-free tomato pasta sauce

1/2 cup fat-free half-and-half or refrigerated fat-free nondairy creamer

1/4 cup grated fat-free Parmesan cheese topping

1/4 cup chopped fresh parsley

Cook and drain ravioli as directed on package; keep warm.

Spray same saucepan with cooking spray; heat over medium heat. Cook mushrooms and onion in saucepan about 5 minutes, stirring frequently, until onion is crisp-tender.

Stir in pasta sauce and half-and-half. Heat to boiling; reduce heat to low. Stir in ravioli, cheese and parsley. Sprinkle with additional cheese if desired.

1 Serving

Calories 215
(Calories from Fat 65)

Fat 7g (Saturated 4g)

Cholesterol 85mg

Sodium 1,100mg

Carbohydrate 30g
(Dietary Fiber 2g)

Protein 12g

% Daily Value

Vitamin A 12%

Vitamin C 10%

Calcium 20%

Iron 10%

Diet Exchanges

2 Starch

1 Very Lean Meat

1/2 Fat

1 Eating Smart • Traditional Alfredo sauce is based on butter, grated Parmesan cheese and heavy cream. Some food manufacturers offer lighter versions of this ultra-rich pasta sauce, or you can make your own using low-fat dairy products like fat-free (skim) milk instead of the cream.

2 Staying Active • One of the most common reasons for giving up on exercise is doing too much too soon, which can leave you feeling discouraged. By setting reasonable, achievable goals, you're more likely to stick with your program. When you reach one of your short-term goals, be sure to set another one. And don't forget to reward yourself!

Ravioli with Tomato-Alfredo Sauce

Pizza
Primavera

PREP: 15 MIN; BAKE: 17 MIN | 6 SERVINGS

1 loaf (1 pound) frozen honey-wheat or white bread dough, thawed

1/4 cup fat-free Italian dressing

1/2 pound asparagus, cut into 1-inch pieces

2 medium carrots, sliced (1 cup)

1 cup small broccoli flowerets

3 medium roma (plum) tomatoes, thinly sliced

1 cup shredded reduced-fat mozzarella cheese (4 ounces)

Heat oven to 450°. Spray cookie sheet with cooking spray. Pat or roll dough into 12-inch circle on cookie sheet. Prick dough thoroughly with fork. Bake 8 minutes (if dough puffs during baking, flatten with spoon).

Heat dressing to boiling in 10-inch nonstick skillet. Stir in asparagus, carrots and broccoli. Heat to boiling; reduce heat to medium. Cover and cook 3 to 4 minutes or until vegetables are crisp-tender.

Place tomato slices on partially baked crust. Spread vegetable mixture evenly over tomatoes. Sprinkle with cheese. Bake 7 to 9 minutes or until cheese is melted and crust is golden brown.

1 **Eating Smart** • Enjoying occasional meatless meals can help you stay slim by reducing the calories, fat and cholesterol in your diet. Other benefits of going meatless include reduced risk of heart disease, cancer and diabetes.

2 **Staying Active** • Be sure to record each and every one of your exercise achievements: walking to the store, taking stairs instead of the elevator, carrying laundry upstairs in three trips instead of one. Congratulate yourself on the many creative ways you find to exercise during a hectic day.

1 Serving

Calories 255
(Calories from Fat 65)

Fat 7g (Saturated 3g)

Cholesterol 10mg

Sodium 600mg

Carbohydrate 41g
(Dietary Fiber 7g)

Protein 14g

% Daily Value

Vitamin A 38%

Vitamin C 16%

Calcium 20%

Iron 16%

Diet Exchanges

2 Starch

2 Vegetable

1 Fat

Potato and Tomato
Pizza

PREP: 15 MIN; BAKE: 25 MIN | 8 SERVINGS

1 can (10 ounces) refrigerated pizza crust dough

2 cups frozen potato wedges with skins, thawed (about 32 pieces)

1 tablespoon Dijon mustard

3 medium roma (plum) tomatoes, coarsely chopped (1 1/2 cups)

1 medium zucchini, cut lengthwise in half, then cut crosswise into slices

1/2 teaspoon dried basil leaves

1/4 teaspoon coarsely ground pepper

1 cup shredded reduced-fat mozzarella cheese (4 ounces)

Heat oven to 425°. Spray 14-inch pizza pan with cooking spray. Press pizza crust dough into pan.

Toss potatoes and mustard until potatoes are coated; arrange on crust. Top with tomatoes, zucchini, basil, pepper and cheese. Bake 20 to 25 minutes or until cheese is melted and crust is golden brown.

1 Serving

Calories 170 (Calories from Fat 25)

Fat 3g (Saturated 2g)

Cholesterol 8mg

Sodium 270mg

Carbohydrate 29g (Dietary Fiber 2g)

Protein 8g

% Daily Value

Vitamin A 4%

Vitamin C 10%

Calcium 12%

Iron 10%

Diet Exchanges

2 Starch

1 Eating Smart • When shopping in the produce section of your supermarket, purchase extra fresh vegetables to chop and add as a last-minute topper to pizza or pasta. The best part? You can approach fresh veggies with reckless abandon. With the exception of avocados, they are virtually fat free.

2 Staying Active • "I'm too tired to exercise." Sound familiar? You should know that working out actually boosts your energy. It also helps you cope with the stresses that drag you down. And exercising can help you sleep better, giving you more energy for the next day.

White Bean and
Spinach Pizza

PREP: 15 MIN; BAKE: 10 MIN | 8 SERVINGS

1/2 cup sun-dried tomato halves (not oil-packed)

1 can (15 to 16 ounces) great northern or navy beans, rinsed and drained

2 medium cloves garlic, finely chopped

1 ready-to-serve thin pizza crust (12 inches in diameter)

1/4 teaspoon dried oregano leaves

1 cup firmly packed spinach leaves, shredded

1/2 cup shredded reduced-fat Colby–Monterey Jack cheese (2 ounces)

Heat oven to 425°. Pour enough boiling water over dried tomatoes to cover. Let stand 10 minutes; drain. Cut into thin strips; set aside.

Place beans and garlic in food processor. Cover and process until smooth.

Spread beans over pizza crust. Sprinkle with oregano, tomatoes, spinach and cheese. Place on ungreased cookie sheet. Bake about 10 minutes or until cheese is melted.

1 Serving

Calories 155
(Calories from Fat 10)

Fat 1g (Saturated 0g)

Cholesterol 0mg

Sodium 270mg

Carbohydrate 31g
(Dietary Fiber 4g)

Protein 10g

% Daily Value

Vitamin A 4%

Vitamin C 2%

Calcium 8%

Iron 18%

Diet Exchanges

2 Starch

1 **Eating Smart** • When picking out your pizza crust, think thin. The thick-crust variety is higher in calories and has almost double the fat grams per serving.

2 **Staying Active** • Has lifting weights left you wondering how much weight is too much? You know you're lifting too much weight if you can't complete ten to twelve repetitions in good form. To make sure you're using good form, consider meeting with a trainer or attend a weight room orientation at your health club.

White Bean and Spinach Pizza

The Vegetarian Pantry

Going vegetarian or meatless? Keeping your kitchen well-stocked with a variety of low-fat, high-flavor ingredients makes meatless meal planning a snap.

On the Shelf

- Canned or jarred sauces: chutney, mustards, relishes, salsa
- Canned tomato products: plain and seasoned
- Canned whole beans: black, butter, cannellini, great Northern, kidney, pinto
- Dried fruit: apricots, cranberries, dates, diced dried fruits, raisins
- Dried legumes: beans, lentils, split peas
- Fat-free vegetable broth
- Grains: barley, bulgur, quinoa, rice
- Pasta
- Ready-to-eat cereals
- Whole grain breads and rolls
- Whole grain crackers

In the Refrigerator

- Fat-free or low-fat milk or soy milk
- Fat-free or low-fat yogurt
- Flour and corn tortillas
- Fresh fruits and vegetables
- Hummus
- Reduced-fat cheeses
- Reduced-fat tofu

In the Freezer

- Fruit juices
- Frozen fruits and vegetables
- Frozen meat substitutes (vegetable burgers, vegetarian hot dogs and breakfast meats)

Creamy Mushroom–Topped
Baked Potatoes

PREP: 15 MIN; COOK: 8 MIN | 4 SERVINGS

4 medium unpeeled baking potatoes

1 tablespoon margarine or butter

4 cups sliced mushrooms (10 ounces)

1 clove garlic, finely chopped

1 cup fat-free (skim) milk

3 tablespoons all-purpose flour

1 teaspoon freeze-dried chives

1/2 teaspoon vegetable or chicken bouillon granules

1/4 teaspoon salt

1/4 teaspoon pepper

1/4 cup shredded Parmesan cheese

Pierce potatoes. Arrange potatoes about 1 inch apart in circle on microwavable paper towel in microwave oven. Microwave uncovered on High about 8 minutes or until tender.

While potatoes are microwaving, melt margarine in 10-inch nonstick skillet over medium heat. Cook mushrooms and garlic in skillet about 3 minutes, stirring frequently, until mushrooms are tender.

Mix remaining ingredients except cheese; stir into mushrooms. Heat to boiling, stirring constantly. Boil and stir 1 minute; remove from heat.

Place each potato on dinner plate. Cut potatoes lengthwise in half. Spoon mushroom sauce over potatoes. Sprinkle with cheese.

1 Serving

Calories 235
(Calories from Fat 45)

Fat 5g (Saturated 2g)

Cholesterol 5mg

Sodium 480mg

Carbohydrate 42g
(Dietary Fiber 4g)

Protein 9g

% Daily Value

Vitamin A 8%

Vitamin C 16%

Calcium 16%

Iron 16%

Diet Exchanges

2 Starch

2 Vegetable

1/2 Fat

1 **Eating Smart** • To get the most nutrients from your baked potato, be sure to eat the skin. Ounce for ounce, the skin has more fiber, iron, potassium and B vitamins than the flesh.

2 **Staying Active** • A treadmill tip: Look straight ahead. Because your feet tend to follow your eyes, focusing on what's in front of you will put you on a straight path. Turning your head for conversation or to look around the room can easily throw you off balance.

Savory Breads Vegetables and Side Dishes

7

Cheesy Mexican Corn Bread, 190

Cheddar and Green Onion Biscuits, 191

Savory Currant Wedges, 192

Carrots and Zucchini with Herbs, 194

Grilled Veggies, 196

Spaghetti with Squash, 197

Caramelized Onion and Sweet Potato Skillet, 198

Horseradish Mashed Potatoes, 200

Triple-Cabbage Slaw, 202

Mediterranean Vegetable Salad, 204

Antipasto Pasta Salad, 205

French Bread Salad, 206

Orzo Parmesan, 207

Spaetzle in Herbed Tomato Cream Sauce, 208

Onion and Mushroom Quinoa, 210

Pine Nut and Green Onion Pilaf, 212

Confetti Wild Rice, 213

Cheddar and Green Onion Biscuits (page 191)

Cheesy
Mexican Corn Bread

PREP: 10 MIN; BAKE: 30 MIN | 12 SERVINGS

1 1/2 cups yellow cornmeal

1/2 cup all-purpose flour

1/2 cup shredded reduced-fat Monterey Jack or Cheddar cheese (2 ounces)

1 cup buttermilk

3 tablespoons vegetable oil or shortening

2 teaspoons baking powder

1 teaspoon sugar

1 teaspoon salt

1 teaspoon chili powder

1/2 teaspoon baking soda

1/2 cup fat-free cholesterol-free egg product or 2 eggs

1 can (8 ounces) cream-style corn

1 can (4 ounces) chopped green chilies, well drained

Heat oven to 450°. Grease round pan, 9 × 1 1/2 inches, square pan, 8 × 8 × 2 inches, or 10-inch ovenproof skillet.

Mix all ingredients. Beat vigorously 30 seconds. Pour batter into pan.

Bake round or square pan 25 to 30 minutes, skillet about 20 minutes, or until golden brown. Serve warm.

1 Serving

Calories 150
(Calories from Fat 45)

Fat 5g (Saturated 1g)

Cholesterol 5mg

Sodium 460mg

Carbohydrate 23g
(Dietary Fiber 2g)

Protein 6g

% Daily Value

Vitamin A 2%

Vitamin C 6%

Calcium 8%

Iron 12%

Diet Exchanges

1 1/2 Starch

1 Fat

1 **Eating Smart** • Corn, with its subtly sweet flavor, is ideal for those looking for sweetness without mega fat and calories. Corn lovers will never tire of this nutritious veggie. Enjoy it as a side dish, in muffins or bread, on salads, in soups or as the well-loved corn on the cob.

2 **Staying Active** • Being an active participant instead of an observer can help burn calories. At a party, an hour of dancing will burn about 470 calories. If you sat on the sidelines, you'd have to watch the dance floor for 6 hours to burn that many calories.

Cheddar and Green Onion
Biscuits

PREP: 15 MIN; BAKE: 11 MIN | 8 BISCUITS

1 1/3 cups all-purpose flour

1 1/2 teaspoons baking
    powder

1/2 teaspoon salt

1/4 teaspoon baking soda

1/4 teaspoon ground mustard

4 medium green onions,
    sliced (1/4 cup)

1/3 cup shredded reduced-fat
    Cheddar cheese

3/4 cup buttermilk

3 tablespoons vegetable oil

Heat oven to 450°. Spray cookie sheet with cooking spray. Mix flour, baking powder, salt, baking soda and mustard in medium bowl. Stir in onions and cheese. Mix buttermilk and oil; stir into flour mixture until soft dough forms.

Drop dough by 8 spoonfuls onto cookie sheet. Bake 9 to 11 minutes or until golden brown. Serve warm.

1 Biscuit

Calories 120
(Calories from Fat 45)

Fat 5g (Saturated 1g)

Cholesterol 0mg

Sodium 300mg

Carbohydrate 16g
(Dietary Fiber 1g)

Protein 4g

% Daily Value

Vitamin A 0%

Vitamin C 0%

Calcium 8%

Iron 6%

Diet Exchanges

1 Starch

1 Fat

1 **Eating Smart** • You wouldn't know by the name, but buttermilk contains no butter and has very little fat. (For 0 fat grams, buy fat-free buttermilk.) Buttermilk is a calcium-rich, refreshing beverage. It also adds tang and great flavor to salad dressings, dips and baked goods.

2 **Staying Active** • Those who have achieved their fitness goals often credit role models for their success. Find others who have attained the goals you want to reach. When your enthusiasm wanes, remind yourself of what they've achieved and remember that you can achieve it, too!

Currant Wedges

PREP: 10 MIN; BAKE: 35 MIN; COOL: 10 MIN | 12 WEDGES

1 1/2 cups all-purpose flour

1/2 cup currants or raisins

1 teaspoon baking powder

1/2 teaspoon salt

1/4 teaspoon baking soda

1 cup shredded reduced-fat mozzarella cheese (4 ounces)

3/4 cup buttermilk

1/4 cup fat-free cholesterol-free egg product or 1 egg

2 tablespoons olive or vegetable oil

Heat oven to 375°. Spray round pan, 9 × 1 1/2 inches, with cooking spray.

Mix flour, currants, baking powder, salt and baking soda in large bowl. Stir in remaining ingredients. Spread in pan.

Bake 30 to 35 minutes or until golden brown. Cool 10 minutes. Cut into wedges. Serve warm.

1 Wedge	
Calories 125 (Calories from Fat 35)	
Fat 4g (Saturated 1g)	
Cholesterol 5mg	
Sodium 240mg	
Carbohydrate 18g (Dietary Fiber 1g)	
Protein 5g	

% Daily Value

Vitamin A 2%	
Vitamin C 0%	
Calcium 12%	
Iron 6%	

Diet Exchanges

1 Starch

1 Fat

1 **Eating Smart** • Even though they look like baby raisins, currants are actually a different variety of dried fruit. Currants are dried Zante grapes—most raisins are dried from Thompson or Muscat grapes. Dried fruits are concentrated sources of many nutrients. Include them in baked goods for a sweet, low-fat burst of flavor.

2 **Staying Active** • The next time you pass a play-ground, steal a few seconds for yourself. Return to your childhood by swinging, sliding and climbing. When you're playing and having fun, you don't even realize that you're also working out and burning calories.

Savory Currant Wedges

Carrots and
Zucchini with Herbs

PREP: 10 MIN; COOK: 15 MIN | 4 SERVINGS

2 medium carrots, sliced
(1 cup)

4 medium zucchini, cut into
julienne strips

2 tablespoons margarine or
butter

1 tablespoon chopped fresh
or 1 teaspoon dried sage
leaves

1 teaspoon chopped fresh or
1/4 teaspoon dried dill
weed

2 teaspoons lemon juice

1/4 teaspoon salt

1/4 teaspoon pepper

Place steamer basket in 1/2 inch water in saucepan (water should not touch bottom of basket). Place carrots in basket. Cover tightly and heat to boiling; reduce heat. Steam carrots 3 minutes. Add zucchini. Steam 4 to 6 minutes or until carrots and zucchini are crisp-tender.

Melt margarine in 12-inch skillet over medium heat. Stir in carrots, zucchini and remaining ingredients. Cook uncovered 2 to 3 minutes, stirring gently, until hot.

1 Serving

Calories 90
(Calories from Fat 55)

Fat 6g (Saturated 1g)

Cholesterol 0mg

Sodium 240mg

Carbohydrate 9g
(Dietary Fiber 3g)

Protein 3g

% Daily Value

Vitamin A 62%

Vitamin C 16%

Calcium 4%

Iron 6%

Diet Exchanges

2 Vegetable

1 Fat

1 Eating Smart • Zucchini is a summer squash variety that offers a mere nine calories per half-cup. A colorful addition to many cooked dishes, zucchini can also be enjoyed raw. For a low-calorie snack, dip zucchini sticks into salsa or a nonfat sour cream dip.

2 Staying Active • When lifting weights, slow-and-steady wins the muscle building race. Lifting weights quickly enlists the aid of your momentum—and your muscles get less of a workout. By lifting slowly, you rely solely on the strength of your muscles.

Carrots and Zucchini with Herbs

Grilled
Veggies

PREP: 15 MIN; GRILL: 20 MIN | 4 SERVINGS

1 tablespoon margarine or butter, melted

2 tablespoons lemon pepper

1 large potato, cut lengthwise into fourths

1 medium zucchini, cut lengthwise in half

1 medium yellow summer squash, cut lengthwise in half

2 large bell peppers, cut lengthwise into fourths and seeded

1 medium onion, cut into 1/2-inch slices

Bibb lettuce, if desired

1/4 cup fat-free Italian dressing

Mix margarine and lemon pepper. Brush on potato, zucchini, squash, bell peppers and onion.

Heat coals or gas grill for direct heat. Cover and grill vegetables 4 inches from medium heat 10 to 20 minutes, turning frequently, until tender.

Line platter with lettuce. As vegetables become done, remove from grill to platter. Sprinkle with dressing. Serve warm.

1 Serving

Calories 120 (Calories from Fat 25)

Fat 3g (Saturated 1g)

Cholesterol 0mg

Sodium 700mg

Carbohydrate 25g (Dietary Fiber 5g)

Protein 3g

% Daily Value

Vitamin A 12%

Vitamin C 74%

Calcium 4%

Iron 10%

Diet Exchanges

5 Vegetable

1 Eating Smart • Reach for your toothbrush after a meal. Brushing immediately after eating signals the end of your mealtime, making it less likely that you'll continue eating. After all, no food tastes good once your mouth is minty fresh!

2 Staying Active • Mile for mile, walking and running burn the same number of calories. Because running 1 mile takes less time than walking the same distance, you can run farther in the same amount of time and burn more total calories. Don't discount walking, though. Running stresses leg muscles and joints; walking is easier on your hips, knees, ankles and feet—plus it offers a greater opportunity to enjoy your surroundings.

Spaghetti with
Squash

PREP: 15 MIN; COOK: 20 MIN; STAND: 10 MIN | 6 SERVINGS

1 medium spaghetti squash (about 3 pounds)

4 ounces uncooked spaghetti, broken in half

1/4 cup chopped fresh parsley

2 tablespoons grated Parmesan cheese

2 tablespoons margarine or butter, melted

1 tablespoon chopped fresh or 1 teaspoon dried oregano leaves

1/2 teaspoon garlic salt

Prick squash with fork; place on microwavable paper towel in microwave oven. Microwave on High 8 minutes; turn squash over. Microwave 8 to 11 minutes longer or until tender. Let stand 10 minutes.

Meanwhile, cook and drain spaghetti as directed on package. Cut squash lengthwise in half; remove seeds and fibers. Reserve one half for another use. Remove spaghetti-like strands with 2 forks.

Toss squash, spaghetti and remaining ingredients. Return spaghetti mixture to squash shell to serve.

Conventional Directions: Heat oven to 400°. Prick squash with fork; place in ungreased square baking dish, 8 × 8 × 2 inches. Bake uncovered about 1 1/2 hours or until tender. Continue as directed.

1 Serving

Calories 140 (Calories from Fat 25)

Fat 3g (Saturated 1g)

Cholesterol 0mg

Sodium 170mg

Carbohydrate 28g (Dietary Fiber 4g)

Protein 5g

% Daily Value

Vitamin A 8%

Vitamin C 8%

Calcium 6%

Iron 8%

Diet Exchanges

1 Starch

2 Vegetable

1 **Eating Smart** • Diets rich in carotenoids, notably beta-carotene, may play a role in preventing cancer. Beta-carotene-rich foods are given away by their orange color—squash, sweet potatoes, carrots and cantaloupe are examples. Non-orange sources include kale, spinach and dandelion greens.

2 **Staying Active** • Fit stretching into your busy day by combining it with other activities. When you watch TV or read a book, sit on the floor or in bed and place the soles of your feet together. Let your knees drop gently out to the sides to lengthen inner-thigh muscles.

Caramelized Onion and
Sweet Potato Skillet

PREP: 10 MIN; COOK: 20 MIN | 4 SERVINGS

1 teaspoon vegetable oil

1/4 large sweet onion
  (Bermuda, Maui, Spanish
  or Vidalia), sliced

3 medium sweet potatoes,
  peeled and sliced
  (3 1/2 cups)

2 tablespoons packed brown
  sugar

1/2 teaspoon jerk seasoning

1 tablespoon chopped fresh
  parsley

Heat oil in 10-inch skillet over medium heat. Cook onion and sweet potatoes in oil about 5 minutes, stirring occasionally, until light brown; reduce heat to low. Cover and cook 10 to 12 minutes, stirring occasionally, until potatoes are tender.

Stir in brown sugar and jerk seasoning. Cook uncovered about 3 minutes, stirring occasionally, until glazed. Sprinkle with parsley.

1 Serving

Calories 115
(Calories from Fat 10)

Fat 1g (Saturated 0g)

Cholesterol 0mg

Sodium 10mg

Carbohydrate 28g
(Dietary Fiber 3g)

Protein 2g

% Daily Value

Vitamin A 100%

Vitamin C 18%

Calcium 2%

Iron 2%

Diet Exchanges

1/2 Starch

1 Vegetable

1 Fruit

1 **Eating Smart** • Despite their extra sweetness, sweet potatoes have only a few more calories per ounce than white potatoes. A 3 1/2-ounce portion of baked sweet potato contains about 100 calories and four times the RDA for Vitamin A.

2 **Staying Active** • Running rookies: The best way to start running is by alternating periods of walking and running. Start with 2 minutes walking and 1 minute running. Gradually decrease your walking intervals until you can run continuously for 20 minutes, and build from there.

Caramelized Onion and Sweet Potato Skillet

Horseradish
Mashed Potatoes

PREP: 10 MIN; COOK: 20 MIN | 4 SERVINGS

4 medium unpeeled boiling potatoes (about 1 1/2 pounds), cut into 1/2-inch slices

1/3 cup plain low-fat or fat-free yogurt

1 tablespoon prepared horseradish

1/2 teaspoon salt

2 to 4 tablespoons fat-free (skim) milk

Chopped fresh parsley, if desired

Heat 1 inch water to boiling in 3-quart saucepan. Add potatoes. Heat to boiling. Reduce heat to low and cook about 15 minutes or until tender; drain. Return potatoes to saucepan. Shake pan with potatoes over low heat to dry; remove from heat.

Mash potatoes until no lumps remain. Beat in yogurt, horseradish and salt. Add milk in small amounts, beating after each addition (amount of milk needed to make potatoes smooth and fluffy depends on the kind of potatoes used). Beat vigorously until potatoes are light and fluffy. Sprinkle with parsley.

1 **Eating Smart** • Not only are they a terrific source of carbohydrates, eating potatoes is a good way to get more Vitamin C and fiber, particularly when eating the skin. Potatoes are also essentially fat-free, and studies have shown that they keep you "filled up" longer than most any other food.

2 **Staying Active** • Just taking a break and going for a walk helps clear body, mind and spirit. Instead of eating lunch at your desk every day, make it a goal to get up, stretch, go for a walk, and return to your desk refreshed and ready for the afternoon!

1 Serving

Calories 130 (Calories from Fat 0)

Fat 0g (Saturated 0g)

Cholesterol 0mg

Sodium 330mg

Carbohydrate 31g (Dietary Fiber 3g)

Protein 4g

% Daily Value

Vitamin A 0%

Vitamin C 12%

Calcium 6%

Iron 8%

Diet Exchanges

2 Starch

Salad Strategies—Cutting the Calories

With a wide array of salad add-ons, what should you choose if you want to lose?

- **Pile on the plain veggies!** Choose greens, cucumbers, tomatoes, carrots, celery, broccoli, cauliflower, mushrooms, sprouts, peppers, water chestnuts and onions.
- **Choose fresh fruit.** Pineapple, melon, bananas and apples are satisfying, low-fat options.
- **Avoid high-fat and high-calorie dressing.** Pick low-fat or fat-free salad dressing, vinegar or lemon juice. If full-fat dressing is your only option, limit it to 1 tablespoon.

Salad Bars—The Calories Add Up

All those delicious toppings are tempting. But look out! Some of your favorites may be loaded with calories and fat.

	Calories	Fat (g)
1/2 cup creamy coleslaw	200	15
1/2 cup potato salad	200	15
2 tablespoons ranch dressing	140	14
1/4 cup Cheddar cheese	114	9
2 tablespoons sunflower seeds	100	8
1/4 cup bacon bits	100	6
1/4 cup flavored croutons	85	6
1/4 cup chopped egg	75	5

Triple-Cabbage
Slaw

PREP: 15 MIN | 4 SERVINGS

2 cups thinly sliced Chinese (napa) cabbage

1 1/2 cups shredded green cabbage

1/2 cup shredded red cabbage

1 tablespoon chopped fresh chives

3 tablespoons orange marmalade

2 tablespoons rice vinegar

1 teaspoon grated gingerroot

Mix cabbage and chives in large glass or plastic bowl. Stir marmalade, vinegar and gingerroot until blended. Add to cabbage; toss lightly.

1 Eating Smart • Nearly fat and calorie free, cabbage is a cruciferous vegetable that contains nitrogen compounds that may protect against certain cancers. Other cruciferous veggies include broccoli, cauliflower, kale, collards, mustard greens and Brussels sprouts.

2 Staying Active • Getting a massage can benefit your fitness program. Massage loosens up kinks in your muscles, relieves stress and helps you relax. Scheduling periodic massages is also a good way to reward yourself for all of those short-term fitness goals you're reaching!

1 Serving

Calories 50
(Calories from Fat 0)

Fat 0g (Saturated 0g)

Cholesterol 0mg

Sodium 35mg

Carbohydrate 13g
(Dietary Fiber 1g)

Protein 1g

% Daily Value

Vitamin A 10%

Vitamin C 48%

Calcium 6%

Iron 2%

Diet Exchanges

1 Vegetable

1/2 Fruit

Triple-Cabbage Slaw

Mediterranean
Vegetable Salad

PREP: 10 MIN; CHILL: 1 HR | 6 SERVINGS

1/3 cup tarragon or white wine vinegar

3 tablespoons olive or vegetable oil

2 tablespoons chopped fresh or 2 teaspoons dried oregano leaves

1/2 teaspoon sugar

1/2 teaspoon ground mustard

1/2 teaspoon salt

1/2 teaspoon pepper

2 cloves garlic, finely chopped

2 large yellow bell peppers, sliced into thin rings

3 large tomatoes, sliced

6 ounces spinach leaves

1/2 cup crumbled feta cheese (2 ounces)

Kalamata olives, if desired

Mix vinegar, oil, oregano, sugar, mustard, salt, pepper and garlic. Place bell peppers and tomatoes in glass or plastic container. Pour vinegar mixture over vegetables. Cover and refrigerate at least 1 hour to blend flavors.

Line serving platter with spinach. Drain vegetables; place on spinach. Sprinkle with cheese. Garnish with olives.

1 Serving

Calories 135
(Calories from Fat 80)

Fat 9g (Saturated 2g)

Cholesterol 10mg

Sodium 360mg

Carbohydrate 12g
(Dietary Fiber 3g)

Protein 4g

% Daily Value

Vitamin A 56%

Vitamin C 100%

Calcium 12%

Iron 12%

Diet Exchanges

2 Vegetable

2 Fat

Eating Smart • Vegetable salads are a great way to make a dent in the recommended 3 to 5 daily servings of fresh vegetables. With all the health benefits fresh veggies offer, some experts say we should aim for as high as 7 to 9 daily servings.

Staying Active • Even taking out the trash can be an opportunity for activity. Carry the trash receptacle out instead of dragging or rolling it. Or carry less trash each time and make more trips—exercise doesn't need to be limited to a special reserved time in your schedule.

Antipasto
Pasta Salad

PREP: 15 MIN; CHILL: 6 HR | 4 SERVINGS

1 cup sliced mushrooms
(3 ounces)

1 cup sliced quartered
zucchini

1 cup chopped cauliflower

1/2 cup shredded carrot

1/2 cup chopped red bell
pepper

1/4 cup sliced ripe olives

2 medium green onions,
sliced (2 tablespoons)

2/3 cup fat-free Italian
dressing

1/4 teaspoon salt

1 1/2 cups uncooked medium
pasta shells

Mix all ingredients except pasta in large glass or plastic
bowl. Cover and refrigerate at least 6 hours to blend
flavors.

Cook and drain pasta as directed on package. Rinse with
cold water; drain. Mix pasta and vegetable mixture.
Refrigerate up to 1 hour if desired.

1 Serving

Calories 225
(Calories from Fat 20)

Fat 2g (Saturated 0g)

Cholesterol 0mg

Sodium 620mg

Carbohydrate 45g
(Dietary Fiber 4g)

Protein 8g

% Daily Value

Vitamin A 34%

Vitamin C 88%

Calcium 4%

Iron 16%

Diet Exchanges

2 Starch

3 Vegetable

Eating Smart • Fat-free Italian dressing can play
many roles in a low-fat kitchen. Use your favorite brand
to marinate poultry or raw veggies, toss with salads,
pasta or cooked veggies, or stir into low-fat sour cream
for a tasty dip.

Staying Active • Although a few days of inactivity is OK, being inactive for too long can cause you to
lose ground. Experts say that most aerobic benefits are
lost within 2 weeks to 3 months of inactivity. The good
news? You can maintain your fitness level during especially hectic times by merely cutting back instead of
cutting out.

French Bread
Salad

6 slices day-old French or Italian bread, 1 inch thick

2 medium tomatoes, chopped (1 1/2 cups)

1 medium cucumber, peeled and chopped (1 1/4 cups)

1 small onion, thinly sliced

1/3 cup fat-free red wine vinegar dressing

2 tablespoons chopped fresh or 2 teaspoons dried basil leaves

1/4 teaspoon pepper

Tear bread into 1-inch pieces. Mix bread and remaining ingredients in glass or plastic bowl.

Cover and refrigerate, stirring once, at least 1 hour to blend flavors and soften bread. Stir before serving.

1 Serving
Calories 105 (Calories from Fat 10)
Fat 1g (Saturated 0g)
Cholesterol 0mg
Sodium 210mg
Carbohydrate 22g (Dietary Fiber 2g)
Protein 4g

% Daily Value
Vitamin A 4%
Vitamin C 18%
Calcium 4%
Iron 8%

Diet Exchanges

1 Starch

1 Vegetable

1 Eating Smart • Contrary to the teachings of some diet gurus, bread is not fattening. Weight gain is caused by eating more calories than your body needs. Overindulging in bread or spreading slices thick with high-fat, high-calorie toppings can cause you to put on pounds. Including bread in a well-balanced diet is part of most successful weight-loss programs.

2 Staying Active • Pop quiz: To burn 100 calories, would you rather jump rope or read the paper? If you want to burn more calories in less time, you'll opt for jumping rope. You'd have to read the paper for 80 minutes to burn 100 calories. Ten minutes of jumping rope accomplishes the same thing.

Orzo
Parmesan

PREP: 10 MIN; COOK: 15 MIN | 6 SERVINGS

1 can (14 1/2 ounces) fat-free chicken broth

1/2 cup water

1/4 teaspoon salt

1 1/3 cups uncooked rosa-marina (orzo) pasta

2 cloves garlic, finely chopped

8 medium green onions, sliced (1/2 cup)

1/3 cup grated fat-free Parmesan cheese topping

1 tablespoon chopped fresh or 1 teaspoon dried basil leaves

1/8 teaspoon freshly ground pepper

Heat broth, water and salt to boiling in 2-quart saucepan. Stir in pasta, garlic and onions. Heat to boiling; reduce heat. Cover and simmer about 12 minutes, stirring occasionally, until most of the liquid is absorbed. Stir in remaining ingredients.

1 Serving

Calories 145
(Calories from Fat 20)

Fat 2g (Saturated 1g)

Cholesterol 0mg

Sodium 510mg

Carbohydrate 28g
(Dietary Fiber 2g)

Protein 6g

% Daily Value

Vitamin A 0%

Vitamin C 2%

Calcium 4%

Iron 8%

Diet Exchanges

2 Starch

1 **Eating Smart** • Italian for "barley," orzo is a tiny, rice-shaped pasta. Add variety to your meals by substituting this small, complex carbohydrate-rich pasta for rice in pilafs, salads, soups and casseroles.

2 **Staying Active** • When you start an exercise program, you'll be replacing fat with muscle. And because muscle weighs more than fat, your weight may not drop much at first. Rather than falsely discouraging yourself by using the scale, go by how well your clothes fit or how much more energy you have, or most importantly, by how you feel overall.

Spaetzle in
Herbed Tomato Cream Sauce

PREP: 10 MIN; COOK: 10 MIN | 4 SERVINGS

1 teaspoon olive or vegetable oil

4 roma (plum) tomatoes, cut into fourths and sliced (2 cups)

2 cloves garlic, finely chopped

2 tablespoons chopped fresh chives

1 tablespoon chopped fresh or 1 teaspoon dried basil leaves

1/4 cup fat-free sour cream

2 tablespoons fat-free mayonnaise or salad dressing

1 package (12 ounces) frozen cooked spaetzle (4 cups)

Heat oil in 10-inch nonstick skillet over medium heat. Cook tomatoes and garlic in oil 5 to 7 minutes, stirring occasionally, until tomatoes are tender; reduce heat to low. Stir in chives, basil, sour cream and mayonnaise. Cook 2 to 3 minutes, stirring occasionally, until sauce is hot.

Meanwhile, heat spaetzle as directed on package. Add hot spaetzle to skillet; toss to coat with sauce.

1 Serving

Calories 110
(Calories from Fat 25)

Fat 3g (Saturated 1g)

Cholesterol 50mg

Sodium 220mg

Carbohydrate 17g
(Dietary Fiber 1g)

Protein 5g

% Daily Value

Vitamin A 8%

Vitamin C 10%

Calcium 6%

Iron 6%

Diet Exchanges

1 Starch

1/2 Fat

1 **Eating Smart** • Meaning "little sparrow" in German, spaetzle is a dish of tiny noodles or dumplings often served with butter, gravy or a cream sauce. For a tasty side dish that isn't loaded with fat, toss spaetzle with bottled spaghetti sauce or another favorite low-fat pasta sauce.

2 **Staying Active** • Create a list of activities that your entire family enjoys. Post this list on the refrigerator, and make a point to do at least one activity each week. Suggestions for your list: bowling, ice skating, playing catch, walking the dog, visiting an amusement park.

Spaetzle in Herbed Tomato Cream Sauce

Onion and
Mushroom Quinoa

PREP: 10 MIN; COOK: 20 MIN | 6 SERVINGS

1 teaspoon vegetable oil

1 cup uncooked quinoa

1 small onion, cut into
   fourths and sliced

1 medium carrot, shredded
   (2/3 cup)

1 small green bell pepper,
   chopped (1/2 cup)

1 cup sliced mushrooms
   (3 ounces)

1 teaspoon chopped fresh or
   1/4 teaspoon dried thyme
   leaves

1/4 teaspoon salt

1 can (14 1/2 ounces) fat-
   free vegetable broth

Heat oil in 2-quart saucepan over medium heat. Cook
   quinoa and onion in oil 4 to 5 minutes, stirring occasionally, until light brown.

Stir in remaining ingredients. Heat to boiling; reduce
   heat. Cover and simmer about 15 minutes or until
   liquid is absorbed. Fluff with fork.

1 Serving

Calories 125
(Calories from Fat 25)

Fat 3g (Saturated 0g)

Cholesterol 0mg

Sodium 410mg

Carbohydrate 24g
(Dietary Fiber 3g)

Protein 4g

% Daily Value

Vitamin A 20%

Vitamin C 10%

Calcium 2%

Iron 16%

Diet Exchanges

1 Starch

2 Vegetable

1/2 Fat

1 Eating Smart • Quinoa has been hailed as a
"supergrain" because it contains more protein than any
other grain. Tiny and bead-shaped, ivory-colored quinoa
takes only 20 minutes to cook. Like other whole grains,
it's low in fat and provides a rich, balanced source of
vital nutrients.

2 Staying Active • Is it time to rearrange your
furniture? You might think so when you learn that 30
minutes of moving furniture can burn nearly 180 calories! Experiment with new arrangements and get your
heart pumping at the same time.

Onion and Mushroom Quinoa

Pine Nut and
Green Onion Pilaf

PREP: 20 MIN; COOK: 25 MIN | 6 SERVINGS

1 tablespoon margarine or butter

1 cup uncooked regular long-grain rice

12 medium green onions, sliced (3/4 cup)

3 tablespoons pine nuts

2 1/2 cups fat-free chicken broth

1 teaspoon grated lemon peel

1/4 teaspoon salt

Melt margarine in 3-quart saucepan over medium-high heat. Cook rice, 1/2 cup of the onions and the nuts in margarine about 5 minutes, stirring occasionally, until nuts are light brown.

Stir in broth, lemon peel and salt. Heat to boiling, stirring once or twice; reduce heat. Cover and simmer 15 minutes. (Do not lift cover or stir.) Remove from heat; fluff rice lightly with fork. Sprinkle with remaining 1/4 cup onions.

1 Serving
Calories 175 (Calories from Fat 45)
Fat 5g (Saturated 1g)
Cholesterol 0mg
Sodium 560mg
Carbohydrate 29g (Dietary Fiber 1g)
Protein 5g

% Daily Value
Vitamin A 2%
Vitamin C 2%
Calcium 2%
Iron 8%

Diet Exchanges
2 Starch
1/2 Fat

1 **Eating Smart** • Green onions belong to the onion family along with garlic, leeks, scallions (a distinct variety of green onion) and shallots. Members of the onion family contain a fair amount of vitamin C with traces of other vitamins and minerals. One of their greatest contributions to a low-fat kitchen is the tremendous flavor they give food, without adding fat.

2 **Staying Active** • Dress for success. You'll feel better about exercising and be more likely to stick with it when you know you look good. Even if you're working out at home, wear workout clothes you love.

Confetti
Wild Rice

PREP: 10 MIN; COOK: 55 MIN | 6 SERVINGS

1 tablespoon margarine or butter

1/2 cup uncooked wild rice

1 1/2 cups sliced mushrooms (4 ounces)

2 medium green onions, thinly sliced (2 tablespoons)

1 1/4 cups water

1/2 teaspoon salt

1/4 teaspoon pepper

1 package (10 ounces) frozen chopped broccoli, thawed and drained

1 tablespoon lemon juice

Melt margarine in 10-inch nonstick skillet over medium heat. Cook wild rice, mushrooms and onions in margarine about 3 minutes, stirring occasionally, until onions are tender.

Stir in water, salt and pepper. Heat to boiling, stirring occasionally; reduce heat. Cover and simmer 40 to 50 minutes or until rice is tender; drain if necessary.

Stir in broccoli and lemon juice. Heat uncovered, stirring occasionally, until hot.

1 Serving

Calories 75 (Calories from Fat 10)

Fat 1g (Saturated 0g)

Cholesterol 0mg

Sodium 220mg

Carbohydrate 15g (Dietary Fiber 3g)

Protein 4g

% Daily Value

Vitamin A 10%

Vitamin C 16%

Calcium 2%

Iron 4%

Diet Exchanges

1 Starch

1 **Eating Smart** • To lose 1 pound a week, you need to create a 500-calorie daily deficit. Well-balanced weight-loss plans recommend eating 250 fewer calories each day and burning an additional 250 calories through exercise. Remember, a healthy weight-loss plan includes a healthy diet plus exercise, rather than focusing too much on one or the other.

2 **Staying Active** • It's all in the attitude. Telling yourself that you *have to* exercise in order to lose weight takes the fun out of your workout. Instead, focus on positive outcomes: the extra energy you'll get from working out and the well-toned body you'll have.

Delicious Desserts

8

Apple-Maple Bundt Cake, 216

Mocha Angel Cake, 217

Chocolate Soufflé Cakes, 218

Almond Cheesecake with Raspberry Sauce, 220

Mini Pumpkin Cheesecakes, 221

Pear and Cherry Crisp, 222

Blueberry-Lemon Tart, 224

Banana Split Ice–Cream Dessert, 225

Frosty Margarita Pie, 226

Strawberry-Rhubarb Frozen-Yogurt Parfaits, 228

Triple-Chocolate Malts, 229

Orange Cappuccino Brownies, 230

Ginger Gems Cookies, 232

Cherry–Chocolate Chip Cookies, 234

Almond Cheesecake with Raspberry Sauce (page 220)

Apple-Maple
Bundt Cake

PREP: 30 MIN; BAKE: 55 MIN; COOL: 1 HR 15 MIN | 16 SERVINGS

3 cups all-purpose flour

1 cup packed brown sugar

2 teaspoons baking soda

1/2 teaspoon salt

1/2 teaspoon ground nutmeg

1/4 teaspoon ground allspice

1 cup applesauce

1/2 cup fat-free cholesterol-free egg product or 2 eggs

1/4 cup maple-flavored syrup

1/4 cup vegetable oil

2 medium all-purpose apples, peeled and diced (2 cups)

1/3 cup golden raisins

1/3 cup chopped dates

Maple Glaze (right)

Heat oven to 350°. Lightly grease and flour 12-cup bundt cake pan. Mix flour, brown sugar, baking soda, salt, nutmeg and allspice in large bowl. Stir in applesauce, egg product, maple syrup and oil. Beat 2 minutes with electric mixer on medium speed. Stir in apples, raisins and dates. Pour into pan.

Bake 50 to 55 minutes or until toothpick inserted in center comes out clean. Cool 15 minutes; remove from pan to wire rack. Cool completely, about 1 hour. Drizzle with Maple Glaze.

Maple Glaze

1/4 cup powdered sugar

1 to 2 tablespoons maple-flavored syrup

Mix ingredients until smooth and thin enough to drizzle.

1 Serving

Calories 230
(Calories from Fat 35)

Fat 4g (Saturated 1g)

Cholesterol 0mg

Sodium 260mg

Carbohydrate 46g
(Dietary Fiber 1g)

Protein 3g

% Daily Value

Vitamin A 0%

Vitamin C 0%

Calcium 2%

Iron 8%

Diet Exchanges

1 Starch

2 Fruit

1 Fat

1 **Eating Smart** • Having a little of a "forbidden" food is sometimes better than denying yourself and continuing to think about it. Serve yourself a small portion, put the rest away, then sit down and enjoy your treat. A small taste of what you're craving may satisfy your urge, letting you get on with life.

2 **Staying Active** • Do you have a favorite TV show you can't miss? Turn your date with the tube into a weekly exercise session by working out while watching. This is a great time to use your stationary bike or treadmill. No machines? You can still run in place, stretch or do crunches, push-ups and leg lifts.

Mocha
Angel Cake

PREP: 15 MIN; BAKE: 45 MIN; COOL: 1 HR | 12 SERVINGS

1 package (1 pound) one-
    step white angel food
    cake mix

1 tablespoon baking cocoa

1 1/4 cups cold coffee

Mocha Topping (below)

Chocolate shot, if desired

Bake and cool cake as directed on package for two 9-inch loaf pans—except stir cocoa into cake mix (dry) and substitute cold coffee for the water.

Serve cake with Mocha Topping. Sprinkle with chocolate shot. Store covered in refrigerator.

Mocha Topping

1/2 package (2.8-ounce size) whipped topping mix (1 envelope)

1/2 cup cold fat-free (skim) milk

1/2 teaspoon vanilla

2 tablespoons powdered sugar

2 teaspoons baking cocoa

Make topping mix as directed on package, using fat-free milk and vanilla; add powdered sugar and cocoa for the last minute of beating.

1 **Eating Smart** • Made with egg whites, angel food cake is lower in fat than other sweets. Why? Egg whites contain only about 20 of an egg's 75 calories. The white is also fat and cholesterol free. Two whites can often be substituted for one whole egg in baking recipes.

2 **Staying Active** • Research has found that exercise is one of the most effective ways to lift poor spirits. Instead of reaching for chocolate next time you're down, try a 10-minute walk or bike ride.

1 Serving

Calories 165
(Calories from Fat 10)

Fat 1g (Saturated 0g)

Cholesterol 0mg

Sodium 260mg

Carbohydrate 35g
(Dietary Fiber 0g)

Protein 4g

% Daily Value

Vitamin A 0%

Vitamin C 0%

Calcium 0%

Iron 4%

Diet Exchanges

2 Starch

Chocolate
Soufflé Cakes

PREP: 20 MIN; BAKE: 22 MIN; COOL: 20 MIN | 8 SERVINGS

1 ounce sweet baking
  chocolate

1 tablespoon margarine or
  butter

1 teaspoon instant espresso
  coffee (dry)

2 egg whites

2 eggs, separated

1 container (8 ounces) vanilla
  low-fat yogurt

1/2 cup granulated sugar

1/4 cup packed brown sugar

1/4 cup all-purpose flour

1/4 cup baking cocoa

1/4 teaspoon ground
  cinnamon

Mocha Topping (below)

Frozen (thawed) fat-free
  whipped topping, if
  desired

Heat oven to 375°. Spray bottoms only of 8 jumbo muffin cups, 3 3/4 × 1 7/8 inches, with cooking spray. Heat chocolate, margarine and espresso in 1-quart saucepan over low heat, stirring constantly, until melted and smooth; cool slightly.

Beat 4 egg whites in medium bowl with electric mixer on high speed until stiff peaks form; set aside.

Beat egg yolks and yogurt in another medium bowl on medium speed until blended. Gradually beat in granulated sugar, brown sugar and chocolate mixture. Stir in flour, cocoa and cinnamon just until blended. Fold in egg whites. Spoon into muffin cups.

Bake 20 to 22 minutes or until firm to the touch. Cool 5 minutes (centers of cakes will sink slightly). Remove from muffin cups to wire rack. Cool 15 minutes.

Make Mocha Topping. Place cakes on individual plates. Drizzle with topping. Serve with whipped topping.

Mocha Topping

1/4 cup chocolate-flavored syrup

4 teaspoons powdered sugar

1/2 teaspoon instant espresso coffee (dry)

Heat all ingredients in 1-quart saucepan over low heat, stirring constantly, until smooth.

1 **Eating Smart** • Dress up this dessert without adding a lot of fat or calories with a sprinkling of baking cocoa, ground cinnamon or powdered sugar.

2 **Staying Active** • You can fall into an exercise rut by finding one favorite activity and "sticking to it." Instead, find several activities you enjoy, and mix them up depending on your mood and schedule. Forcing yourself to do things you don't enjoy will only leave you discouraged.

Chocolate Soufflé Cakes

1 Serving	
Calories 215 (Calories from Fat 45)	
Fat 5g (Saturated 2g)	
Cholesterol 55mg	
Sodium 80mg	
Carbohydrate 38g (Dietary Fiber 1g)	
Protein 5g	

% Daily Value	
Vitamin A 4%	
Vitamin C 0%	
Calcium 6%	
Iron 6%	

Diet Exchanges	
2 Starch	
1/2 Fruit	
1 Fat	

Almond Cheesecake with
Raspberry Sauce

PREP: 20 MIN; BAKE: 1 HR; COOL: 45 MIN; CHILL: 3 HR | 16 SERVINGS

1/2 cup crushed reduced-fat graham crackers (8 squares)

2 packages (8 ounces each) reduced-fat cream cheese (Neufchâtel), softened

2/3 cup sugar

1/2 cup fat-free cholesterol-free egg product or 2 eggs

1/2 teaspoon almond extract

2 cups vanilla low-fat yogurt

2 tablespoons all-purpose flour

Raspberry Sauce (below)

1 tablespoon sliced almonds, if desired

Fresh raspberries, if desired

Heat oven to 300°. Spray springform pan, 9 × 3 inches, with cooking spray. Sprinkle crushed crackers over bottom of pan.

Beat cream cheese in medium bowl with electric mixer on medium speed until smooth. Add sugar, egg product and almond extract. Beat on medium speed about 2 minutes or until smooth. Add yogurt and flour. Beat on low speed until smooth. Carefully spread batter over crackers in pan.

Bake 1 hour. Turn off oven; cool in oven 30 minutes with door closed. Remove from oven; cool on wire rack 15 minutes. Carefully remove side of pan. Cover and refrigerate at least 3 hours.

Serve cheesecake with Raspberry Sauce. Garnish with almonds and fresh raspberries. Store covered in refrigerator.

Raspberry Sauce

2 cups fresh or frozen (thawed and drained) raspberries

2 tablespoons water

3 tablespoons sugar

1/4 teaspoon almond extract

Place all ingredients in food processor. Cover and process until smooth. Press through sieve to remove seeds.

1 Serving

Calories 170
(Calories from Fat 65)

Fat 7g (Saturated 4g)

Cholesterol 20mg

Sodium 160mg

Carbohydrate 24g
(Dietary Fiber 2g)

Protein 5g

% Daily Value

Vitamin A 8%

Vitamin C 6%

Calcium 8%

Iron 2%

Diet Exchanges

1 Starch

1 Fruit

1 1/2 Fat

1 Eating Smart • Cheesecake doesn't have to be high in fat to be delicious. By replacing full-fat cream cheese and sour cream with their low-fat counterparts, you can have your cheesecake and eat it, too.

2 Staying Active • When stretching, don't hold your breath. Rather, breathe slowly and deeply, inhaling through your nose and exhaling through your mouth, to keep oxygen flowing to your muscles.

Mini
Pumpkin Cheesecakes

PREP: 15 MIN; BAKE: 35 MIN; COOL: 15 MIN; CHILL: 1 HR | 8 SERVINGS

2 soft molasses cookies
(3 inches in diameter)

1 package (8 ounces) fat-free
cream cheese, softened

1/3 cup packed brown sugar

1/2 cup fat-free cholesterol-
free egg product or 2 eggs

1/2 teaspoon vanilla

2/3 cup canned pumpkin
(not pumpkin pie mix)

1/2 teaspoon pumpkin pie
spice

1 cup frozen (thawed)
reduced-fat whipped
topping

Heat oven to 350°. Line 8 medium muffin cups, 2 1/2 ×
1 1/4 inches, with aluminum foil or paper baking cups.
Break cookies into fine crumbs. Reserve 2 teaspoons
cookie crumbs for topping. Divide remaining crumbs
among muffin cups.

Beat cream cheese and brown sugar in medium bowl with
electric mixer on medium speed until smooth. Stir in
egg product and vanilla just until blended. Stir in
pumpkin and pumpkin pie spice. Spoon evenly into
muffin cups.

Bake 30 to 35 minutes or until edges are set; cool 15
minutes. Remove cheesecakes from pan. Refrigerate
about 1 hour or until completely chilled. Serve each
cheesecake topped with 2 tablespoons whipped topping.
Sprinkle with reserved cookie crumbs. Store covered
in refrigerator.

1 Serving

Calories 110
(Calories from Fat 20)

Fat 2g (Saturated 1g)

Cholesterol 0mg

Sodium 190mg

Carbohydrate 18g
(Dietary Fiber 1g)

Protein 6g

% Daily Value

Vitamin A 60%

Vitamin C 0%

Calcium 10%

Iron 4%

Diet Exchanges

1 Starch

1/2 Fat

1 **Eating Smart** • Canned pumpkin is just as nutritious as its fresh counterpart. One-half cup contains
about 40 calories and is free of fat, sodium and cholesterol. The same 1/2 cup also contains 100% of the RDA
for Vitamin A, along with a good amount of fiber, iron
and other minerals.

2 **Staying Active** • Do you want to burn 450 calories? You can: a) swim for an hour; or b) float on a pool
chair for 8 hours. Anyone with a schedule to keep knows
that option "a" is the best bet.

Pear and Cherry
Crisp

PREP: 30 MIN; BAKE: 35 MIN; COOL: 15 MIN | 8 SERVINGS

3/4 cup quick-cooking oats

1/4 cup packed brown sugar

3 tablespoons all-purpose flour

2 tablespoons margarine or butter, melted

2 tablespoons dried cherries

4 medium pears, peeled, cored and sliced (4 cups)

1 cup frozen pitted tart cherries

1/3 cup granulated sugar

3 tablespoons all-purpose flour

1/2 teaspoon almond extract

Almond Custard Sauce (right)

Heat oven to 375°. Mix oats, brown sugar, 3 tablespoons flour and the margarine until crumbly. Stir in dried cherries; set aside.

Mix remaining ingredients except Almond Custard Sauce in square baking dish, 8 × 8 × 2 inches. Sprinkle oat mixture over filling; press slightly.

Bake 30 to 35 minutes or until topping is golden brown and mixture is bubbly. Cool 15 minutes. Serve with Almond Custard Sauce.

Almond Custard Sauce

2 containers (3 to 4 ounces each) refrigerated vanilla fat-free pudding

1/4 cup fat-free half-and-half

1/4 teaspoon almond extract

Mix all ingredients.

1 Serving

Calories 250
(Calories from Fat 35)

Fat 4g (Saturated 1g)

Cholesterol 0mg

Sodium 90mg

Carbohydrate 54g
(Dietary Fiber 4g)

Protein 4g

% Daily Value

Vitamin A 6%

Vitamin C 6%

Calcium 6%

Iron 6%

Diet Exchanges

1 Starch

2 1/2 Fruit

1/2 Fat

1 **Eating Smart** • Fruit is the perfect portable snack! Few foods are easier to throw into a backpack or briefcase than apples, pears, oranges and bananas. Fruit is also low in calories and high in fiber, vitamins and carbohydrates.

2 **Staying Active** • Make spring cleaning a full-fledged workout. Mix and match the following activities: rearranging your wardrobe (2.3 calories per minute), cleaning out the attic (3.4 calories per minute), washing windows (4.4 calories per minute) and scrubbing floors (5.4 calories per minute).

Pear and Cherry Crisp

Blueberry-Lemon
Tart

PREP: 15 MIN; BAKE: 10 MIN; CHILL: 2 HR | 12 SERVINGS

35 reduced-fat vanilla wafer cookies, crushed (1 1/2 cups)

1 egg white, beaten

1 tablespoon margarine or butter, melted

1 1/4 cups fat-free (skim) milk

1 package (4-serving size) lemon instant pudding and pie filling mix

1 1/2 teaspoons grated lemon peel

1 cup frozen (thawed) fat-free whipped topping

Blueberry Topping (right)

Heat oven to 400°. Lightly spray tart pan with removable bottom, 9 × 1 inch, with cooking spray. Mix crushed cookies, egg white and margarine until crumbly. Press in bottom and up side of pan. Bake 8 to 10 minutes or until light golden brown; cool.

Beat milk, pudding mix and lemon peel in medium bowl with electric mixer on low speed about 2 minutes or until smooth. Chill 5 minutes.

Fold in whipped topping. Spread over crust. Cover and refrigerate at least 2 hours until chilled. Serve with Blueberry Topping. Store covered in refrigerator.

Blueberry Topping

2 tablespoons sugar

1 teaspoon cornstarch

3 tablespoons water

1 1/2 cups fresh or frozen blueberries

1 tablespoon lemon juice

Mix sugar, cornstarch and water in 1-quart saucepan. Stir in 1/2 cup of the blueberries. Heat to boiling; reduce heat to medium-low. Cook about 5 minutes or until slightly thickened. Stir in lemon juice; remove from heat. Cool 10 minutes. Stir in remaining 1 cup blueberries. Cover and refrigerate at least 1 hour until chilled.

1 **Eating Smart** • How about a double dessert delight? Double the recipe for Blueberry Topping, and save half for spooning over fat-free ice cream, frozen yogurt or fat-free vanilla pudding.

2 **Staying Active** • Did you know that making your bed can provide a workout? Get more out of this daily chore by increasing the number of times you walk around the bed. Also, try to walk quickly and stretch farther across the bed.

1 Serving

Calories 120 (Calories from Fat 20)

Fat 2g (Saturated 1g)

Cholesterol 0mg

Sodium 200mg

Carbohydrate 25g (Dietary Fiber 1g)

Protein 2g

% Daily Value

Vitamin A 2%

Vitamin C 4%

Calcium 4%

Iron 2%

Diet Exchanges

1/2 Starch

1 Fruit

1/2 Fat

Banana Split
Ice-Cream Dessert

PREP: 15 MIN; FREEZE: 2 HR 20 MIN; STAND: 15 MIN | 15 SERVINGS

1 1/2 cups crushed reduced-
   fat graham crackers
   (24 squares)

2 tablespoons margarine or
   butter, melted

2 ripe medium bananas,
   mashed (1 cup)

1/2 teaspoon lemon juice

1 quart (4 cups) vanilla fat-
   free ice cream, softened

1/4 cup hot fudge fat-free
   topping, warmed

1 1/2 cups frozen (thawed)
   fat-free whipped topping

1 package (10 ounces) frozen
   strawberries in light syrup,
   thawed

Fresh strawberries, if desired

Banana slices, if desired

Spray bottom only of rectangular pan, 13 × 9 × 2 inches,
with cooking spray. Mix crushed crackers and margarine until crumbly. Press in bottom of pan. Cover and
freeze 20 minutes.

Mix bananas and lemon juice in medium bowl. Stir in
ice cream. Beat with electric mixer on low speed about
30 seconds or until well blended. Spoon evenly over
frozen crust. Drizzle hot fudge topping over ice-cream
mixture; swirl with tip of knife. Cover and freeze about
1 hour or until firm.

Mix whipped topping and strawberries until well blended.
Spread over ice-cream mixture. Cover and freeze at
least 1 hour until firm.

Let stand at room temperature 15 minutes before serving.
For servings, cut into 5 rows by 3 rows. Garnish with
fresh strawberries, banana slices and additional hot
fudge topping if desired.

1 Serving

Calories 145
(Calories from Fat 25)

Fat 3g (Saturated 1g)

Cholesterol 0mg

Sodium 105mg

Carbohydrate 30g
(Dietary Fiber 2g)

Protein 2g

% Daily Value

Vitamin A 6%

Vitamin C 16%

Calcium 6%

Iron 2%

Diet Exchanges

2 Fruit

Eating Smart • Bananas are versatile "tools" in a
low-fat kitchen. You can use mashed bananas to partially
replace some of the butter or oil in baked goods. Bananas
also make great snacks. If you're craving something cool
and frosty, a frozen peeled banana is a tasty treat.

Staying Active • Running for 20 minutes 3 times
a week can help you lose as much as 9 pounds in one
year. If you increase your run to 5 times a week, you can
lose up to 15 pounds.

Frosty
Margarita Pie

PREP: 20 MIN; FREEZE: 6 HR | 8 SERVINGS

1 cup graham cracker crumbs (12 squares)

3 tablespoons powdered sugar

1/4 cup frozen (thawed) margarita mix concentrate

1 pint (2 cups) lime sherbet, softened

1/3 cup frozen (thawed) margarita mix concentrate

3 tablespoons tequila, if desired

1 pint (2 cups) vanilla fat-free ice cream, softened

Mix cracker crumbs and powdered sugar. Stir in 1/4 cup margarita mix until crumbly. Press mixture firmly against bottom and side of pie plate, 9 × 1 1/4 inches.

Mix sherbet, 1/3 cup margarita mix and the tequila in large bowl. Gently swirl in ice cream. Spoon mixture into crust; spread evenly. Cover and freeze 4 to 6 hours or until firm.

1 Serving	
Calories 200 (Calories from Fat 20)	
Fat 2g (Saturated 1g)	
Cholesterol 5mg	
Sodium 105mg	
Carbohydrate 45g (Dietary Fiber 2g)	
Protein 2g	

% Daily Value

Vitamin A 4%

Vitamin C 8%

Calcium 8%

Iron 2%

Diet Exchanges

1 Starch

1 **Eating Smart** • Garnish this spectacular no-bake dessert with sugared lime slices. Brush corn syrup onto lime slices and sprinkle with sugar.

2 **Staying Active** • Surround yourself with a fitness-friendly environment. Keep your walking shoes by your bed, another pair in your car and a pair of dumbbells or resistance bands at work so you can exercise in spare moments.

Frosty Margarita Pie

Strawberry-Rhubarb
Frozen-Yogurt Parfaits

PREP: 10 MIN; COOK: 10 MIN | 8 SERVINGS

4 cups cut-up rhubarb

1/3 cup water

1/2 package (4-serving size)
strawberry-flavored
gelatin (1/4 cup)

1 cup chopped fresh or frozen
(thawed) strawberries

1/2 gallon vanilla fat-free
frozen yogurt

Heat rhubarb and water to boiling in 2-quart saucepan. Boil 5 minutes, stirring occasionally; remove from heat. Stir in gelatin until dissolved. Boil 5 minutes longer, stirring constantly; remove from heat.

Stir in strawberries. Serve sauce warm or cold, layering frozen yogurt and sauce in parfait glasses.

1 Serving

Calories 235
(Calories from Fat 0)

Fat 0g (Saturated 0g)

Cholesterol 5mg

Sodium 115mg

Carbohydrate 54g
(Dietary Fiber 1g)

Protein 6g

% Daily Value

Vitamin A 8%

Vitamin C 34%

Calcium 30%

Iron 2%

Diet Exchanges

1 Starch

2 Fruit

1/2 Skim Milk

1 **Eating Smart** • Rhubarb, considered a fruit because it's usually found in sweets such as pies, muffins and quick breads, is really a vegetable. Although extremely low in calories (about 25 per cup), rhubarb does not need to be cooked with a sweetener. Rhubarb also contains some vitamin A, which is vital for healthy eyes, hair and skin.

2 **Staying Active** • Make time to exercise on your busiest day. Accomplishing a workout when you didn't think it was possible will boost your confidence and subconsciously affirm that exercise is a priority. Workouts will also seem much more doable on your less-busy days!

Triple-Chocolate
Malts

PREP: 5 MIN | 2 SERVINGS

3/4 cup fat-free (skim)
chocolate milk

1/4 cup reduced-calorie
chocolate-flavored syrup

1 tablespoon natural-flavor
malted milk powder

1 1/2 cups chocolate fat-free
frozen yogurt

Place milk, chocolate syrup and malted milk powder in blender. Cover and blend on high speed 2 seconds.

Add frozen yogurt. Cover and blend on low speed about 5 seconds or until smooth. Pour into glasses.

1 Serving

Calories 245
(Calories from Fat 10)

Fat 1g (Saturated 0g)

Cholesterol 5mg

Sodium 145mg

Carbohydrate 52g
(Dietary Fiber 0g)

Protein 7g

% Daily Value

Vitamin A 18%

Vitamin C 14%

Calcium 26%

Iron 4%

Diet Exchanges

2 1/2 Fruit

1 Skim Milk

1 **Eating Smart** • Everyone knows that premium ice creams are packed with calories. But what about low-fat ice creams and frozen yogurts? Check the nutrition label because some frozen treats contain as many as 400 calories in a couple of scoops!

2 **Staying Active** • By working out at the same time every day, you may be more likely to stick with your fitness program. On the other hand, some people enjoy the variety that comes with working out at different times. You'll burn calories regardless of when you exercise. Just do what you most enjoy and when you most enjoy doing it!

Orange
Cappuccino Brownies

PREP: 20 MIN; BAKE: 20 MIN; COOL: 15 MIN | 16 BROWNIES

1 cup all-purpose flour

1 cup sugar

1/2 cup baking cocoa

2 teaspoons instant espresso coffee (dry)

1/4 teaspoon baking powder

1/2 cup fat-free cholesterol-free egg product or 2 eggs

1/4 cup margarine or butter, melted

2 tablespoons water

Orange–Cream Cheese Glaze (right)

Grated orange peel, if desired

Heat oven to 350°. Spray square pan, 9 × 9 × 2 inches, with cooking spray. Mix flour, sugar, cocoa, espresso and baking powder in medium bowl. Stir in egg product, margarine and water. Spread in pan.

Bake 18 to 20 minutes or until center is set and brownies begin to pull away from sides of pan. Cool 15 minutes. Drizzle Orange–Cream Cheese Glaze over brownies. Sprinkle with orange peel. For brownies, cut into 4 rows by 4 rows.

Orange–Cream Cheese Glaze

1/3 cup powdered sugar

1/2 teaspoon frozen (thawed) orange juice concentrate or orange juice

1/2 teaspoon grated orange peel

1 ounce fat-free cream cheese, softened

Mix all ingredients until smooth.

1 Eating Smart • Mocha fans, beware: A large mocha topped with whipped cream can contain as many as 400 calories and 25 fat grams! You can easily reduce fat and calories without sacrificing taste by switching to plain coffee and adding a packet of sugar-free hot cocoa mix. Or downsize to a regular latte made with fat-free milk.

2 Staying Active • True or false? Lifting weights turns fat into muscle. False. Fat and muscle tissue are distinctly different. Weight training increases your muscle tissue. Although more muscle means a faster metabolism, the best way to burn fat is through aerobic exercise.

1 Brownie

Calories 125
(Calories from Fat 25)

Fat 3g (Saturated 1g)

Cholesterol 0mg

Sodium 65mg

Carbohydrate 23g
(Dietary Fiber 1g)

Protein 2g

% Daily Value

Vitamin A 4%

Vitamin C 0%

Calcium 2%

Iron 4%

Diet Exchanges

1 Starch

1/2 Fruit

1/2 Fat

Orange Cappuccino Brownies

Ginger Gems
Cookies

PREP: 15 MIN; CHILL: 2 HR; BAKE: 10 MIN PER SHEET; COOL: 30 MIN | ABOUT 5 DOZEN COOKIES

1 cup sugar

1/4 cup margarine or butter, softened

1/4 cup fat-free cholesterol-free egg product or 1 egg

1/4 cup molasses

1 3/4 cups all-purpose flour

1 teaspoon baking soda

1/2 teaspoon ground cinnamon

1/2 teaspoon ground ginger

1/4 teaspoon ground cloves

1/4 teaspoon salt

2 tablespoons orange marmalade

2 tablespoons finely chopped crystallized ginger

Beat 3/4 cup of the sugar, the margarine, egg product and molasses in medium bowl with electric mixer on medium speed, or mix with spoon. Stir in flour, baking soda, cinnamon, ground ginger, cloves and salt. Cover and refrigerate at least 2 hours until firm.

Heat oven to 350°. Lightly spray cookie sheet with cooking spray. Shape dough into 3/4-inch balls; roll in remaining 1/4 cup sugar. Place about 2 inches apart on cookie sheet. Make indentation in center of each ball, using finger. Fill each indentation with about 1/4 teaspoon of the marmalade. Sprinkle with about 1/4 teaspoon of the crystallized ginger.

Bake 8 to 10 minutes or until set. Immediately remove from cookie sheet to wire rack. Cool completely, about 30 minutes.

1 Cookie

Calories 40
(Calories from Fat 10)

Fat 1g (Saturated 0g)

Cholesterol 0mg

Sodium 45mg

Carbohydrate 8g
(Dietary Fiber 0g)

Protein 0g

% Daily Value

Vitamin A 0%

Vitamin C 0%

Calcium 0%

Iron 2%

Diet Exchanges

1/2 Fruit

1 **Eating Smart** • If you haven't switched from 2 percent milk to the fat-free variety because you think it tastes watery, add a tablespoon of nonfat dried milk to each cup of fat-free milk. The milk will taste thicker and richer, and you'll get an extra protein and calcium boost.

2 **Staying Active** • Don't make exercise out to be the bad guy. Our bodies are designed to move and be active. By becoming a couch potato, we defy nature. Think of exercise as play, and celebrate your body as it continues to get slimmer, stronger and healthier.

Super-Simple Sweets

Sometimes a meal just doesn't feel complete without a taste of something sweet at the end. Rather than cheat your tastebuds out of dessert, satisfy your sweet tooth with these easy-to-assemble ideas weighing in at **150 calories or less:**

- **Strawberry Shortcake:** Top a slice of angel food with fresh strawberries and a dollop of fat-free whipped topping.
- **Cool Lemon-Ginger Treat:** Top 1/2 cup lemon sorbet or sherbet with crushed ginger-snap cookies and grated lemon peel.
- **Hot Fudge Sundae:** Drizzle 1 tablespoon fat-free fudge topping over 1/2 cup fat-free vanilla frozen yogurt. Top with a maraschino cherry.
- **Berry Crunch Parfait:** Layer 1/2 cup fat-free yogurt or frozen yogurt and 1/4 cup fresh berries in a parfait glass. Top with 1 tablespoon granola.
- **Maple-Frosted Pound Cake:** Stir 1 teaspoon maple-flavored syrup into 1 tablespoon fat-free cream cheese, softened. Spread over a slice of fat-free pound cake and sprinkle with ground cinnamon.
- **Frosty Mocha Cappuccino:** Place 1/4 cup cold, very strong coffee, 1/2 cup vanilla fat-free ice cream and 2 teaspoons chocolate-flavored syrup in blender or food processor. Cover and blend on high speed until smooth.

Nature's Tempting Treats

Fresh fruits are perfect for dessert. Their natural sweetness is a fat-free way to end a meal.

	Calories
Apple (medium)	80
Cherries (1/2 cup)	50
Grapes (1/2 cup)	55
Honeydew melon (1/2 cup cubed pieces)	30
Nectarine (medium)	35
Peach (medium)	40
Pear (medium)	100
Pineapple (1/2 cup)	40
Plum (medium)	35
Strawberries (1/2 cup)	25
Watermelon (10-inch × 1-inch slice)	115

Cherry–Chocolate Chip
Cookies

PREP: 20 MIN; BAKE: 12 MIN PER SHEET; COOL: 30 MIN | ABOUT 2 DOZEN COOKIES

1/4 cup margarine or butter, melted

1 cup packed brown sugar

1 tablespoon milk

1/2 teaspoon vanilla

1/4 cup fat-free cholesterol-free egg product or 1 egg

1 cup all-purpose flour

1 cup old-fashioned oats

1/2 teaspoon baking soda

1/4 teaspoon salt

1/4 cup dried cherries, chopped

1/4 cup miniature semisweet chocolate chips

Heat oven to 350°. Grease cookie sheet. Mix margarine and brown sugar in large bowl. Stir in milk, vanilla and egg product. Stir in flour, oats, baking soda and salt. Stir in cherries and chocolate chips.

Drop dough by tablespoonfuls 2 inches apart onto cookie sheet. Bake 10 to 12 minutes or until golden brown (cookies will be slightly soft). Cool 3 minutes before removing from cookie sheet to wire rack. Cool completely, about 30 minutes.

1 Cookie

Calories 100
(Calories from Fat 25)

Fat 3g (Saturated 1g)

Cholesterol 0mg

Sodium 85mg

Carbohydrate 18g
(Dietary Fiber 1g)

Protein 1g

% Daily Value

Vitamin A 2%

Vitamin C 0%

Calcium 0%

Iron 4%

Diet Exchanges

1 Starch

1/2 Fat

1 **Eating Smart** • A healthy attitude about food and weight loss dispels the notion of "good" and "bad" foods. All foods—even chocolate chip cookies—are acceptable to some extent. The key lies in balancing portion size, calorie intake and variety.

2 **Staying Active** • Do you have exercise equipment collecting dust in your garage or basement? Move the equipment to a place you're more likely to use it, such as the TV room. If you still can't get yourself to use the machine, sell it and buy yourself the equipment (or gym membership or running shoes) that you really want.

A Week's Worth of Menus

Meal and menu planning doesn't have to be difficult or time consuming, even if you are trying to lose weight. On the next pages you'll find plenty of ideas for healthy, quick meals that meet a reduced-calorie and reduced-fat eating plan. These menus vary from 1,300 to 1,600 calories and 17 to 40 grams of total fat per day. You don't have to follow these menus in any particular order. Feel free to mix and match meals from different days to add variety to your eating plan. Just keep track of your total calories and grams of fat to make sure you're not eating too much or too little.*

Menu 1

BREAKFAST

1/2 cup bran cereal

1/2 grapefruit

1 cup fat-free (skim) milk

Calories 195 • Total Fat 3g
• Saturated Fat 0g • Fiber 4g

LUNCH

1 serving Veggie Focaccia
Sandwiches (page 85)

1 cup grapes

1 cup fat-free (skim) milk

Calories 440 • Total Fat 10g
• Saturated Fat 3g • Fiber 14g

DINNER

1 serving Marinated Tuna Steaks
with Cucumber Sauce (page 118)

1 cup cooked frozen snap peas,
cauliflower and carrots

1/2 cup cooked brown rice

1/2 cup frozen fruit-flavored sorbet or
sherbet with 1/4 cup blackberries

Calories 460 • Total Fat 7g
• Saturated Fat 2g • Fiber 8g

SNACK

1/3 cup raisins

1 ounce peanuts

Calories 325 • Total Fat 14g
• Saturated Fat 2g • Fiber 5g

TOTAL

Calories 1,420 • Total Fat 34g
• Saturated Fat 7g • Fiber 31g

*The average recommended caloric intake for healthy adults is 2,000 calories and 65 grams of fat per day. Your needs may be higher or lower depending on your height, weight, gender and activity level. If you are trying to lose weight, you will want to decrease your calorie and fat intake and increase your activity level.

Menu 2

BREAKFAST

2 shredded whole wheat
cereal biscuits

1 banana

1 cup fat-free (skim) milk

Calories 360 • Total Fat 2g
• Saturated Fat 1g • Fiber 6g

LUNCH

1 serving Flank Steak Sandwiches
(page 79)

1 medium pear

1 cup fat-free (skim) milk

Calories 500 • Total Fat 8g
• Saturated Fat 3g • Fiber 5g

DINNER

1 serving Seafood and Vegetables
with Rice (page 124)

1/2 cup oyster crackers

1 cup cooked frozen broccoli,
cauliflower and carrots

Romaine salad with 1 Tbsp
reduced-fat Caesar dressing

1 Mini Pumpkin Cheesecake
(page 221)

Calories 490 • Total Fat 10g
• Saturated Fat 2g • Fiber 6g

SNACK

3 cups air-popped popcorn

1 medium orange

Calories 155 • Total Fat 2g
• Saturated Fat 0g • Fiber 8g

TOTAL

Calories 1505 • Total Fat 22g
• Saturated Fat 6g • Fiber 25g

Menu 3

BREAKFAST

1 serving Cinnamon-Raisin French
Toast (page 48) sprinkled with
2 Tbsp wheat germ

1 Tbsp maple-flavored syrup

1 medium orange

1 cup fat-free (skim) milk

Calories 245 • Total Fat 4g
• Saturated Fat 1g • Fiber 6g

LUNCH

1 serving Zesty Autumn Pork Stew
(page 74)

1 corn muffin with 1 tsp margarine

1 cup fat-free (skim) milk

Calories 495 • Total Fat 14g
• Saturated Fat 5g • Fiber 4g

DINNER

1 serving Pizza Casserole
(page 140)

1 small dinner roll with 1 tsp
margarine

1 cup cooked peas

Mixed-greens salad with 1 Tbsp
reduced-fat dressing

1 tomato, sliced

Calories 595 • Total Fat 18g
• Saturated Fat 5g • Fiber 14g

SNACK

1 serving Pear and Cherry Crisp
(page 222)

Calories 250 • Total Fat 4g
• Saturated Fat 2g • Fiber 4g

TOTAL

Calories 1,585 • Total Fat 40g
• Saturated Fat 13g • Fiber 28g

Menu 4

BREAKFAST

1 scrambled egg

2 slices whole wheat bread,
toasted, with 1 Tbsp jam or jelly

1/2 grapefruit

1 cup fat-free (skim) milk

Calories 400 • Total Fat 9g
• Saturated Fat 3g • Fiber 6g

LUNCH

1 serving Turkey–Wild Rice Salad
(page 88)

1 small whole wheat dinner roll
with 1 tsp margarine

1 cup fat-free (skim) milk

Calories 530 • Total Fat 10g
• Saturated Fat 2g • Fiber 9g

DINNER

1 serving Vegetarian Paella
(page 164)

1 cup steamed green beans

1/2 cup melon cubes

1 serving Mocha Angel cake
(page 217)

Calories 510 • Total Fat 3g
• Saturated Fat 0g • Fiber 15g

SNACK

1/2 English muffin with 1 tsp
peanut butter

1/2 cup apple juice

Calories 160 • Total Fat 3g
• Saturated Fat 1g • Fiber 1g

TOTAL

Calories 1,600 • Total Fat 25g
• Saturated Fat 6g • Fiber 31g

Menu 5

BREAKFAST

1 bagel with 1 Tbsp fat-free
cream cheese

1 cup orange juice

Calories 280 • Total Fat 2g
• Saturated Fat 0g • Fiber 2g

LUNCH

1 serving Cuban Spicy Bean Salad
with Oranges and Cilantro
(page 93)

1 serving Lime Tortilla Chips
(page 37)

1 cup fat-free (skim) milk

Calories 515 • Total Fat 2g
• Saturated Fat 0g • Fiber 19g

DINNER

1 serving Skillet Ham and
Vegetables au Gratin (page 151)

1 slice French bread with
1 tsp margarine

Mixed-greens salad with 1 Tbsp
reduced-fat dressing

1 cup sliced cucumbers and
tomatoes

1/2 cup mixed fresh fruit

Calories 315 • Total Fat 10g
• Saturated Fat 4g • Fiber 5g

SNACK

1 Cherry–Chocolate Chip Cookie
(page 234)

1 cup fat-free (skim) milk

Calories 190 • Total Fat 3g
• Saturated Fat 1g • Fiber 1g

TOTAL

Calories 1,300 • Total Fat 17g
• Saturated Fat 5g • Fiber 27g

Menu 6

BREAKFAST

1 Old-Fashioned Blueberry Muffin
(page 60)

1 cup raspberries

1 cup fat-free (skim) milk

Calories 245 • Total Fat 5g
• Saturated Fat 1g • Fiber 9g

LUNCH

1 serving Barley-Burger Stew
(page 73)

1 slice whole wheat bread with
1 tsp margarine

Celery sticks

1 cup fat-free (skim) milk

Calories 415 • Total Fat 7g
• Saturated Fat 2g • Fiber 8g

DINNER

1 serving Mediterranean Chicken
with Rosemary Orzo (page 107)

1 cup steamed broccoli

1 whole-grain dinner roll with 1 tsp
margarine

1/2 cup reduced-fat frozen yogurt with
1 Tbsp chocolate fudge fat-free topping

Calories 610 • Total Fat 11g
• Saturated Fat 3g • Fiber 11g

SNACK

1 Savory Currant Wedge
(page 192) with 1 tsp margarine

1/2 cup cranberry juice

Calories 195 • Total Fat 4g
• Saturated Fat 2g • Fiber 1g

TOTAL

Calories 1,515 • Total Fat 26g
• Saturated Fat 7g • Fiber 29g

Menu 7

BREAKFAST

1 serving Triple-Fruit Yogurt
Smoothie (page 66)

1 scrambled egg

1 cup fresh blueberries

Calories 335 • Total Fat 10g
• Saturated Fat 3g • Fiber 7g

LUNCH

1 serving Honey Ham Bagels
(page 80)

10 reduced-fat potato chips

1 cup grapes

Carrot and celery sticks

1 cup fat-free (skim) milk

Calories 450 • Total Fat 9g
• Saturated Fat 3g • Fiber 5g

DINNER

1 serving Herbed Baked Chicken
Breasts (page 98)

1 serving Orzo Parmesan (page 207)

Mixed-greens salad with 1 Tbsp
reduced-fat dressing

1 medium tomato, sliced

1 cup steamed broccoli

1/2 cup fresh cherries

Calories 480 • Total Fat 10g
• Saturated Fat 3g • Fiber 9g

SNACK

1 serving Chai Tea (page 63)

3 cups air-popped popcorn

Calories 190 • Total Fat 3g
• Saturated Fat 2g • Fiber 4g

TOTAL

Calories 1,455 • Total Fat 32g
• Saturated Fat 11g • Fiber 25g

Extra Charts, Tables and Helpful Hints

Gerontology Research Center Table

Use the following table, which has been created for both women and men, as a guide to healthy weight ranges, but pay attention to how you feel at specific weights. Find a weight range where you feel energetic and self-confident, and use that as your guide as to what you should weigh. Check with your doctor if you have questions about your desired body weight.

Height	Age 20–29	Age 30–39	Age 40–49	Age 50–59	Age 60–69
4'10"	84–111	92–119	99–127	107–135	115–142
4'11"	87–115	95–123	103–131	111–139	119–147
5'0"	90–119	98–127	106–135	114–143	123–152
5'1"	93–123	101–131	110–140	118–148	127–157
5'2"	96–127	105–136	113–144	122–153	131–163
5'3"	99–131	108–140	117–149	126–158	135–168
5'4"	102–135	112–145	121–154	130–163	140–173
5'5"	106–140	115–149	125–159	134–168	144–179
5'6"	109–144	119–154	129–164	138–174	148–184
5'7"	112–148	122–159	133–169	143–179	153–190
5'8"	116–153	126–163	137–174	147–184	158–196
5'9"	119–157	130–168	141–179	151–190	162–201
5'10"	122–162	134–173	145–184	156–195	167–207
5'11"	126–167	137–178	149–190	160–201	172–213
6'0"	129–171	141–183	153–195	165–207	177–219
6'1"	133–176	145–188	157–200	169–213	182–235
6'2"	137–181	149–194	162–206	174–219	187–232
6'3"	141–186	153–199	166–212	179–225	192–238
6'4"	144–191	157–205	171–218	184–231	197–244

All heights without shoes, weights in pounds without clothes.

Body Mass Index (BMI) Table

BMIs ranging from 19 to 25 are considered healthy. A BMI between 27 and 30 is considered moderately overweight; anything over 30 is considered seriously overweight. BMIs of 27 or more are associated with increased risk of developing weight-related problems such as diabetes or high cholesterol. Because the BMI doesn't account for the increased weight of those who carry a lot of muscle weight, it's possible to be physically fit and have a relatively high BMI without added health risk. Check with your doctor if you're unsure.

Weight (pounds)	Height (feet and inches)										
	5'0"	5'2"	5'4"	5'6"	5'8"	5'10"	6'0"	6'2"	6'4"	6'6"	6'8"
100	20	18	17	16	15	14	14	13	12	12	11
105	21	19	18	17	16	15	14	14	13	12	12
110	22	20	19	18	17	16	15	14	13	13	12
115	23	21	20	19	18	17	16	15	14	13	13
120	23	22	21	19	18	17	16	15	14	14	13
125	24	23	22	20	19	18	17	16	15	14	14
130	25	24	22	21	20	19	18	17	16	15	14
135	26	25	23	22	21	19	18	17	16	16	15
140	27	26	24	23	21	20	19	18	17	16	15
145	28	27	25	23	22	21	20	19	18	17	16
150	29	27	26	24	23	22	20	19	18	17	17
155	30	28	27	25	24	22	21	20	19	18	17
160	31	29	28	26	24	23	22	21	20	19	18
165	32	30	28	27	25	24	22	21	20	19	18
170	33	31	29	27	26	24	23	22	21	20	19
175	34	32	30	28	27	25	24	23	21	20	19
180	35	33	31	29	27	26	24	23	22	21	20
185	36	34	32	30	28	27	25	24	23	21	20
190	37	35	33	31	29	27	26	24	23	22	21
195	38	36	34	32	30	28	27	25	24	23	21
200	39	37	34	32	30	29	27	26	24	23	22
205	40	38	35	33	31	29	28	26	25	24	23
210	41	38	36	34	32	30	29	27	26	24	23
215	42	39	37	35	33	31	29	28	26	25	24
220	43	40	38	36	34	32	30	28	27	25	24
225	44	41	39	36	34	32	30	29	27	26	25
230	45	42	40	37	35	33	31	30	28	27	25
235	46	43	40	38	36	34	32	30	29	27	26
240	47	44	41	39	37	35	33	31	29	28	26
245	48	45	42	40	37	35	33	32	30	28	27
250	49	46	43	40	38	36	34	32	30	29	28
255	50	47	44	41	39	37	35	33	31	30	28
260	51	48	45	42	40	37	35	33	32	30	29
265	52	49	46	43	40	38	36	34	32	31	29
270	53	49	46	44	41	39	37	35	33	31	30
275	54	50	47	44	42	40	37	35	34	32	30
280	55	51	48	45	43	40	38	36	34	32	31
285	56	52	49	46	43	41	39	37	35	33	31
290	57	53	50	47	44	42	39	37	35	34	32
295	58	54	51	48	45	42	40	38	36	34	32
300	59	55	52	49	46	43	41	39	37	35	33

You can also determine your BMI using the following equation:

Weight (in pounds) x 704 ÷ Height (in inches)^2 = BMI

Food Guide Pyramid

A Guide to Daily Food Choices

The Food Guide Pyramid is your road map for eating well. It emphasizes variety in your food choices from the five major food groups and shows you the proportions in which to eat them. For example, the base of the pyramid—bread, cereal, rice and pasta—is the foundation of a well-balanced diet. Featuring fats, oils and sweets at the top, the pyramid advises us to use these foods "sparingly." Sandwiched in between are four remaining food groups: fruits, vegetables, dairy products and protein sources.

Experts suggest that at least three different food groups be represented at each meal. Do your best to estimate numbers of servings in foods that contain several different groups. Healthy snacks can also balance your intake.

The food pyramid is easier to use when you have a handle on serving sizes. It's also important to read labels on packaged foods. A bakery bagel or muffin, for instance, may be as many as two or three servings.

What Counts As a Serving?

Breads, Cereal, Rice and Pasta: 1 slice (1 ounce) bread; 1 tortilla; 1/2 cup cooked rice, pasta, or cereal; 1 ounce ready-to-eat cereal (usually between 2/3 and 3/4 cup); 1/2 hamburger bun, bagel or English muffin; 4 small crackers.

Vegetables: 1 cup raw leafy greens; 1/2 cup fresh, cooked or canned chopped vegetables; 3/4 cup vegetable juice.

Fruits: 1 medium piece of fruit; 1/2 cup fresh, cooked or canned cut-up fruit; 3/4 cup fruit juice.

Milk, Yogurt and Cheese: 1 cup milk or yogurt; 2 cups cottage cheese; 1 1/2 ounces natural cheese; 2 ounces processed American cheese; 1 cup frozen yogurt.

Meat, Poultry, Fish, Dry Beans, Eggs and Nuts: 2 1/2 to 3 ounces lean beef, pork, lamb, veal, poultry or fish; 1/2 cup cooked beans; 1 egg or 2 tablespoons peanut butter count as 1 ounce lean meat.

Food Guide Pyramid

Fats, Oils and Sweets
USE SPARINGLY

Milk, Yogurt and Cheese Group
2–3 SERVINGS

Vegetable Group
3–5 SERVINGS

KEY
● Fat (naturally occurring and added)
▼ Sugars (added)
These symbols show fats, oils and added sugar in foods.

Meat, Poultry, Fish, Dry Beans, Eggs and Nuts Group
2–3 SERVINGS

Fruit Group
2–4 SERVINGS

Bread, Cereal, Rice and Pasta Group
6–11 SERVINGS

Source: U.S. Department of Agriculture, U.S. Department of Health and Human Services

Health and Nutrition Claims

What Can Labels Say?

As foods continue to move closer to the realm of medicine, it's easy to wonder if what we eat may prevent disease. Will certain foods prevent osteoporosis? Reduce cholesterol levels? Prevent cancer? Packages that carry health claims must meet certain standards to earn their claims. Current health claims allowed on food packages include:

What Do Nutrition Claims Mean?

Do you wonder what it really means when a product label says light, sodium free, or low fat? The following definitions will help you understand the meaning of these claims when you read them on packages and in advertising. Claims can only be used if a food meets strict government definitions. Here are some of the meanings:

Label Health Claims

A diet that is:	May help to reduce the risk of:
High in calcium	Osteoporosis
High in fiber-containing grain products, fruits and vegetables	Cancer
High in fruits or vegetables (high in dietary fiber or vitamins A or C)	Cancer
High in fiber from fruits, vegetable and grain products	Heart disease
Low in fat	Cancer
Low in saturated fat and cholesterol	Heart disease
Low in sodium	High blood pressure
High in soy protein (25 grams/day), low in saturated fat and cholesterol	Heart disease

Label Nutrition Claims

Label Claim	Definition (per serving)
Low Calorie	40 calories or fewer
Light (or Lite)	1/3 fewer calories or 50 percent less fat than the original product; if more than half the calories are from fat, fat content must be reduced by 50 percent or more
Light in Sodium	50 percent less sodium
Fat Free	Less than 0.5 gram of fat
Low Fat	3 grams or fewer of fat
Cholesterol Free	Fewer than 2 milligrams of cholesterol and 2 grams or fewer of saturated fat
Low Cholesterol	20 milligrams or fewer of cholesterol and 2 grams or fewer of saturated fat
Sodium Free	Fewer than 5 milligrams of sodium
Very Low Sodium	35 milligrams or fewer of sodium
Low Sodium	140 milligrams or fewer of sodium
High Fiber	5 grams or more of fiber

Low-Fat Shopping and Stocking

While traveling the aisles of your favorite grocery store or supermarket, it's easy to feel overwhelmed by the hundreds of food choices that face you. How can you be sure to shop smart and healthy? Use the following helpful tips and strategies the next time you are stocking your fridge or pantry:

Shopping Smart

- Grocery shop after you've eaten, instead of when hungry; you'll be less tempted and will make better food choices.

- Prepare a shopping list and stick to it as closely as possible.

- Don't clip coupons for high-fat or novelty foods. They may cost you more in the long run!

- Buy just the low-fat foods you love. Foods you won't enjoy are a waste of money and calories.

- Learn how to read food labels (see Understanding Nutrition Labels on page 241). You can use this information to comparison shop.

- While waiting in line, glance at the food in your cart. Have you made choices that affirm your desire to lose weight?

Aisle by Aisle

Meats, Poultry and Fish

- "Prime" grades of meat are heavily marbled with fat, making them a higher-fat choice.

- Lean cuts of beef include round steak, sirloin tip, tenderloin and extra-lean or diet-lean ground beef.

- Lean cuts of pork include tenderloin, loin chops, center-cut ham and Canadian bacon.

- Other lean choices? Wild game, such as buffalo, venison, rabbit, squirrel and pheasant.

- Limit fowl such as duck and goose, which are extremely high in fat.

- Beware: Turkey and chicken hot dogs are not necessarily low in fat. Read labels.

- Half of chicken's calories are in the skin! Buy skinless chicken parts, or remove skin and visible fat before eating.

- Most fish and shellfish contain less fat than meat and poultry.

Dairy Case

- Plain fat-free yogurt is high in protein and calcium. Use it to replace mayo in salads and dips.

- Replace full-fat cream, sour cream, cottage cheese and cream cheese with their low-fat counterparts.

- A bit of sharp cheese adds more flavor and less fat than a larger amount of milder cheese. Other high-flavor cheeses include blue and feta.

- Buttermilk, made from cultured skim milk, is actually quite low in fat.

Produce Section

- Learn to love fresh fruits and vegetables. Except for avocados and coconut, most produce is virtually fat free.

- Add chopped veggies to stir-fries, casseroles, soups, salads and pasta dishes. Chop fresh veggies at home, or buy them already cut to save time.

- Curb between-meal hunger by snacking on fresh fruits and veggies.

- Craving ice cream? Frozen bananas make a great-tasting, low-fat alternative.

- Exotic fruits and vegetables are finding their way into grocery stores. Expand your horizons by trying one new fresh fruit or vegetable each week.

Freezer Case

- Marinate frozen vegetable mixes in reduced-calorie Italian dressing and cook as directed.

- Use frozen "meal-in-a-bag" products to cut down on kitchen time. Just remember to combine the frozen veggies with lean cuts of meat, poultry or seafood.

- Frozen chopped spinach is a fat-free, time-saving addition to lasagna, pizza, quesadillas, egg dishes and dips.

- Add frozen berries to muffin and pancake batter. Or puree berries with a bit of liquid for a dessert sauce. You can also blend them with yogurt and juice for a smoothie or enjoy as an out-of-hand snack.

- Frozen fruit and juice bars can satisfy a craving for sweets without the fat found in ice cream.
- Read the labels on fat-free ice creams and frozen yogurts. Some have just as many—or more—calories as the full-fat versions. Buying a little bit of the real thing may satisfy your craving more than buying fat-free versions that don't satisfy.

Stocking the Shelves

- **Canned beans:** Fiber-rich and fat-free, beans are great pantry staples. Use in soups, salads, stir-fries and pasta dishes. Another option: puree beans for rich-tasting dips or spreads. Rinse canned beans before using them if you are watching your sodium intake.
- **Canned chopped chilies:** These chilies make quick work of enhancing flavor in many dishes. Use canned chipotle chilies in adobo sauce to lend a rich, smoky flavor to food.
- **Fat-free chicken broth:** Refrigerate canned or shelf-stable boxes of broth after opening. (Transfer leftover canned broth to a nonmetal container.) Dry bouillon cubes or granules will keep in tightly covered containers at room temperature. Check labels; not all brands are fat-free.
- **Chutney:** An intensely sweet condiment that often comes in exotic flavors such as mango and tamarind.
- **Low-calorie, low-fat dressings:** The Italian varieties are great for marinating raw veggies and lean pork or chicken. Other low-cal dressings add flavor (without fat) to potato, pasta and vegetable salads.
- **Fat-free cholesterol-free egg products:** Made mostly from egg whites, these are good substitutes for whole eggs in baked products, omelets and scrambled eggs.
- **Canned evaporated fat-free milk:** A good substitute for half-and-half and cream in sauces and soups. Use instead of full-fat evaporated milk in pies. Refrigerate leftover evaporated milk.
- **Garlic:** An aromatic addition to nearly any savory food. Buy it by the bulb or already chopped in a jar. One clove equals about 1/2 teaspoon of chopped or minced garlic.
- **Fresh gingerroot:** Bring a wonderfully complex flavor to stir-fries and marinades by adding grated or chopped fresh gingerroot. Refrigerate up to a week, or wrap tightly and freeze if you're storing it for longer.
- **Dried herbs and spices:** Add a little or a lot, depending on the flavor intensity you're looking for. Herbs and spices are a great way to add plenty of fat-free flavor to food.
- **Lemons and limes:** Freshly squeezed lemon or lime juice adds flavor without fat to plain or carbonated water. The juice of these citrus fruits also brightens up salad dressings, fish and cooked veggies. Grate the peel (or zest) to add a flavor boost to baked goods.
- **Pasta, noodles and rice:** Fat-free; cooks up in minutes; comes in many sizes, shapes, and colors; goes well with many foods; rich in complex carbohydrates, fiber and some vitamins and minerals. What's not to love?!
- **Pasta sauce:** Use flavorful, low-fat bottled sauces to make spaghetti, lasagna and manicotti. Or toss with veggies and serve over hot cooked noodles. Pasta sauce is also a good stand-in for pizza sauce. Read labels: some brands of pasta sauce are higher in fat than others.
- **Rice vinegar:** Made from fermented rice and sugar, this vinegar adds great flavor to salad dressings and stir-fries. Seasoned rice vinegar is flavored with ginger and garlic; plain rice vinegar is not. Look for both in the Asian-foods section of your grocery store.
- **Roasted red bell peppers:** A must-have for low-fat cooking, they add deep, savory flavor to salads and sandwiches. Can also puree for use in dressings, dips and soups.
- **Salsa:** Salsa is a perfect fat-free topping for potatoes, chicken, fish, eggs and veggies.
- **Sesame oil:** This Asian ingredient has a fat and calorie content equal to that of any other oil. Its deliciously nutty taste means you need only a bit to boost flavor in stir-fries and salads. Once opened, store sesame oil in the refrigerator.
- **Stewed or chopped tomatoes:** Use these canned veggies as a base for tomato sauce, soup and chili. Look for flavor varieties such as Southwestern, Italian and Cajun. You can also buy plain canned tomatoes and add your own herbs.

Cooking Information

Nutrition Guidelines

We provide nutrition information for each recipe that includes calories, fat, cholesterol, sodium, carbohydrate, fiber and protein. Individual food choices can be based on this information.

Recommended intake for a daily diet of 2,000 calories as set by the Food and Drug Administration

Total Fat	Less than 65g
Saturated Fat	Less than 20g
Cholesterol	Less than 300mg
Sodium	Less than 2,400mg
Total Carbohydrate	300g
Dietary Fiber	25g

Criteria Used for Calculating Nutrition Information

- The first ingredient was used wherever a choice is given (such as 1/3 cup sour cream or plain yogurt).

- The first ingredient amount was used wherever a range is given (such as 3- to 3-1/2–pound cut-up broiler-fryer chicken).

- The first serving number was used wherever a range is given (such as 4 to 6 servings).

- "If desired" ingredients and recipe variations were not included (such as sprinkle with brown sugar, if desired).

- Only the amount of a marinade or frying oil that is estimated to be absorbed by the food during preparation or cooking was calculated.

Ingredients Used in Recipe Testing and Nutrition Calculations

- Ingredients used for testing represent those that the majority of consumers use in their homes: large eggs, 2% milk, 80%-lean ground beef, canned ready-to-use chicken broth and vegetable oil spread containing not less than 65 percent fat.

- Fat-free, low-fat or low-sodium products were not used, unless otherwise indicated.

- Solid vegetable shortening (not butter, margarine, nonstick cooking sprays or vegetable oil spread as they can cause sticking problems) was used to grease pans, unless otherwise indicated.

Equipment Used in Recipe Testing

We use equipment for testing that the majority of consumers use in their homes. If a specific piece of equipment (such as a wire whisk) is necessary for recipe success, it is listed in the recipe.

- Cookware and bakeware without nonstick coatings were used, unless otherwise indicated.

- No dark-colored, black or insulated bakeware was used.

- When a pan is specified in a recipe, a metal pan was used; a baking dish or pie plate means ovenproof glass was used.

- An electric hand mixer was used for mixing only when mixer speeds are specified in the recipe directions. When a mixer speed is not given, a spoon or fork was used.

Cooking Terms Glossary

Beat: Mix ingredients vigorously with spoon, fork, wire whisk, hand beater or electric mixer until smooth and uniform.

Boil: Heat liquid until bubbles rise continuously and break on the surface and steam is given off. For rolling boil, the bubbles form rapidly.

Chop: Cut into coarse or fine irregular pieces with a knife, food chopper, blender or food processor.

Cube: Cut into squares 1/2 inch or larger.

Dice: Cut into squares smaller than 1/2 inch.

Grate: Cut into tiny particles using small rough holes of grater (citrus peel or chocolate).

Grease: Rub the inside surface of a pan with shortening, using pastry brush, piece of waxed paper or paper towel, to prevent food from sticking during baking (as for some casseroles).

Julienne: Cut into thin, matchlike strips, using knife or food processor (vegetables, fruits, meats).

Mix: Combine ingredients in any way that distributes them evenly.

Sauté: Cook foods in hot oil or margarine over medium-high heat with frequent tossing and turning motion.

Shred: Cut into long thin pieces by rubbing food across the holes of a shredder, as for cheese, or by using a knife to slice very thinly, as for cabbage.

Simmer: Cook in liquid just below the boiling point on top of the stove; usually after reducing heat from a boil. Bubbles will rise slowly and break just below the surface.

Stir: Mix ingredients until uniform consistency. Stir once in a while for stirring occasionally, often for stirring frequently and continuously for stirring constantly.

Toss: Tumble ingredients lightly with a lifting motion (such as green salad), usually to coat evenly or mix with another food.

Conversion Guide

Volume

U.S. Units	Canadian Metric	Australian Metric
1/4 teaspoon	1 mL	1 ml
1/2 teaspoon	2 mL	2 ml
1 teaspoon	5 mL	5 ml
1 tablespoon	15 mL	20 ml
1/4 cup	50 mL	60 ml
1/3 cup	75 mL	80 ml
1/2 cup	125 mL	125 ml
2/3 cup	150 mL	170 ml
3/4 cup	175 mL	190 ml
1 cup	250 mL	250 ml
1 quart	1 liter	1 liter
1 1/2 quarts	1.5 liters	1.5 liters
2 quarts	2 liters	2 liters
2 1/2 quarts	2.5 liters	2.5 liters
3 quarts	3 liters	3 liters
4 quarts	4 liters	4 liters

Weight

U.S. Units	Canadian Metric	Australian Metric
1 ounce	30 grams	30 grams
2 ounces	55 grams	60 grams
3 ounces	85 grams	90 grams
4 ounces (1/4 pound)	115 grams	125 grams
8 ounces (1/2 pound)	225 grams	225 grams
16 ounces (1 pound)	455 grams	500 grams
1 pound	455 grams	1/2 kilogram

Measurements

Inches	Centimeters
1	2.5
2	5.0
3	7.5
4	10.0
5	12.5
6	15.0
7	17.5
8	20.5
9	23.0
10	25.5
11	28.0
12	30.5
13	33.0

Temperatures

Fahrenheit	Celsius
32°	0°
212°	100°
250°	120°
275°	140°
300°	150°
325°	160°
350°	180°
375°	190°
400°	200°
425°	220°
450°	230°
475°	240°
500°	260°

Note: The recipes in this cookbook have not been developed or tested using metric measures. When converting recipes to metric, some variations in quality may be noted.

Index

Note: *Italicized* page references indicate photographs.

A

Activity Pyramid, 12
Aioli and Vegetable Appetizer, Layered, *16,* 21
alcoholic beverages, 9
Almond Cheesecake with Raspberry Sauce, *214,* 220
Almond Custard Sauce, 222, *223*
Antipasto Pasta Salad, 205
appetizers and snacks, 18–41
   Asiago Cheese and Artichoke Dip, 33
   Black Bean–Corn Wonton Cups, 25
   Caramelized-Sugar Popcorn, 39
   Caribbean Salsa Bites, 26, *27*
   Crunchy Fruit Snack Mix, 40, *41*
   Easy Salmon Pâté, 30, *31*
   Gingered Caramel and Yogurt Dip, 34, *35*
   Herbed Seafood Spread, 32
   high-energy, low-cal, 38
   Layered Vegetable and Aioli Appetizer, *16,* 21
   Lime Tortilla Chips, 37
   Oven-Fried Chicken Chunks with Peanut Sauce, 18
   Roasted Red Pepper Bruschetta, *22, 23*
   Rosemary Focaccia Wedges, 24
   Spinach Quesadillas with Feta Cheese, 20
   Sun-Dried Tomato Biscotti with Basil–Cream Cheese Topping, 28, *29*
   Sweet-Hot Salsa, 36
   Thai-Spiced Cocktail Shrimp, 19

Apple-Kiwi Smoothie, 64, *65*
Apple-Maple Bundt Cake, 216
Apples, Glazed Salmon with, 114, *115*
Artichoke(s)
   and Asiago Cheese Dip, 33
   Vegetarian Paella, 164, *165*
Asiago Cheese and Artichoke Dip, 33
Asian Noodle Bowl, 175
Asparagus
   Chicken and Pasta Stir-Fry, 105
   Pizza Primavera, 182
   Sea Scallop Stir-Fry, 126, *127*

B

Bagel and Cream Cheese Morning Mix, *65,* 67
Bagels, Honey Ham, 80
Banana(s)
   frozen, 242
   Muffins, Tropical, 62
   Split Ice-Cream Dessert, 225
   -Strawberry Filling, Cocoa Crepes with, 52, *53*
   Triple-Fruit Yogurt Smoothie, *59,* 66
Barley and Lentil Casserole, Curried, 160
Barley-Burger Stew, 73
Basil–Cream Cheese Topping, 28, *29*
Bean(s)
   adding to recipes, 243
   Black, –Chipotle Burritos, 171
   Black, –Corn Wonton Cups, 25
   Butter, Patties with Southwestern Sauce, 170
   Cannellini, Vegetarian Lasagna, 172, *173*
   Chicken Chili with Cheese, 106

   Curried Lentil and Barley Casserole, 160
   Garbanzo, Tabbouleh with, 158, *159*
   Red Pepper–Lentil Soup, 72
   and Rice, Confetti, 169
   Salad, Cuban Spicy, with Oranges and Cilantro, 93
   Saucy Italian Steak, 134
   Southwest Fettuccine Bowl, 176, *177*
   Soy, and Rice, Creole, 168
   Turkey Burritos, 78
   Tuscan Pasta and, 174
   White, and Spinach Pizza, 184, *185*
Beef
   Barley-Burger Stew, 73
   Flank Steak Sandwiches, 79
   Garlic Shepherds Pie, 142
   Giant Oven Burger, 143
   lean cuts of, 135, 242
   Medallions with Pear-Cranberry Chutney, 132, *133*
   Orange-Teriyaki, with Noodles, 136, *137*
   Philly Cheese Steak Casserole, 138
   Pizza Casserole, 140, *141*
   Saucy Italian Steak, 134
   Spicy Pepper Steak, 139
bell peppers. *See* Pepper(s)
beverages
   Apple-Kiwi Smoothie, 64, *65*
   Chai Tea, 63
   Triple-Chocolate Malts, 229
   Triple-Fruit Yogurt Smoothie, *59,* 66
Biscotti, Sun-Dried Tomato, with Basil–Cream Cheese Topping, 28, *29*

Biscuits, Cheddar and Green Onion, *188,* 191

Black Bean(s)
    Cuban Spicy Bean Salad with Oranges and Cilantro, 93
    –Chipotle Burritos, 171
    –Corn Wonton Cups, 25
    Southwest Fettuccine Bowl, 176, *177*

Blueberry
    -Lemon Tart, 224
    Muffins, Old-Fashioned, 60
    Topping, 224

Body Mass Index (BMI), 6–7, 239

Bread Pudding, Fruited, with Eggnog Sauce, 56, *57*

Bread(s). *See also* Pizza; Sandwiches; Tortilla(s)
    Carrot-Pineapple, 55
    Cheddar and Green Onion Biscuits, *188,* 191
    Cinnamon-Raisin French Toast, 48
    Corn, Cheesy Mexican, 190
    French Bread Salad, 206
    Old-Fashioned Blueberry Muffins, 60
    Orange-Cranberry Scones, 58, *59*
    Roasted Red Pepper Bruschetta, 22, *23*
    Rosemary Focaccia Wedges, 24
    Savory Currant Wedges, 192, *193*
    Tropical Banana Muffins, 62

breakfast dishes, 44–67
    Apple-Kiwi Smoothie, 64, *65*
    Bagel and Cream Cheese Morning Mix, *65,* 67
    Carrot-Pineapple Bread, 55
    Chai Tea, 63
    Cinnamon-Raisin French Toast, 48
    Cocoa Crepes with Strawberry-Banana Filling, 52, *53*
    Country Eggs in Tortilla Cups, 46, *47*
    Fruited Bread Pudding with Eggnog Sauce, 56, *57*
    Ginger Pancakes with Lemon–Cream Cheese Topping, 50, *51*
    healthy choices for, 61
    Mediterranean Eggs, 45
    Old-Fashioned Blueberry Muffins, 60
    Orange-Cranberry Scones, 58, *59*
    Peach-Almond Coffee Cake, 54
    Spring Vegetable Frittata, *42,* 44
    Triple-Fruit Yogurt Smoothie, *59,* 66
    Tropical Banana Muffins, 62
    Whole Wheat Waffles, 49

Broccoli
    Asian Noodle Bowl, 175
    Cheesy Turkey, Rice, and, 109
    Confetti Wild Rice, 213
    Pizza Primavera, 182

broth, chicken, 243

Brownies, Orange Cappuccino, 230, *231*

Bruschetta, Roasted Red Pepper, 22, *23*

Burger, Giant Oven, 143

Burgers, Spicy Turkey, 108

Burritos, Chipotle–Black Bean, 171

Burritos, Turkey, 78

Butter Bean Patties with Southwestern Sauce, 170

buttermilk, 242

C

Cabbage
    Crab Tortilla Roll-Ups, 82, *83*
    Slaw, Triple-, 202, *203*
    Zesty Autumn Pork Stew, 74, *75*

Caesar Chicken Paninis, 76, *77*

Cake(s)
    Almond Cheesecake with Raspberry Sauce, *214,* 220
    Angel, Mocha, 217
    Bundt, Apple-Maple, 216
    Chocolate Soufflé, 218, *219*
    Coffee, Peach-Almond, 54
    Mini Pumpkin Cheesecakes, 221

Cannellini Bean Lasagna, Vegetarian, 172, *173*

Cappuccino Brownies, Orange, 230, *231*

Caramel and Yogurt Dip, Gingered, 34, *35*

Caramelized Onion and Sweet Potato Skillet, 198, *199*

Caramelized-Sugar Popcorn, 39

Caribbean Pork Roast, 146

Caribbean Salsa Bites, 26, *27*

Carrot(s)
    Creamy Ham and Pasta, 152, *153*
    Cuban Spicy Bean Salad with Oranges and Cilantro, 93
    -Pineapple Bread, 55
    Pizza Primavera, 182
    and Zucchini with Herbs, 194, *195*

Cashew Chicken, Sichuan, 100, *101*

Catfish, Crispy Baked, 113

Cauliflower
    Antipasto Pasta Salad, 205
    Creamy Pesto–Pasta Salad, 92

Chai Tea, 63

Cheddar and Green Onion Biscuits, *188,* 191

Cheese. *See also* Cream Cheese; Pizza
    Asiago, and Artichoke Dip, 33
    Cheddar and Green Onion Biscuits, *188,* 191
    Cheesy Mexican Corn Bread, 190
    Cheesy Turkey, Rice and Broccoli, 109
    Chicken Chili with, 106
    Creamy Corn and Garlic Risotto, 161
    Easy Mac 'n, 179
    Feta, Spinach Quesadillas with, 20
    high-flavor, varieties of, 242
    Honey Ham Bagels, 80

low-fat varieties of, 242
Orzo Parmesan, 207
Parmesan Perch, 121
Ratatouille Polenta Bake, 162, *163*
Rosemary Focaccia Wedges, 24
Savory Currant Wedges, 192, *193*
Spread, Chili-, 108
Steak Casserole, Philly, 138
Vegetarian Cannellini Bean Lasagna, 172, *173*
Cheesecake, Almond, with Raspberry Sauce, *214,* 220
Cheesecakes, Mini Pumpkin, 221
Cherry and Pear Crisp, 222, *223*
Cherry–Chocolate Chip Cookies, 234
Chicken
    Breasts, Herbed Baked, 98
    broth, buying, 243
    Chili with Cheese, 106
    Chunks, Oven-Fried, with Peanut Sauce, 18
    with Couscous and Chili Sauce, 96, *97*
    Garlic-Ginger, with Fettuccine, 104
    lean parts of, 99, 242
    Mediterranean, with Rosemary Orzo, *94,* 107
    Niçoise, 102, *103*
    Paninis, Caesar, 76, *77*
    and Pasta Stir-Fry, 105
    Sichuan Cashew, 100, *101*
    and Strawberry-Spinach Salad, 86, *87*
Chili, Chicken, with Cheese, 106
Chili-Cheese Spread, 108
Chili Sauce, Green, 96, *97*
Chipotle–Black Bean Burritos, 171
Chips, Lime Tortilla, 37
Chocolate
    Chip–Cherry Cookies, 234
    Cocoa Crepes with Strawberry-Banana Filling, 52, *53*
    Orange Cappuccino Brownies, 230, *231*

Soufflé Cakes, 218, *219*
Triple-, Malts, 229
cholesterol, 8
Cinnamon-Raisin French Toast, 48
Cocoa Crepes with Strawberry-Banana Filling, 52, *53*
Coffee Cake, Peach-Almond, 54
Confetti Beans and Rice, 169
Confetti Wild Rice, 213
Cookies, Cherry-Chocolate Chip, 234
Cookies, Ginger Gems, 232
cooking terms glossary, 244–45
Corn
    Asian Noodle Bowl, 175
    Bread, Cheesy Mexican, 190
    and Garlic Risotto, Creamy, 161
    –Black Bean Wonton Cups, 25
Country Eggs in Tortilla Cups, 46, *47*
Couscous
    Chicken with, and Chili Sauce, 96, *97*
    Spanish Lamb and, *130,* 154
Crab
    Herbed Seafood Spread, 32
    Tortilla Roll-Ups, 82, *83*
Cranberry-Orange Scones, 58, *59*
Cranberry-Pear Chutney, Beef Medallions with, 132, *133*
Cream Cheese
    Almond Cheesecake with Raspberry Sauce, *214,* 220
    and Bagel Morning Mix, *65,* 67
    low-fat varieties of, 242
    –Basil Topping, 28, *29*
    –Lemon Topping, 50, *51*
    Mini Pumpkin Cheesecakes, 221
    –Orange Glaze, 230, *231*
Creamy Corn and Garlic Risotto, 161
Creamy Ham and Pasta, 152, *153*
Creamy Mushroom–Topped Baked Potatoes, 187
Creamy Pesto–Pasta Salad, 92
Creole Soy Beans and Rice, 168

Crepes, Cocoa, with Strawberry-Banana Filling, 52, *53*
Crisp, Pear and Cherry, 222, *223*
Crispy Baked Catfish, 113
Crunchy Fruit Snack Mix, 40, *41*
Cuban Spicy Bean Salad with Oranges and Cilantro, 93
Cucumber(s)
    French Bread Salad, 206
    Gazpacho Pasta Salad with Tomato-Lime Dressing, 90, *91*
    Jicama Salsa, 120
    Sauce, 118, *119*
    Sweet-Hot Salsa, 36
Currant Wedges, Savory, 192, *193*
Curried Lentil and Barley Casserole, 160

D

desserts, 216–34
    Almond Cheesecake with Raspberry Sauce, *214,* 220
    Apple-Maple Bundt Cake, 216
    Banana Split Ice-Cream Dessert, 225
    Blueberry-Lemon Tart, 224
    Cherry-Chocolate Chip Cookies, 234
    Chocolate Soufflé Cakes, 218, *219*
    Frosty Margarita Pie, 226, *227*
    Ginger Gems Cookies, 232
    low-fat, easy ideas for, 233
    Mini Pumpkin Cheesecakes, 221
    Mocha Angel Cake, 217
    Orange Cappuccino Brownies, 230, *231*
    Pear and Cherry Crisp, 222, *223*
    Strawberry-Rhubarb Frozen-Yogurt Parfaits, 228
    Triple-Chocolate Malts, 229
diet, healthy, food choices for, 11
diet, healthy, guidelines for, 8–9
diets. *See* weight-loss plans

Dip
    Asiago Cheese and Artichoke, 33
    Gingered Caramel and Yogurt,
        34, *35*
    Sweet-Hot Salsa, 36
    Yogurt Salsa, 82, *83*
Dressing. *See also specific salad*
      recipes
    Lemon-Garlic, 158, *159*
    low-cal, uses for, 243
    Strawberry, 86, *87*
    Tomato-Lime, 90, *91*

E

Easy Mac 'n Cheese, 179
Easy Salmon Pâté, 30, *31*
eating disorders, 10
Eggnog Sauce, 56, *57*
Eggplant
    Ratatouille Polenta Bake, 162, *163*
    Sauce, Spicy, Whole Wheat
        Spaghetti with, 178
Egg(s)
    Country, in Tortilla Cups, 46, *47*
    egg substitute products, 243
    Mediterranean, 45
    Spring Vegetable Frittata, *42,* 44
evaporated milk, 243
exercise, 12–15

F

fad diets, 9–10
fat, body weight from, 6
fat, dietary, 8
Feta Cheese, Spinach Quesadillas
    with, 20
Fettuccine, Garlic-Ginger Chicken
    with, 104
Fettuccine Bowl, Southwest, 176,
    177
Fish. *See also* shellfish
    Crispy Baked Catfish, 113
    Easy Salmon Pâté, 30, *31*
    Glazed Salmon with Apples, 114,
        115

Grilled, with Jicama Salsa, 120
Marinated Tuna Steaks with
    Cucumber Sauce, 118, *119*
Parmesan Perch, 121
Red Snapper with Mango Relish,
    112
Rolls, Spinach-Filled, 116, *117*
Seafood and Vegetables with
    Rice, 124, *125*
F.I.T. Principle, 13
Five-Spice Tofu Stir-Fry, 166, *167*
Flank Steak Sandwiches, 79
Focaccia Sandwiches, Veggie,
    68, 85
Focaccia Wedges, Rosemary, 24
Food Guide Pyramid, 8, 240, *240*
French Bread Salad, 206
French Toast, Cinnamon-Raisin, 48
Frittata, Spring Vegetable, *42,* 44
Frosty Margarita Pie, 226, *227*
Fruit. *See also specific fruit*
    Fruited Bread Pudding with
        Eggnog Sauce, 56, *57*
    in healthy diet, 8, 242
    as low-calorie dessert, 233
    Snack Mix, Crunchy, 40, *41*
    Triple-, Yogurt Smoothie, *59,* 66

G

Garbanzo Beans, Tabbouleh with,
    158, *159*
Garlic, 243
    and Corn Risotto, Creamy, 161
    -Ginger Chicken with Fettuccine,
        104
    -Lemon Dressing, 158, *159*
    Shepherds Pie, 142
    Shrimp, 122, *123*
Gazpacho Pasta Salad with
    Tomato-Lime Dressing,
        90, *91*
Giant Oven Burger, 143
ginger, for flavoring, 243
Gingered Caramel and Yogurt Dip,
    34, *35*
Ginger Gems Cookies, 232

Ginger Pancakes with
        Lemon–Cream Cheese
        Topping, 50, *51*
Glaze, Maple, 216
Glaze, Orange, 58, *59*
Glaze, Orange–Cream Cheese, 230,
    231
Glazed Salmon with Apples, 114, *115*
glossary of cooking terms, 244–45
grains. *See also* Rice
    Barley-Burger Stew, 73
    Chicken with Couscous and Chili
        Sauce, 96, *97*
    Curried Lentil and Barley
        Casserole, 160
    in healthy diet, 8
    Onion and Mushroom Quinoa,
        210, *211*
    Spanish Lamb and Couscous,
        130, 154
    Tabbouleh with Garbanzo Beans,
        158, *159*
Green Chili Sauce, 96, *97*
Grilled Fish with Jicama Salsa, 120
Grilled Shrimp Kabobs, 129
Grilled Southwestern Pork Chops,
    150
Grilled Veggies, 196

H

Ham
    Honey, Bagels, 80
    lean cuts of, 242
    and Pasta, Creamy, 152, *153*
    and Vegetables au Gratin, Skillet,
        151
health claims, on labels, 241
heart rate, target, 13
herbal supplements, 10
Herbed Baked Chicken Breasts, 98
Herbed Seafood Spread, 32
herbs, for flavoring, 243
Honey Ham Bagels, 80
Honey-Mustard Turkey with Snap
    Peas, 110, *111*
Horseradish Mashed Potatoes, 200

I–J–K

Ice Cream
Dessert, Banana Split, 225
low-fat alternatives to, 242–43
Italian Roasted Pork Tenderloin, 147
Italian Sausage Soup, 70

Jicama Salsa, 120

Kabobs, Grilled Shrimp, 129
Kiwi-Apple Smoothie, 64, *65*

L

Lamb and Couscous, Spanish,
130, 154
Lamb Chops, Mustard, 155
Lasagna, Vegetarian Cannellini
Bean, 172, *173*
Layered Vegetable and Aioli
Appetizer, *16*, 21
Lemon
-Garlic Dressing, 158, *159*
juice, for flavoring, 243
–Cream Cheese Topping, 50, *51*
Lentil and Barley Casserole, Curried,
160
Lentil–Red Pepper Soup, 72
Lime
juice, for flavoring, 243
-Tomato Dressing, 90, *91*
Tortilla Chips, 37
low-fat shopping strategies, 242–43

M

Mac 'n Cheese, Easy, 179
main dishes (meat)
Beef Medallions with Pear-
Cranberry Chutney, 132,
133
Caribbean Pork Roast, 146
Creamy Ham and Pasta, 152, *153*
Garlic Shepherds Pie, 142
Giant Oven Burger, 143
Grilled Southwestern Pork Chops,
150

Italian Roasted Pork Tenderloin,
147
Mustard Lamb Chops, 155
Orange-Teriyaki Beef with
Noodles, 136, *137*
Philly Cheese Steak Casserole,
138
Pizza Casserole, 140, *141*
Roasted Pork Chops and
Vegetables, 148, *149*
Saucy Italian Steak, 134
Skillet Ham and Vegetables au
Gratin, 151
Spanish Lamb and Couscous,
130, 154
Spicy Pepper Steak, 139
Veal and Potato Strata with
Roasted Peppers, 144, *145*
main dishes (meatless)
Asian Noodle Bowl, 175
Butter Bean Patties with
Southwestern Sauce, 170
Chipotle–Black Bean Burritos, 171
Confetti Beans and Rice, 169
Creamy Corn and Garlic Risotto,
161
Creamy Mushroom–Topped Baked
Potatoes, 187
Creamy Pesto–Pasta Salad, 92
Creole Soy Beans and Rice, 168
Cuban Spicy Bean Salad with
Oranges and Cilantro, 93
Curried Lentil and Barley
Casserole, 160
Easy Mac 'n Cheese, 179
Five-Spice Tofu Stir-Fry, 166,
167
Gazpacho Pasta Salad with
Tomato-Lime Dressing,
90, *91*
Pizza Primavera, 182
Potato and Tomato Pizza, *156*,
183
Ratatouille Polenta Bake, 162,
163
Ravioli with Tomato-Alfredo
Sauce, 180, *181*

Southwest Fettuccine Bowl, 176,
177
Tabbouleh with Garbanzo Beans,
158, *159*
Tuscan Pasta and Beans, 174
Vegetarian Cannellini Bean
Lasagna, 172, *173*
Vegetarian Paella, 164, *165*
White Bean and Spinach Pizza,
184, *185*
Whole Wheat Spaghetti with
Spicy Eggplant Sauce, 178
main dishes (poultry)
Cheesy Turkey, Rice and Broccoli,
109
Chicken and Pasta Stir-Fry, 105
Chicken and Strawberry–Spinach
Salad, 86, *87*
Chicken Chili with Cheese, 106
Chicken Niçoise, 102, *103*
Chicken with Couscous and Chili
Sauce, 96, *97*
Garlic-Ginger Chicken with
Fettuccine, 104
Herbed Baked Chicken Breasts, 98
Honey-Mustard Turkey with Snap
Peas, 110, *111*
Mediterranean Chicken with
Rosemary Orzo, *94*, 107
Sichuan Cashew Chicken, 100,
101
Spicy Turkey Burgers, 108
Turkey-Wild Rice Salad, 88
main dishes (seafood)
Crispy Baked Catfish, 113
Garlic Shrimp, 122, *123*
Glazed Salmon with Apples, 114,
115
Grilled Fish with Jicama Salsa,
120
Grilled Shrimp Kabobs, 129
Marinated Tuna Steaks with
Cucumber Sauce, 118, *119*
Parmesan Perch, 121
Red Snapper with Mango Relish,
112
Savory Scallops and Shrimp, 128

main dishes (seafood) *(cont.)*
  Seafood and Vegetables with
    Rice, 124, *125*
  Sea Scallop Stir-Fry, 126, *127*
  Spinach-Filled Fish Rolls, 116,
    117
  Spinach-Shrimp Salad with Hot
    Bacon Dressing, 89
Malts, Triple-Chocolate, 229
Mango Relish, 112
Maple Glaze, 216
Margarita Pie, Frosty, 226, *227*
Marinated Tuna Steaks with
    Cucumber Sauce, 118, *119*
meat. *See* Beef; Ham; Lamb; Pork;
    Veal
Mediterranean Chicken with
    Rosemary Orzo, *94*, 107
Mediterranean Eggs, 45
Mediterranean Vegetable Salad, 204
menus, for one week, 235–37
Mini Pumpkin Cheesecakes, 221
Mocha Angel Cake, 217
Mocha Topping, 217, 218, *219*
Muffins, Old-Fashioned Blueberry, 60
Muffins, Tropical Banana, 62
Mushroom(s)
  Antipasto Pasta Salad, 205
  Confetti Wild Rice, 213
  Grilled Shrimp Kabobs, 129
  Layered Vegetable and Aioli
    Appetizer, *16*, 21
  –Topped Baked Potatoes, Creamy,
    187
  and Onion Quinoa, 210, *211*
  Seafood and Vegetables with
    Rice, 124, *125*
  Spinach-Shrimp Salad with Hot
    Bacon Dressing, 89
Mustard Lamb Chops, 155

N

Noodle(s), 243
  Bowl, Asian, 175
  Orange-Teriyaki Beef with, 136,
    137

Philly Cheese Steak Casserole,
    138
Sea Scallop Stir-Fry, 126, *127*
nutrition claims, on labels, 241

O

Old-Fashioned Blueberry Muffins, 60
Onion(s)
  Green, and Cheddar Biscuits,
    188, 191
  Green, and Pine Nut Pilaf, 212
  and Mushroom Quinoa, 210,
    211
  Rosemary Focaccia Wedges, 24
  and Sweet Potato Skillet,
    Caramelized, 198, *199*
Orange(s)
  Cappuccino Brownies, 230, *231*
  and Cilantro, Cuban Spicy Bean
    Salad with, 93
  -Cranberry Scones, 58, *59*
  –Cream Cheese Glaze, 230, *231*
  Glaze, 58, *59*
  -Teriyaki Beef with Noodles, 136,
    137
Orzo, Rosemary, Mediterranean
    Chicken with, *94*, 107
Orzo Parmesan, 207
Oven-Fried Chicken Chunks with
    Peanut Sauce, 18

P–Q

Pâté, Easy Salmon, 30, *31*
Paella, Vegetarian, 164, *165*
Pancakes, Ginger, with
    Lemon–Cream Cheese
    Topping, 50, *51*
Paninis, Caesar Chicken, 76, *77*
pantry items, low-fat, 243
pantry items, vegetarian, 186
papayas, 36
Parfaits, Strawberry-Rhubarb
    Frozen-Yogurt, 228
Parmesan, Orzo, 207
Parmesan Perch, 121

Pasta, 243. *See also* Noodle(s)
  and Beans, Tuscan, 174
  and Chicken Stir-Fry, 105
  Creamy Ham and, 152, *153*
  Easy Mac 'n Cheese, 179
  Garlic-Ginger Chicken with
    Fettuccine, 104
  Italian Sausage Soup, 70
  –Pesto Salad, Creamy, 92
  Mediterranean Chicken with
    Rosemary Orzo, *94*, 107
  Orzo Parmesan, 207
  Pizza Casserole, 140, *141*
  Ravioli with Tomato-Alfredo
    Sauce, 180, *181*
  Rio Grande Turkey Soup, *4*, 71
  Salad, Antipasto, 205
  Salad, Gazpacho, Salad with
    Tomato-Lime Dressing,
    90, *91*
  sauce, bottled, 243
  Southwest Fettuccine Bowl, 176,
    177
  Spaghetti with Squash, 197
  Vegetarian Cannellini Bean
    Lasagna, 172, *173*
  Whole Wheat Spaghetti with
    Spicy Eggplant Sauce, 178
Peach-Almond Coffee Cake, 54
Peanut Sauce, 18
Pear and Cherry Crisp, 222, *223*
Pear-Cranberry Chutney, Beef
    Medallions with, 132, *133*
Peas, Snap
  Honey-Mustard Turkey with, 110,
    111
  Orange-Teriyaki Beef with
    Noodles, 136, *137*
Pepper(s)
  Chicken Niçoise, 102, *103*
  chili, for flavoring, 243
  Chili-Cheese Spread, 108
  Chipotle–Black Bean Burritos, 171
  Creamy Pesto–Pasta Salad, 92
  Gazpacho Pasta Salad with
    Tomato-Lime Dressing,
    90, *91*

Green Chili Sauce, 96, *97*
Grilled Veggies, 196
Layered Vegetable and Aioli
    Appetizer, *16*, 21
Mediterranean Vegetable Salad,
    204
Ratatouille Polenta Bake, 162,
    163
Red, –Lentil Soup, 72
Roasted, Veal and Potato Strata
    with, 144, *145*
Roasted Red, Bruschetta, 22, *23*
roasted red, for flavoring, 243
Sea Scallop Stir-Fry, 126, *127*
Spring Vegetable Frittata, *42*, 44
Steak, Spicy, 139
Vegetables and Pork in Pitas, 81
Veggie Focaccia Sandwiches,
    68, 85
Perch, Parmesan, 121
Pesto–Pasta Salad, Creamy, 92
Philly Cheese Steak Casserole, 138
Pie, Frosty Margarita, 226, *227*
Pie, Garlic Shepherds, 142
Pilaf, Pine Nut and Green Onion,
    212
Pineapple
  -Carrot Bread, 55
  Tropical Banana Muffins, 62
Pine Nut and Green Onion Pilaf,
    212
Pizza, Potato and Tomato, *156*,
    183
Pizza, White Bean and Spinach,
    184, *185*
Pizza Casserole, 140, *141*
Pizza Primavera, 182
Polenta Bake, Ratatouille, 162, *163*
Popcorn, Caramelized-Sugar, 39
Pork
  Chops, Grilled Southwestern, 150
  Chops and Vegetables, Roasted,
    148, *149*
  Creamy Ham and Pasta, 152,
    153
  Honey Ham Bagels, 80
  lean cuts of, 135, 242

Roast, Caribbean, 146
Skillet Ham and Vegetables au
    Gratin, 151
Stew, Zesty Autumn, 74, *75*
Tenderloin, Italian Roasted, 147
and Vegetables in Pitas, 81
Potato(es). *See also* Sweet Potato(es)
  Baked, Creamy
    Mushroom–Topped, 187
  Country Eggs in Tortilla Cups,
    46, *47*
  Grilled Veggies, 196
  Mashed, Horseradish, 200
  and Tomato Pizza, *156*, 183
  and Veal Strata with Roasted
    Peppers, 144, *145*
poultry. *See* Chicken; Turkey
Pudding, Fruited Bread, with
    Eggnog Sauce, 56, *57*
Pumpkin Cheesecakes, Mini, 221

Quesadillas, Spinach, with Feta
    Cheese, 20
Quinoa, Onion and Mushroom,
    210, *211*

R

Raspberry(ies)
  Sauce, *214*, 220
  Triple-Fruit Yogurt Smoothie,
    59, 66
Ratatouille Polenta Bake, 162, *163*
Ravioli with Tomato-Alfredo Sauce,
    180, *181*
red peppers. *See* Pepper(s)
Red Snapper with Mango Relish,
    112
Relish, Mango, 112
Rhubarb-Strawberry Frozen-Yogurt
    Parfaits, 228
Rice, 243
  Cheesy Turkey, Broccoli and, 109
  Confetti Beans and, 169
  Creamy Corn and Garlic Risotto,
    161
  Creole Soy Beans and, 168

Pine Nut and Green Onion Pilaf,
    212
  Seafood and Vegetables with,
    124, *125*
  Vegetarian Paella, 164, *165*
  Wild, Confetti, 213
  Wild, –Turkey Salad, 88
rice vinegar, 243
Rio Grande Turkey Soup, *4*, 71
Risotto, Corn and Garlic, Creamy, 161
Roasted Pork Chops and Vegetables,
    148, *149*
Roasted Red Pepper Bruschetta, 22, *23*
Rosemary Focaccia Wedges, 24
Rosemary Orzo, Mediterranean
    Chicken with, *94*, 107

S

Salad (main dish)
  Chicken and Strawberry–Spinach,
    86, *87*
  Cuban Spicy Bean, with Oranges
    and Cilantro, 93
  deli, calories and fat in, 84
  Gazpacho Pasta, with Tomato-
    Lime Dressing, 90, *91*
  Pesto–Pasta, Creamy, 92
  Spinach-Shrimp, with Hot Bacon
    Dressing, 89
  toppings, calories and fat in, 201
  Turkey–Wild Rice, 88
Salad (side dish)
  Antipasto Pasta, 205
  deli, calories and fat in, 84
  French Bread, 206
  Mediterranean Vegetable, 204
  toppings, calories and fat in, 201
  Triple-Cabbage Slaw, 202, *203*
Salmon, Glazed, with Apples, 114,
    115
Salmon Pâté, Easy, 30, *31*
Salsa
  Jicama, 120
  Sweet-Hot, 36
  used as topping, 243
  Yogurt, 82, *83*

Salsa Bites, Caribbean, 26, *27*
salt, in healthy diet, 9
Sandwiches
    Caesar Chicken Paninis, 76, *77*
    Crab Tortilla Roll-Ups, 82, *83*
    deli, calories and fat in, 84
    Flank Steak, 79
    Giant Oven Burger, 143
    Honey Ham Bagels, 80
    Spicy Turkey Burgers, 108
    Turkey Burritos, 78
    Vegetables and Pork in Pitas, 81
    Veggie Focaccia, *68,* 85
saturated fats, 8
Sauce. *See also* Relish; Salsa
    Almond Custard, 222, *223*
    Blueberry Topping, 224
    Cream Cheese–Lemon Topping,
        50, *51*
    Cucumber, 118, *119*
    Eggnog, 56, *57*
    Green Chili, 96, *97*
    Mocha Topping, 217, 218, *219*
    Peanut, 18
    Raspberry, *214,* 220
Saucy Italian Steak, 134
Sausage Soup, Italian, 70
Savory Currant Wedges, 192, *193*
Savory Scallops and Shrimp, 128
Scallop(s)
    Sea, Stir-Fry, 126, *127*
    Seafood and Vegetables with
        Rice, 124, *125*
    and Shrimp, Savory, 128
Scones, Orange-Cranberry, 58, *59*
seafood. *See* Fish; Shellfish
sea scallops. *See* Scallop(s)
serving sizes, recommended, 240
sesame oil, 243
shellfish
    Crab Tortilla Roll-Ups, 82, *83*
    Garlic Shrimp, 122, *123*
    Grilled Shrimp Kabobs, 129
    Herbed Seafood Spread, 32
    Savory Scallops and Shrimp,
        128

Seafood and Vegetables with
    Rice, 124, *125*
Sea Scallop Stir-Fry, 126, *127*
Spinach-Shrimp Salad with Hot
    Bacon Dressing, 89
Thai-Spiced Cocktail Shrimp, 19
Shepherds Pie, Garlic, 142
shopping strategies, 242–43
Shrimp
    Garlic, 122, *123*
    Grilled, Kabobs, 129
    Herbed Seafood Spread, 32
    and Scallops, Savory, 128
    Seafood and Vegetables with
        Rice, 124, *125*
    -Spinach Salad with Hot Bacon
        Dressing, 89
    Thai-Spiced Cocktail, 19
Sichuan Cashew Chicken, 100, *101*
side dishes, 190–213
    Antipasto Pasta Salad, 205
    Caramelized Onion and Sweet
        Potato Skillet, 198, *199*
    Carrots and Zucchini with Herbs,
        194, *195*
    Cheddar and Green Onion
        Biscuits, *188,* 191
    Cheesy Mexican Corn Bread, 190
    Confetti Wild Rice, 213
    French Bread Salad, 206
    Grilled Veggies, 196
    Horseradish Mashed Potatoes, 200
    Mediterranean Vegetable Salad,
        204
    Onion and Mushroom Quinoa,
        210, *211*
    Orzo Parmesan, 207
    Pine Nut and Green Onion Pilaf,
        212
    Savory Currant Wedges, 192, *193*
    Spaetzle in Herbed Tomato Cream
        Sauce, 208, *209*
    Spaghetti with Squash, 197
    Triple-Cabbage Slaw, 202, *203*
Skillet Ham and Vegetables au
    Gratin, 151

Slaw, Triple-Cabbage, 202, *203*
Smoothie, Apple-Kiwi, 64, *65*
Smoothie, Triple-Fruit Yogurt,
    59, 66
snacks and appetizers. *See* appetizers
    and snacks
Snap Peas
    Honey-Mustard Turkey with, 110,
        111
    Orange-Teriyaki Beef with
        Noodles, 136, *137*
sodium, in healthy diet, 9
Soup, Italian Sausage, 70
Soup, Red Pepper–Lentil, 72
Soup, Turkey, Rio Grande, *4,* 71
Southwest Fettuccine Bowl, 176, *177*
Soy Beans and Rice, Creole, 168
Spaetzle in Herbed Tomato Cream
    Sauce, 208, *209*
Spaghetti, Whole Wheat, with Spicy
    Eggplant Sauce, 178
Spaghetti with Squash, 197
Spanish Lamb and Couscous, *130,*
    154
spices, for flavoring, 243
Spicy Pepper Steak, 139
Spicy Turkey Burgers, 108
Spinach
    adding to recipes, 242
    -Filled Fish Rolls, 116, *117*
    –Strawberry Salad, Chicken and,
        86, *87*
    Quesadillas with Feta Cheese, 20
    -Shrimp Salad with Hot Bacon
        Dressing, 89
    Vegetarian Cannellini Bean
        Lasagna, 172, *173*
    and White Bean Pizza, 184, *185*
Spread(s)
    Basil–Cream Cheese Topping,
        28, *29*
    Chili-Cheese, 108
    Easy Salmon Pâté, 30, *31*
    Herbed Seafood, 32
    Layered Vegetable and Aioli
        Appetizer, *16,* 21

Spring Vegetable Frittata, *42*, 44
Squash. *See also* Zucchini
    Mini Pumpkin Cheesecakes, 221
    Spaghetti with, 197
Stew
    Barley-Burger, 73
    Chicken Chili with Cheese, 106
    Pork, Zesty Autumn, 74, *75*
Strawberry(ies)
    -Banana Filling, Cocoa Crepes
        with, 52, *53*
    Banana Split Ice-Cream Dessert,
        225
    Dressing, 86, *87*
    –Spinach Salad, Chicken and,
        86, *87*
    -Rhubarb Frozen-Yogurt Parfaits,
        228
strength training, 15
stretching exercises, 15
sugar, in healthy diet, 8
Sun-Dried Tomato Biscotti with
        Basil–Cream Cheese
        Topping, 28, *29*
Sweet-Hot Salsa, 36
Sweet Potato(es)
    and Onion Skillet, Caramelized,
        198, *199*
    Zesty Autumn Pork Stew, 74, *75*

T

Tabbouleh with Garbanzo Beans,
        158, *159*
target heart rate, 13, 14
Tart, Blueberry-Lemon, 224
Tea, Chai, 63
Thai-Spiced Cocktail Shrimp, 19
Tofu Stir-Fry, Five-Spice, 166, *167*
Tomato(es)
    canned, 243
    Chicken Chili with Cheese, 106
    Chicken with Couscous and Chili
        Sauce, 96, *97*
    Cream Sauce, Herbed, Spaetzle in,
        208, *209*

French Bread Salad, 206
Green Chili Sauce, 96, *97*
-Alfredo Sauce, Ravioli with, 180,
    181
-Lime Dressing, Gazpacho Pasta
    Salad with, 90, *91*
Mediterranean Eggs, 45
Mediterranean Vegetable Salad,
    204
and Potato Pizza, *156*, 183
Ratatouille Polenta Bake, 162,
    163
Saucy Italian Steak, 134
Seafood and Vegetables with
    Rice, 124, *125*
Sun-Dried, Biscotti with
    Basil–Cream Cheese
    Topping, 28, *29*
Whole Wheat Spaghetti with
    Spicy Eggplant Sauce, 178
toppings. *See* Glaze; Relish; Salsa;
    Sauce; Spread(s)
Tortilla(s)
    Caribbean Salsa Bites, 26, *27*
    Chipotle–Black Bean Burritos,
        171
    Chips, Lime, 37
    Crab, Roll-Ups, 82, *83*
    Cups, Country Eggs in, 46, *47*
    Spinach Quesadillas with Feta
        Cheese, 20
    Turkey Burritos, 78
Triple-Cabbage Slaw, 202, *203*
Triple-Chocolate Malts, 229
Triple-Fruit Yogurt Smoothie,
    59, 66
Tropical Banana Muffins, 62
Tuna Steaks, Marinated, with
    Cucumber Sauce, 118, *119*
Turkey
    Burgers, Spicy, 108
    Burritos, 78
    Honey-Mustard, with Snap Peas,
        110, *111*
    Italian Sausage Soup, 70
    lean parts of, 99, 242

–Wild Rice Salad, 88
Rice, and Broccoli, Cheesy, 109
Soup, Rio Grande, *4*, 71
Tuscan Pasta and Beans, 174

V

Veal and Potato Strata with Roasted
        Peppers, 144, *145*
Vegetable(s). *See also specific*
        vegetables
    adding to recipes, 242
    and Aioli Appetizer, Layered,
        16, 21
    Antipasto Pasta Salad, 205
    Five-Spice Tofu Stir-Fry, 166, *167*
    Garlic Shepherds Pie, 142
    Grilled Veggies, 196
    in healthy diet, 8, 241
    Italian Sausage Soup, 70
    and Pork Chops, Roasted, 148,
        149
    and Pork in Pitas, 81
    Rio Grande Turkey Soup, *4*, 71
    Salad, Mediterranean, 204
    Seafood and, with Rice, 124, *125*
    Sichuan Cashew Chicken, 100,
        101
    Skillet Ham and, au Gratin, 151
    Spring, Frittata, *42*, 44
    Vegetarian Paella, 164, *165*
    Veggie Focaccia Sandwiches,
        68, 85
Vegetarian Cannellini Bean
        Lasagna, 172, *173*
Vegetarian Paella, 164, *165*
vegetarian pantry items, 186
Veggie Focaccia Sandwiches, *68*, 85

W

Waffles, Whole Wheat, 49
weight-height table, 6, 238
weight-loss plans
    exercise and, 12–15
    food choices for, 11

weight-loss plans *(cont.)*
  group support for, 10
  high-protein/low-carbohydrate,
    9–10
  liquid diets, 9
  meal planning and, 10
  setbacks in, 7
  single food diets, 10
  tips for, 10
  very low-calorie, 9
  weight before starting, 6–7
  weight loss goals, setting, 7
White Bean and Spinach Pizza,
    184, *185*

Whole Wheat Spaghetti with Spicy
    Eggplant Sauce, 178
Whole Wheat Waffles, 49
Wild Rice, Confetti, 213
Wild Rice–Turkey Salad, 88
Wonton Cups, Black Bean–Corn, 25

Y–Z

Yogurt
  Apple-Kiwi Smoothie, 64, *65*
  Dip, Gingered Caramel and, 34, *35*
  Frozen, Parfaits, Rhubarb-
    Strawberry, 228
  as mayonnaise substitute, 242

Salsa, 82, *83*
Smoothie, Triple-Fruit, *59*, 66
Triple-Chocolate Malts, 229

Zesty Autumn Pork Stew, 74, *75*
Zucchini
  Antipasto Pasta Salad, 205
  and Carrots with Herbs, 194,
    195
  Grilled Veggies, 196
  Ratatouille Polenta Bake, 162,
    163
  Spring Vegetable Frittata, *42*, 44
  Vegetables and Pork in Pitas, 81

Activity Chart

Activity	Calories Burned per Minute	Activity	Calories Burned per Minute
Aerobics	3–10	Racquetball	8–12
Baseball	5	Reclining (watching TV)	2
Basketball	6–9	Running, 12-minute mile (5 mph)	9
Bowling (while active)	7	Running, 8-minute mile (7.5 mph)	11
Calisthenics	6–8	Skating, in-line or ice (moderate to vigorous)	5–15
Canoeing (3–4 mph)	3–7	Skipping rope	10–15
Cleaning	3	Sleeping	1
Cooking	3	Soccer	9
Cross-country skiing (4 mph)	11–20	Spinning	7
Cycling (5–15 mph)	4–12	Stair climber, light to moderate	8
Dancing (moderate to vigorous)	4–8	Standing, light activity	3
Downhill skiing	8–12	Step aerobics	5–7
Driving car	3	Surfing	3
E-mailing and faxing	2	Swimming	6–14
Eating	3	Tai chi	4
Football (while active)	13	Talking	1
Gardening	6–9	Tennis	7–11
Golf	3	Volleyball	4–8
Gymnastics	4	Walking (3 mph)	4–5
Handball	10	Walking (4 mph)	6–7
Hiking, uphill 5–15 percent grade (3–4 mph)	8–16	Washing and dressing	3
Horseback riding	2–5	Water skiing	8
Judo and karate	13	Weight training	4
Kick-boxing	6	Wrestling	14
Mowing lawn	6	Writing	1
Piano playing	2	Yoga	4